MOVING IDEAS

Colin Lankshear and Michele Knobel
General Editors

Vol. 65

The New Literacies and Digital Epistemologies series
is part of the Peter Lang Education list.
Every volume is peer reviewed and meets
the highest quality standards for content and production.

PETER LANG
New York • Washington, D.C./Baltimore • Bern
Frankfurt • Berlin • Brussels • Vienna • Oxford

MOVING IDEAS

MULTIMODALITY AND EMBODIED LEARNING IN COMMUNITIES AND SCHOOLS

EDITED BY MIRA-LISA KATZ

PETER LANG
New York • Washington, D.C./Baltimore • Bern
Frankfurt • Berlin • Brussels • Vienna • Oxford

Library of Congress Cataloging-in-Publication Data

Moving ideas: Multimodality and embodied learning
in communities and schools / edited by Mira-Lisa Katz.
pages cm. — (New literacies and digital epistemologies; v. 65)
Includes bibliographical references.
1. Movement education. 2. Movement, Psychology of.
3. Dance—Study and teaching. 4. Dance—Psychological aspects.
5. Learning—Physiological aspects. 6. Body image. I. Katz, Mira-Lisa.
GV452.M85 372.86—dc23 2013003342
ISBN 978-1-4331-2208-8 (hardcover)
ISBN 978-1-4331-2207-1 (paperback)
ISBN 978-1-4539-1092-4 (e-book)
ISSN 1523-9543

Bibliographic information published by **Die Deutsche Nationalbibliothek**.
Die Deutsche Nationalbibliothek lists this publication in the "Deutsche Nationalbibliografie"; detailed bibliographic data is available on the Internet at http://dnb.d-nb.de/.

The paper in this book meets the guidelines for permanence and durability of the Committee on Production Guidelines for Book Longevity of the Council of Library Resources.

© 2013 Peter Lang Publishing, Inc., New York
29 Broadway, 18th floor, New York, NY 10006
www.peterlang.com

All rights reserved.
Reprint or reproduction, even partially, in all forms such as microfilm, xerography, microfiche, microcard, and offset strictly prohibited.

Printed in the United States of America

For my mom, Millie

Contents

Acknowledgments   ix

Foreword: Ideas Do Move   xi
James Paul Gee

Poem: "The Body Is the Text"   xiv
Elizabeth Carothers Herron

Introduction   1
Mira-Lisa Katz

1. Growth in Motion: Supporting Young Women's Embodied Identity   31
   and Cognitive Development Through Dance After School
   Mira-Lisa Katz

2. Chroma Harmonia: Multimodal Pedagogy Through Universal   47
   Design for Learning
   Catherine Kroll

3. "All the World's a Stage": Musings on Teaching Dance to People   61
   With Parkinson's
   David Leventhal

4. The Communicative Body in Women's Self-Defense Courses   81
   Keli Yerian

5. Pasture Pedagogy: Field and Classroom Reflections on   109
   Embodied Teaching
   Erica Tom with Mira-Lisa Katz

6. 36 Jewish Gestures   139
   Nina Haft

7. Thinking with Your Skin: Paradoxical Ideas in Physical Theater 157
   Eliot Fintushel

8. Visceral Literature: Multimodal Theater Activities for Middle   171
   and High School English Language Arts
   Tori Truss with Mira-Lisa Katz

9. A Trio: Combining Language, Literacy and Movement in   187
   Preschool and Kindergarten Community-Based Dance Classes
   Jill Homan Randall

10. The Paramparic Body: Gestural Transmission in Indian Music   209
    Matt Rahaim

11. Literacies of Touch: Massage Therapy and the Body Composed   229
    Cory Holding & Hannah Bellwoar

12. The Embodiment of Real and Digital Signs: From the   243
    Sociocultural to the Intersemiotic
    Julie Cheville

Conributors   257

Acknowledgments

Just as literacies are social, books are collaborative. This volume owes its existence to the guidance, hard work and faith of many colleagues, friends, mentors and family members.

First and foremost, I appreciate my co-authors' insightful contributions, which promise to broaden and enliven future studies of multimodality and literacies. I am especially grateful to my colleague and friend, Cathy Kroll, who offered invaluable feedback and intellectual companionship throughout the writing process and conceived the book's title, *Moving Ideas*, which so elegantly captures the collection's intentions. Eve Sweetser, Dor Abrahamson, Katharine Young and Matt Rahaim as well as other members of the U.C. Berkeley Gesture Research Group provided lively and provocative discussions of gesture, language, multimodality and embodied cognition. Heartfelt thanks to my colleague and friend, Noelle Oxenhandler, for offering steadfast encouragement and long term vision, and to fellow members of the California State University ERWC Advisory Committee, especially Nancy Brynelson, John Edlund, Norm Unrau and Nelson Graff, who really walk the walk of collaborative thinking and scholarship.

Dance colleagues Jill Homan Randall, Nina Haft, Frank Shawl, Victor Anderson, Rebecca Johnson, Katie Faulkner, Randee Paufve, David Leventhal, Beth Hoge, Ernesta Corvino, Mercy Sidbury and many other dedicated movers made chapters 1, 3, 6 and 9 possible.

I owe a great deal to the brilliant literacy scholars and teacher educators who continue to inspire me and create access for so many. They include Glynda Hull, Mike Rose, Jim Gee, Anne Haas Dyson, Cyndy Greenleaf, Kathy Schultz, Michele Knobel, Colin Lankshear and Mark Davis. Outstanding graduates of Sonoma State University's M.A. program in English, Erica Tom and Christy Davids, provided immensely helpful commentary on earlier versions of the manuscript. Everyone at Peter Lang Publishing has been a pleasure to work with—thank you.

My family members—Dean Katz, Marian Wachter, Teri Katz and Curran Kennedy—were encouraging and supportive throughout. Most of all, though, I thank my mom, Millie Katz, extraordinary mother of three, who taught high school science for 30 years and treasured every single day she spent in the classroom. Her unbridled passion for teaching and learning is an ongoing source of inspiration to me as well as to thousands of others who have been touched by her curiosity, joy and humor. This book is for her.

IMAGE CREDITS:

Chapters 1, 5, 6, 8: Mira-Lisa Katz

Chapter 2: Catherine Kroll

Chapter 3: Katsuyoshi Tanaka

Chapter 4: Claudia Sims

Chapter 7: Frank Kitus

Chapter 9: Rob Kunkle

Chapter 10: Figure 1 drawing by Douglas Leonard

Chapter 11: Hannah Bellwoar

Foreword

Ideas Do Move

James Paul Gee

Both communication and learning are about moving ideas. Moving ideas from one person to another and moving people to act and feel in certain ways. But how do ideas move?

Ideas move because humans make pictures for each other. A picture of a tree is an invitation to engage in interpretation. It is an invitation to make the picture mean something. What the picture means will depend on what people do with it and that in turn depends on what they want to do with it—how they imagine its purpose. In one context of interpretation it may be made to mean—that is, taken to be a sign for—a forest. In another context, it may mean nature, and in yet another, it may mean a particular species of tree or even a specific tree. It all depends on context, and context is shaped by intention.

If we know people's intentions or can make a good guess about them, we also consider how these manifest in their representation of a tree. But the person who made the picture can never completely control what is made of it. And, in any case, that person, in trying to use the picture to communicate, must carefully consider how people in specific communities and contexts engage in the work and play of interpretation.

Although we don't often think about them as such, words are types of pictures. They, too, exist physically as sound waves or inscriptions. They, too, are invitations to interpretation. Like pictures, words constrain the work of interpretation in certain ways and ask that interpreters consider intentions as far as they can, but they do not and cannot restrict interpretation completely. Active meaning making is always something both speakers (writers) and listeners (readers) do.

Even a mundane request like "Can you get me some coffee?" requires the listener to judge whether it is a cup of coffee, coffee beans, or a pound of coffee that is wanted. We use context to make such judgments. If we are sitting together at the kitchen table, we get a cup of coffee; if the person wants to grind coffee, we get coffee beans; and if one of us is on the way to the store, we buy a pound of coffee.

Now, the realization that the word "coffee" requires context for its interpretation does not seem very exciting or consequential. But, alas, the more important a word is to us, the more it requires interpretation that goes well beyond the producer's control. It is highly consequential what someone takes words like "love," "democracy," "work," "honor," and "marry" to mean in utterances like: "I love you," "The United States is not a real democracy," "Relationships take work," "There is honor among thieves," and "John married his partner, Sam."

Using a word like "democracy" is like holding up a picture; the words around "democracy" in an utterance seek to make the picture more explicit, just as the details around the drawing of a tree do. But, in the end, there is still the work of interpretation to accomplish.

Communication always and everywhere for humans is a matter of making something—a picture, a gesture or movement, a sound or song, an object or artifact—and then telling others to make something out of it, to make it mean something. Producers of these "signs," broadly conceived, always attempt to control aspects of interpretation. They always seek to get their intentions respected to the extent that they even fully know them themselves. And consumers or recipients of these messages always attempt to produce meanings that make sense to them, that are "meaningful." Both producers and consumers negotiate, create, and seek to sustain shared contexts of interpretation. Such contexts are not mental; rather, they are shared through practices, social arrangements, physical orientations and "forms of life."

Meaning is made by using things (words, images, sounds, gestures, movements, objects) that serve as invitations to meaning making—invitations that must be taken up if meaning is to be consummated. When a person is new to a context of interpretation—for example when someone enters a new academic field or community—the person has to learn how to construct and react appropriately to invitations made with words, images, movements or objects that may have varied potential for meaning in other areas or endeavors.

But how do we humans go about attributing meaning to words, movements, sounds, objects and images? We do so based primarily on the experiences we have had in life to date. Confronted with a sign we call up how such signs have worked in previous situations and try to guess how they are working here and now. What did we, and others, do and feel in the past? Sometimes we have to "reach"—to imagine, surmise, estimate, predict, infer. Our previous experiences do not contain any "exact match," and we have to go out on a limb about what things might mean. As we get reactions back from others, as we work with them to make meaning-making mutual, we climb back down the limb to shared understanding and often learn something new and sometimes even create new meanings all together. Meaning making is a dance and dancing too is meaning making.

Although we humans interpret based on experiences we have had in the world, we often forget that our experiences are things our bodies, emotions, and minds have usually come to know in the presence of others; they are "embodied" and often "social," not just "individual" and "mental."

This collection asks (and answers) the question: what do the various modalities have to do with meaning and learning? The answer is: everything. *Moving Ideas* helps educators working in school and community contexts with people of varied ages to consider how our traditional and preconceived ideas about communication and meaning are, in fact, strange. And because our traditional ideas about communication and meaning are strange, our schools are not as conducive as they might be to helping young people find pathways to active engagement in and with the world. It will do us all a wealth of good to consider anew, as does this book, how ideas move within and across modalities, how they shift and are repurposed as people share them among continents and generations, and how they are, at their very core, rooted in the body.

"The Body Is the Text"
Elizabeth Carothers Herron

Without the body there is no text
There is no text without breath
No breath without the body
The body is the text
This is about landscape and psyche
This is about language and earth
Breathing together we are the text
We are speaking even when we are silent

Introduction

> To say that we read—the world, a book, the body—is not enough. The metaphor of reading solicits in turn another metaphor, demands to be explained in images that lie outside the reader's library and yet within the reader's body, so that the function of reading is associated with our other essential bodily functions. (Alberto Manguel, *A History of Reading*, p. 170)

Early one rainy Saturday morning in the summer of 1975, my father picked me up at my mom's house, and together we drove silently across town to a yoga class at Seattle's biggest post-secondary institution, the University of Washington. In a classroom on the third floor of an otherwise quiet building, empty desks shoved haphazardly back against the walls, we stretched ourselves out on the cool linoleum, breathing deeply as we saluted the sun hidden behind the pearly gray clouds of a faithful Northwestern sky.

In high school during the same period of time, I sat daily in neatly ordered desks facing the fronts of numerous classrooms where teachers hurled questions at those whose eyes roamed too far from the chalkboard or page. Hostage to school furnishings, architecture, and social organization, I tucked my legs up underneath myself, my attention toggling between teachers' voices and the physical discomfort of so much stillness. Halfway through senior year, troubled by what I then perceived as the stagnant and narrow nature of school life, I dropped out. Everyone who mattered to me—peers, parents and teachers—unequivocally disapproved. But like so many young people hobbled by the constraints of conventional schooling, I sought, and eventually constructed, an alternative pathway into the world outside of high school.

On those early morning trips with my father to the University of Washington to practice yoga (an esoteric curiosity at that time) in a classroom intended for a very different sort of learning, I was struck by the incongruity of seeing desks and chairs pushed to the room's edges, spatially marginalized on the periphery. Although historically the use of chairs can be traced back to Neolithic times (10,000–4,000 B.C.), they have only recently come to exist in the great numbers and uniform designs we encounter today (Cranz, 1998). As UC Berkeley Professor of Architecture Galen Cranz explains, "We touch chairs not just with our hands but with our whole bodies....What is true of the chair is true of all artifacts we create. We design them; but once built, they shape us....The chair offers a glimpse into our collective ideas about status and honor, comfort and order, beauty and efficiency, discipline and relaxation. As our ideas change, so do our chairs" (p. 15). The chairs we find in schools are certainly no exception.

In many but by no means all parts of the world schools are brimming with chairs which not only organize our behavior and communication patterns, our thinking and learning but also larger aspects of our everyday experience, including architecture itself. Standard window heights, for example, are designed to be congruent with typical chair sizes (Cranz, 1998). Since we know that "Arranging seats in rows facing one direction has very different consequences for social interaction and the flow of information than arranging them in a circle" (Cranz, 1998, p. 18), it is no surprise that social scientists and socioculturally minded educators have been exploring the social effects of physical and structural configurations on interaction and learning. Yet classroom organization resists change.

While schools have great potential to empower young people intellectually and psychologically as well as emotionally and physically, educators are well aware that traditional institutions of learning also help "prepare children to reproduce the workforce, with appropriate habits—both physical and mental....[S]ocialization to passivity starts early in schools, where the first task is not to teach children content, but to teach them orderly behavior—specifically, the ability to sit still for long periods of time" (Cranz, p. 60). And although coming of age manifests differently worldwide, in many societies maturity is often signaled by one's ability to remain quietly attentive for extended intervals while seated in the classroom.

But must schools be physically inhospitable places? For numerous people, perhaps especially for children, sitting in chairs is not only tedious and painful, but also counter-productive to learning. Cranz observes that "Having to sit at tables and [in] chairs is the most common source of physical stress for children, and probably for adults too....But children, being young, are particularly deformed by stressful postures" (Cranz, p. 62). Moreover, these socially and culturally ingrained habits seem to grow more entrenched as learners get older. As Sir Ken Robinson (2006) jests, "as children grow up we start to educate them progressively from the waist up. And then we focus on their heads. And slightly to one side."

In contrast, the authors in this collection suggest accessible and engaging educational practices where teachers and learners are literally moving ideas, making use of perhaps the most ubiquitous yet underutilized educational tools we have at our constant disposal—our bodies.

THE PRIMACY OF MOVEMENT

In some fields—somatics, for example—it is commonly understood that humans are born movers and that it is in large part through movement[1] that we encounter, engage with, understand, participate in, and ultimately find our sense of place in the world. And despite educational reformers' repeated calls for more freedom of movement and physical comfort in schools, very little has shifted. It remains a considerable challenge to figure out how to reorient ourselves—to our own bodies and to those of our students; to classroom layout and spatial organization; and to postural configurations as well as physical, gestural and verbal participation structures that could better serve learners' and educators' needs, capacities and natural inclinations. The chapters in this volume offer a variety of thoughtful explorations of what it looks like to teach with the body in mind.

INSIGHTS FROM MULTIMODAL RESEARCH AND PRACTICE

Because multimodality "requires us to take seriously and attend to the whole range of modalities involved in representation and communication" (Jewitt & Kress, 2003, p. 1), such a perspective can help us re-conceptualize education in a number of crucial ways. We are now aware, for example, that modalities almost always occur in concert, rarely alone; that meanings are distributed across modalities in distinctive ways at different times according to social contexts and purposes; that modes of representation interact with a variety of media, "the technologies for making and distributing meanings as messages" (Jewitt & Kress, 2003, p. 4); and that modes shape both what is represented as well as learners' uptake of those representations. We also now understand that various forms of representation and learners' abilities to take them up are in large part the result of (or could, to a greater extent, be the result of) strategic pedagogical choices, hence the vital importance of the orientations that inform our decisions about learning design.

Jewitt and Kress (2003) suggest that all modes are in some sense *equal*, that is, potentially "significant for meaning and communication" (p. 2) (although some modes—print, visual, auditory—are inarguably heavily privileged in school contexts). But while modes may be equal, they are also *partial*, that is, different contexts and communicative purposes make particular modalities more relevant (Jewitt & Kress, 2003, p. 3) (cf. Farnell, 1995, 1999; Finnegan, 2002; Franks, 2003; Hull & Nelson, 2005; Jewitt & Kress, 2003; Kress, 2001; Kress & van Leeuwen, 2001; Kress et al., 2001; Stein, 2008; Urciuoli, 1995). As Jewitt and Kress put it, "different modes have potentials that make them better for certain tasks than others ..." (Jewitt & Kress, 2003, p. 3). Exploring the unique affordances (Gibson, 1979; Kress & van Leeuwen, 2001) and expressive powers of digital stories, Hull & Nelson argue that such multimodally composed texts "can create a different system of signification, one that transcends the collective contribution of its constituent parts" (Hull & Nelson, 2005, p. 225). What's powerful are the "combinatory semiotic contributions" (p. 234) and the unfolding "semiotic tapestry" or "multimodal laminate" that multimodal composing makes possible (p. 239). Taking a "multimodal semiotic perspective," Anton Franks explains that "Different subjects...tend to operate within specific discursive formations and lead to patterns of physical and mental activity that require particular forms of engagement with the world ..." (Franks, 2003, p. 158). Imagine the increased potential for meaning making in educational contexts where bodily engagement and movement are more conscious parts of the mix.

We are only beginning to understand what this might look like (Bresler, 2004; Stein, 2008; Cahnmann-Taylor & Souto-Manning, 2010). In the meantime, we continue to organize learning in schools—and often outside them—in ways that consistently under-resource our corporeal intelligence. Despite all that we know about the powers of multimodality, classrooms and other educational environments, especially those serving learners beyond the elementary grades, still tend to operate according to at least two deep-seated assumptions: first, that language is the most effective (and should therefore be the dominant) mode of communication; and second, that movement and bodily perception are antithetical (and therefore irrelevant) to learning. Together, these suppositions powerfully shape contexts of education and development, especially for adolescents and adults for whom moving around in space or being aware of bodily sensations *as a part of the learning process* are considered childish if not also awkward and unnecessary.

EMBODIED LITERACIES, CORPOREAL PEDAGOGIES

To promote more holistic and robust learning experiences within and across disciplines for people of all ages, this book's authors explore school and community contexts in which educators and learners communicate, comprehend, create and compose with their bodies. The twelve chapters that follow examine learning in women's self-defense courses; dance classes for children and youth, as well as for adults with Parkinson's disease; equine studies; physical theater; Hindustani vocal music lessons; massage therapy; basketball; high presence computer media contexts; college-level basic reading and writing classes; and English Education courses for pre-service English Language Arts teachers. These chapters suggest how multimodal pedagogies can expand the look, feel and efficacy of learning.[2]

Importantly, these scholar-practitioners and artists consciously conceive of their bodies as multimodal material for and sites of pedagogical sense making and organization. Building on leading researchers' broad conceptions of *literacy*, the authors in this volume employ expansive definitions of terms like "text," "image," "composition," "reading" and "writing."[3] For these educators, in addition to print, image and multimedia texts, bodies, too, constitute the 'page' or 'screen' on which information emerges and is written and read. Bodies are also the vehicles for teachers' and learners' formative assessment—enabling us to check for understanding moment to moment throughout the course of complex educative events.

Our physicality is akin to living connective tissue, a porous membrane between inner and outer worlds through which knowledge is at times simultaneously constructed and circulated. In the diverse learning environments these scholars describe, teachers and learners corporeally encode, decode, comprehend, transform, recode, appropriate and repurpose information. And though teachers and learners working in embodied contexts have a modicum of agency, perhaps more agency than those working in more formal educational settings, they too are constrained by the reality that our bodies, alive and evolving like other literate tools, are always saturated with social meanings (Bourdieu, 1977; Butler, 1993; Merleau-Ponty, 1945; Noland & Ness, 2008; Rahaim, this volume).

Embodied literacies and communicative practices are what sustain and enable the corporeal pedagogies described in *Moving Ideas*; authors helpfully recast many dimensions of effective teaching (such as collaborative problem-solving, co-constructing knowledge, strategically modeling and scaffolding activities, fostering safety, creativity and critical thought, and sharing disciplinary modes of thinking and interacting) to build habits of mind/body in domains where learning and teaching are simultaneously corporeal, intellectual, emotional, psychological, and, of course, deeply social.

Through rich descriptive analyses of multimodal learning in community and school environments, these educators reach beyond existing scholarship,[4] which, while valuably expanding our understandings of visual and new media literacies (especially the relationships between writing and image), could benefit from more focused attention to the integral role that the sensing, kinesthetically active body itself can play in learning and instruction. As experienced practitioners of the types of activities they describe, these authors' views add a uniquely self-reflective dimension to the book's overall investigation. The ensemble of perspectives concretely elucidates how instruction via multiple modes can foster cognitive development, physical well-being, creativity, agency and positive identity formation. In keeping with the work of researchers like Franks (2003), the scholarship collected here "is governed by a desire not simply to read through classroom activity for meaning, treating physical activity as if it is transparent, but to focus on the physicalized aspects of the meaning-making process in social and cultural contexts" (p. 172).

BODILY LEARNING AND KNOWING: STRUGGLE AND POSSIBILITY

The habit of disparaging bodily knowledge reflects our well-ingrained Cartesian reluctance to consider cognitive or emotional processes *as embodied* (Csordas, 1994, 1999; Damasio, 1994, 1999, 2003, 2012; Farnell, 1995, 1999; Fraser & Greco, 2005; Ingold, 2011; Lakoff & Johnson, 1980; Leder, 1990; Lehrer, 2007, 2009; Mauss, 1935; Merleau-Ponty, 1945; Welton, 1999). Although such refusals continue to affect education around the world, the historical consequences for some groups have been particularly devastating. Among the Deaf, for example, signed languages in school and at home were forbidden for centuries because hearing people mistakenly viewed a communicative system rooted in movement as animalistic and void of capacity for abstraction (Bayton, 2008; Groce 1985; Katz, 1995; Klima & Bellugi, 1979; Lane 1984; Padden & Humphries, 2005).

However, recent shifts in many disciplines have expanded our capacities to research the embodied dimensions of learning and stretched our repertoires for more artfully describing them.[5] In the spirit of such scholarship, *Moving Ideas* examines the strategic layering of information across semiotic modes (kinesthetic, tactile, vocal, rhythmic, gestural, visual, spatial, verbal and non-verbal) and challenges us to revisit the philosophical, methodological, and ideological underpinnings of our work by ably wrestling language away from its historically privileged place at the center of social science research and educational practice. The following sections explore relevant anthropological and neuroscientific perspectives on the body, emotion and reason.

FEELING AND THOUGHT: EMOTION AND REASON

In *Body and Emotion*, anthropologist Robert Desjarlais (1992) notes a propensity in anthropological writing "to privilege the linguistic, the discursive, and the cognized over the visceral and the tacit" (p. 29). Because we tend to ignore the senses, "We have lost an understanding of the body as an experiencing, soulful being ..." (p. 29). "There is much to experience," Desjarlais asserts, "that eludes the logic of signs" (p. 32).

> In the end we return to the question of empathy. To what extent can a person participate in another's feelings or ideas? How can we best render this knowledge to others?...Empathy rides on the grounds that two people's ways of knowing are similar, such that we can 'know' what another is feeling based on what we ourselves would feel in that situation. Unless we can achieve a basic understanding of how another person makes sense of the most elemental aspects of their being—how he or she experiences body, pain, or gender—any efforts toward empathy with that person will run aground....(p. 35)

Current mirror neuron research (discussed below and in several chapters in this volume) is helping us to understand how empathy actually works, and the insights gained from this emerging field have vital implications for how we design learning in and out of schools.

To understand how people reason, know, and learn we must also have a sense of how they experience feelings and emotions. Our "language, actions and dispositions," argues Desjarlais, constitute "the basic filaments of a given cultural tradition, derive from the way in which social interactions occur, and give form to the most visceral of bodily experiences. In many ways, they constitute the grammars of cultural experience" (Desjarlais, p. 37). If he is correct, then to ignore the embodied dimensions of feelings, thoughts, beliefs or cognition itself would be to disregard some of the most elemental aspects of being human, and perhaps nowhere are these more significant than in education.

EMBODIED THINKING: NEUROSCIENTIFIC UNDERSTANDINGS OF EMOTION AND REASON

To say that *thinking is embodied* is more than a quixotic claim about the material nature of the gray matter between our ears. Neurologist Antonio Damasio, whose research has focused on the connection between emotions and reason (1994)[6] and on the embodied nature of consciousness and the self (1999, 2003, 2012),[7] contends (based on neuroscientific data rather than philosophical grounds) that without emotions and feelings, we cannot reason effectively. "It does not seem sensible to leave emotions and feelings out of any overall concept of the mind. Yet respectable scientific accounts of cognition do precisely that by failing to include emotions and feelings in their treatment of cognitive systems" (1994, p. 158). Damasio argues that,

> *Feelings are just as cognitive as any other perceptual image*, and just as dependent on the cerebral-cortex processing as any image....[F]eelings...are first and foremost about the

body…they offer us *the cognition of our visceral and musculoskeletal state* as it becomes affected by pre-organized mechanisms and by the cognitive structures we have developed under their influence. Feelings let us *mind the body* attentively….(emphasis in original, p. 159)

In helping us monitor our responses to people, events and experience, feelings enable us to think. "Your mind is not a blank at the start of the reasoning process," explains Damasio. "Rather it is replete with a diverse repertoire of images, generated to the tune of the situation you are facing, entering and exiting your consciousness in a show too rich for you to encompass fully" (1994, p. 170). Contrary to the "high-reason" account of rationality espoused by Plato, Descartes, Kant and others, which suggests that "emotions must be kept *out*" of reasoning processes (p. 171), Damasio explains that emotions are, in fact, "somatically marked" (indexed in the body) and that these "adaptive somatic markers" help us strategically sift through the possible consequences of particular choices and actions at lightning speed (also see Lehrer, 2009). It follows that those individuals who have experienced a greater number of healthy opportunities to sift through possible consequences (those who've had more meaningful practice) will have a larger repertoire of adaptive strategies as well as quicker response time (Damasio, 1994).

These guiding emotions, simultaneously rooted in life experience and in bodily sensing and feeling, help us make sound predictions, choices and decisions (p. 173). They also undergird "willpower," or what some in education call perseverance, self-efficacy or motivation (or all three) (see, for example, Jang, Reeve, & Deci, 2010; Naceur & Schiefele, 2005; National Research Council and the Institute of Medicine, 2004). "Willpower," Damasio (1994) explains,

> draws on the evaluation of a prospect, and that evaluation may not take place if attention is not properly driven to both the immediate trouble and the future payoff, to both the suffering *now* and the *future* gratification. Remove the latter and you remove the lift from under your willpower's wings. Willpower is just another name for choosing according to long-term outcomes rather than short-term ones. (emphasis in original, p. 175)

This relationship between cognition and emotion—the gut sense that informs our decision-making in the moment-to-moment contexts of everyday life—has implications for both micro and macro levels of learning in and outside of schools. At the macro level, we hope many young people will choose to stay in school rather than drop out (school being part of a long-term plan or vision). At the micro level, in order to find staying in school (or staying with any long-term learning project outside of it) an appealing proposition, we must feel capable of and thus motivated and willing to persevere, even in the face of difficulties or challenges. When we can connect short-term choices (attending school regularly; acquiring academic literacies; becoming conversant with and able to wield academic discourses, habits of mind, and social practices) with long-term gains (enhancing understandings of self and others; augmenting imaginable options for participating meaningfully in the world), there's likely to be more incentive and increased staying power for young people to remain in school.

If emotions and feelings are the foundation of reasoning processes such as prediction, choice- and decision-making, as Damasio persuasively argues (1994), then we especially need schools that honor our simultaneous needs for physical, emotional and intellectual engagement. While the human organism is one that "comes to life designed with automatic survival mechanisms," Damasio argues that "education and acculturation add a set of socially permissible and desirable decision-making strategies that, in turn, enhance survival, remarkably improve the quality of that survival, and serve as the basis for constructing a person" (Damasio, 1994, p. 126). Such a view has profound implications for how we might re-envision and orchestrate learning with the body, indeed, the whole person, in mind.

Intriguingly, Damasio's (1994, 1999, 2012) notions of the embodied (neural) basis of self parallel those of theorists[8] whose views of the self are neither unitary nor stable (albeit for different reasons).

> In using the notion of self, I am in no way suggesting that *all* the contents of our minds are inspected by a single central knower and owner, and even less that such an entity would reside in a single brain place. I am saying, though, that our experiences tend to have a consistent perspective....I imagine this perspective to be rooted in a relatively stable, endlessly repeating biological state. (p. 238)

The only thing that is stable about such a self, then, is its continually changeable nature. "The current sense of self is a combination of memories as well as imaginings" (what Damasio calls "memory of the possible future" [p. 239]).

> Self is a repeatedly reconstructed biological state....(pp. 236–237) At each moment, the state of self is constructed from the ground up....Present continuously becomes past, and by the time we take stock of it we are in another present, consumed with planning the future, which we do on the stepping-stones of the past. The present is never here. We are hopelessly late for consciousness. (p. 240)

There remains, though, some space for decision-making and action that may at least partially defy both biological and cultural imperatives. As Damasio (1994) asserts, "Humans do have *some* room for freedom, for willing and performing actions that may go against the apparent grain of biology and culture" (p. 177). Such agency, I believe, might be more readily experienced if the body were a purposeful part of our everyday educative processes, as it is in the contexts described by this book's authors.

About connections between self, individual agency and the social, educators Hull and Katz (2006) suggest that, "We enact the selves we want to become in relation to others—sometimes in concert with them, sometimes in opposition to them, but always in relation to them" (p. 47). Our sense of agency at any given moment, then, is constrained by social, cultural, and historical limitations and goals, yet people can exercise a degree of agency by strategically deploying the unique repertoires of cultural resources, relationships, and artifacts available. Embodied engagement overtly exploits an additional set of cultural resources and artifacts that tend to foster agentive learning, which, in turn can support thoughtful and meaningful participation in both public and private spheres. But agency is fragile and at times contradictory, as the following vignette reveals.

In *Identity and Agency in Cultural Worlds*, Holland Lachicotte, Skinner and Cain (1998/2001) recount how one Nepalese villager in their anthropological study had an appointment to meet with two interviewers seated on the balcony of a fellow villager's house. Needing to get to the second floor, but not wanting to 'contaminate' her higher caste neighbor's home, the woman refused to enter through the front door which offered the most direct access to where her interviewers awaited her. To keep her appointment, she scaled the house walls, "climbing up the house," to get to the second floor balcony (Holland et al., 1998/2001). This individual's surprising response to an awkward social situation evokes the indisputable links between cultural beliefs, identity, cognition and embodiment—how we creatively interpret and negotiate personal understandings of social and cultural meanings and imaginatively repurpose resources, including the physical, to problem-solve on the fly. Teaching requires just this kind of emergent capacity building and resourcefulness on a daily basis.

REFRAMING THE DEBATE

Studies of embodiment have a long and esteemed intellectual history.[9] In the field of education, theorists from Dewey (1938) and Vygotsky (1978) to Rogoff (1990, 2003) and Lave and Wenger (1991) have written extensively about apprenticeship (cf. Chaiklin & Lave, 1996; Wenger, 1998), suggesting that we learn and develop as human beings by engaging directly in activities with more experienced practitioners, whether they be lab technicians, factory workers, sculptors, deep sea divers, airplane pilots, basketball players, painters, doctors, gardeners, horse trainers, or actors. Learning in the physical presence of others offers us a means of cultivating varied sources of understanding in worlds where cognition, self-perception, expression, and emotion are filtered through muscle and movement as well as through mind, language, and social interaction.

In his article, "Our Hands Will Know," educator Mike Rose (1999) describes how students of physical therapy use their bodies to make sense of new ideas via feeling and touch, and to "think of the tactile as data" (p. 143). Like dancers and athletes, physical therapists become skilled over time at utilizing the body "as an infor-mation-collecting device" (p. 143). Charles Goodwin's (1994) work on "profes-sional vision" argues similarly for the continued importance of studying the physical and mulitmodal dimensions of complexly orchestrated, skilled activity.

There is also growing evidence from mirror neuron research (Blakeslee & Blakeslee, 2007; Iacoboni, 2008; Rizzolatti & Arbib, 1998; Rizzolatti & Craighero, 2004; Rizzolatti & Sinigaglia, 2008) that we can consciously (as we do subcon-sciously) facilitate learning through specific bodily orientations (Downey, 2008, 2010; Goldin-Meadow, 2003, 2005; Goldin-Meadow, Wagner-Cook & Mitchell, 2009). In the context of teaching, bodily orientations work on many different levels from the cognitive and neuronal to the visual and kinesthetic. Anthropologist Greg Downey (2008), who conducts ethnographic work on the Brazilian martial art form, capoeira, cites recent neuroscientific research showing how imitative learning is both highly strategic and interactive. Teaching physical activities (like martial arts) is based on "complex…movement analysis, abstraction, and selective demonstration" (p. 205). The strategic organization that teachers demonstrate (what some in education call "pedagogical content knowledge" [Shulman, 1987]) enables teachers to maximally sup-port learning through anticipation of concepts or activities likely to be difficult for novices and strategically crafting opportunities for learning accordingly.

In more recent research, Downey (2010) revisits Bourdieu's concept of the *habitus*, "a socially generated…'structuring structure' internalized through interac-tion with people and the social environment" (p. S23). "The habitus, in Bourdieu's model is history made flesh, a corporeal enculturation that assures social and sym-bolic continuity while underwriting an individual's sense of autonomy" (p. S23). The *habitus* concept, he suggests, has been especially attractive to anthropologists (and other social scientists), because it entails a corporeal dimension that concepts like *culture* and *ideology* lack. "[H]abitus has offered an attractive way to operationalize structure, to suggest that everyday action is both strategic and yet imprinted with the actor's past, and thus society's history . . ." (p. S23). Downey's ethnographic research on capoeira and his analysis of neuroscientific studies on imitative learn-ing both suggest that Bourdieu's distinction between mimesis (unconscious learn-ing) and imitation (deliberate learning) and his understanding of body-to-body learning, while immensely insightful, were perhaps somewhat misguided:

> What we find in capoeira is that bodily learning can bring to conscious light some of the movement traits, postures and tendencies that may have once been unconscious, but become problematized in transformative apprenticeship….As the novice seeks to imitate new styles of moving…training may demonstrably affect physiological change in the brain, nervous sys-tem, bones, joints, sensory organs, even endocrine and autonomic systems. Transformation of the habitus is not simply changing an underlying 'structure' but altering the organic architecture of the subject. (2010, p. S27)

So while we tend to think of physical imitation as requiring no conscious effort (after all, as Downey notes, babies and animals imitate effortlessly), "the ethological evidence suggests that imitation is anything but easy" (Downey, p. S27). But as we know, teachers and learners are inventive and strategic. Speaking about capoeira, Downey notes how "the more difficulty a student has, the more resourceful a skilled instructor can be" (p. S28). In addition to benefiting from good teaching we are also biologically wired to support imitative learning:

> [H]umans' extraordinary imitative ability also appears to be facilitated by our neural architecture, specifically the likelihood that one's own actions, the perceived actions of others, and imagined actions are all represented in the brain in similar fashion, using neural systems that substantially overlap. That is, we may perceive others' actions as meaningful by converting them into first-person simulations…'reading' other people's actions at least in part with our own sense of movement. In other words, motor perception is inherently, neuroarchitecturally, intersubjective." (p. S28)

It is as if the intersubjectivity noted by Downey (and by the mirror neuron researchers' work he references) constitutes a form of bodily storytelling or narrative. If so, this potentially adds a persuasive new dimension to Bruner's (1990, 1994) argument that narrative constitutes a fundamental form of human thought; the storied nature of our social, cognitive and psychological processes is, it would seem, profoundly embodied.

Downey ultimately argues that if the neural mechanisms that underlie imitative learning do indeed involve common coding of action and perception at the neuronal level, this would undermine Bourdieu's idea that the habitus is global (pp. S29–S30); rather, the habitus is domain-specific, and individuals acquire concrete skills that make up the habitus in ad hoc and irregular ways (p. S33). Downey concludes that while, "the notion of a unified structuring structure is elegantly modernist and functional; the human brain and body…are baroque, cobbled together by evolution, biological processes, and individual development" (p. S33). Embodied learning is a much more intricate affair than Bourdieu initially supposed. Its complexity is handily revealed in recent research on gesture.

AT OUR FINGERTIPS: THE ROLE OF GESTURE IN TEACHING AND LEARNING

How striking it is that we gesture in the dark; we gesture when our listeners' backs are turned; we gesture when we're talking to ourselves, and congenitally blind individuals gesture when conversing with other blind people. It seems, then, that as gesture researcher David McNeill claims, "lack of vision…does not impede thinking in gestural terms" (2005, p. 26). Interestingly, "Speech and gesture also spontaneously exchange information in memory, so that when something is recalled the speaker cannot tell the original format" (p. 27). Refuting the "gesture first" argument—that humans gestured prior to speech—researchers McNeill (2005), Goldin-Meadow (2003), and Kendon (2004) suggest that gesture is an actual mode of thought co-occurring with speech and providing information that differs from ideas expressed verbally (each modality is 'good at' carrying specific kinds of meaning). "[L]anguage is inseparable from imagery.....It makes no more sense" McNeill quips, "to treat gestures in isolation from speech than to read a book by looking only at the 'g's" (2005, p. 4). These scholars argue that gesture may even lead learning and cognitive change. According to McNeill (2005), gesture and speech form a "dynamic dialectic." If we ignore gesture, we are missing out on valuable opportunities to 'read people's minds'—to pick up on their inner mental processes by tracking their hands' movements and attending to the relationship between what they say (words, stylistic choices, intonation, timing, rhythm) and do (with hands and body).

Moreover, while we tend to think of gestures as additional cues for our listeners, McNeill and Goldin-Meadow also convincingly argue that gesture is equally useful to the speaker. Speakers use their own gestures as a way of (literally) holding an idea in their hands while they piece thoughts together. Greater awareness and understanding of such multimodal processes enhance learning in ways that Susan Goldin-Meadow and her colleagues have been documenting for some time.

In her research with math teachers (Goldin-Meadow, 2003, 2005; Goldin-Meadow, Wagner-Cook, & Mitchell, 2009), Goldin-Meadow reveals how educators alter gestures moment-to-moment to fine-tune information encoded via gestures that co-occur with speech. Thus consciously and subconsciously, teachers gather information about students' understandings of tasks and concepts, and subsequently modify their gestural communication to aid students' evolving comprehension. In this way, teachers not only *read* students' comprehension via a combination of talk and gesture; they also responsively adjust their own subsequent gestural production, *writing* (or inscribing) in ways that better serve learners' needs. If educators focus too narrowly on speech and discourse, we risk overlooking the degree to which other modalities systematically contribute to successful human communication, cognitive growth and development, and how they could be strategically tapped to support (and at times supplant) other dominant modes of classroom literacies, discourses and forms of interaction.

CHAPTER SUMMARIES

In "Growth in Motion: Supporting Young Women's Embodied Identity and Cognitive Development Through Dance After School," Mira-Lisa Katz describes how dance classes for teenage girls in one community-based setting, where making mistakes is rewarded rather than punished, provide a model for considering how embodied modes of teaching and learning can enhance development. In addition to being a powerful means of knowing oneself and communicating with others, learning dance can support social and cognitive development and identity formation. Combining multiple modes of communication with supportive social relationships and varied opportunities for participation offered the young women in her study fertile grounds for agentive learning. If selves have their roots, "not in words but in corporeal consciousness," as Sheets-Johnstone (1998) claims, then chances to enact embodied selves may help educators in and out of schools imagine educational practices that could more successfully support youth development. Multimodal learning environments like those investigated in Katz's multi-year study provide space for a powerful kind of learning that we know far too little about. As school-based and out-of-school curricula are increasingly narrowed during this age of accountability and high-stakes testing, failing to pay adequate attention to the promise of multimodal instruction means forfeiting significant resources for constructing positive educational experiences that are, quite literally, at our fingertips.

In "Chroma Harmonia: Multimodal Pedagogies Through Universal Design for Learning," literary scholar, educator and athlete Catherine Kroll investigates multimodal instruction in a pedagogical grammar course she offers to college-level pre-service English Language Arts teachers. In her classroom, not only does the array of instructional modalities add a welcome element of play to a difficult subject, the variety also offers students ways to reflect meta-cognitively on their learning processes and study practices, sometimes internalizing these learning strategies so thoroughly that they became part of their at-home study sessions.

Kroll suggests that programs like Universal Design for Learning (UDL)—the approach she employed to comprehensively build multimodality into her own curriculum—offer teachers across disciplines concrete ways to broaden learning pathways in their courses. Contending that "teaching is as much about the creation of the ready conditions for learning as it is about the subject matter itself," Kroll's analysis of strategic pedagogical decision-making encourages educators to rethink how they design and 'deliver' instruction.

> When we ask the tough questions about what truly motivates students to want to learn theory (in this chapter, specifically language theory and English grammar), and resituate theory at ground-level—at the level of the sensing and moving body—we revitalize the instructional experiences of teachers and students alike.

Drawing on neuroscientific research (Rizzolatti & Sinigaglia, 2008), Kroll suggests that multimodal learning creates a

> shared awareness of meaningful action [that] is so automatic and so fast that it obviates the brain's need for any preliminary theory building or analysis. Students read teachers' movements as goal-intentions, and they experience these movements not just through the visual sensory system, but through the mirror neuron system, which enables an understanding of the movements' meanings or goals on an immediate physical level.

If, in fact, embodied messages actually precede intellectual understanding (theory building), they certainly merit more serious pedagogical consideration, and Kroll's chapter is a powerful start in this direction. Finally, reflecting on critical connections between mirror neuron theory and literacy processes, Kroll likens multimodal learning to reading:

> The brain's ability to grasp intention is akin to the kind of predictive functions that structure the reading process....Whether reading a text or grasping the action-intentions of others, we are astute readers of the intentions embedded in the movements and events that unfold around us. Prediction entails hypothesizing about the meanings of others, whether those meanings are expressed in print or via the body.

Exploring action-intention from a different angle, in "'All the World's a Stage': Musings on Teaching Dance to People With Parkinson's," professional dancer and dance-educator David Leventhal describes "Dance for PD," a unique program he co-founded to help people living with Parkinson's disease—for whom movement itself is a daily struggle—acquire learning tools that dancers intuitively use to refine and expand their artistic expression. Leventhal explains that

> Professional dancers and people with Parkinson's disease share a challenge: to execute movement in a natural, graceful, controlled way. For dancers the difficulty of the movement is set by a demanding choreographer; for people with PD—a degenerative neurological disease that affects muscle control, balance, and motor coordination—it is established by the daily realities of their condition.

Both populations must use a series of embodied learning tools (tools that dancers implicitly know but rarely analyze) to approach the imposing task of learning movement. By participating in a specialized dance class taught by professional dancers and accompanied by a master dance musician, people with Parkinson's are effectively able to "understand movement in a dancerly way." Taking as point of departure that "movement is first and foremost a mental activity that uses music to make sense of the unfamiliar," Leventhal's chapter examines the ways in which verbal and visual cues, imagery, and music enhance learning. Indeed, "in a powerful reformulation of life imitating art, these classes evince the various ways dance instruction establishes a strong framework for approaching learning challenges of any kind." Finally, defying traditional hierarchies between teachers and students, this chapter explores what professional dancers and Parkinson's movers simultaneously teach one another.

In "The Communicative Body in Women's Self-Defense Courses," linguist, educator, and martial artist Keli Yerian investigates how bodies can be powerful communicative resources allowing us to see (read) and convey (write)—by coordinating gesture and other physical as well as verbal cues—varied conceptual, emotional and pragmatic meanings. For participants in the courses Yerian describes, "The body is an important source of knowledge, perception, and communication." All physical communicative resources, however, may not be equally accessible for all people to use.

> Social roles and identities involving gender may shape and limit how bodily practices such as gesture and stance are employed (Kunene & Brookes, 2010) because boys and girls may develop differing ranges of 'sex-class linked' physical practices (Goffman, 1977; Tannen, 1996) that shape the ways they communicate throughout their lives.

Based on a fine-grained analysis of a self-defense course for women, this chapter examines an educational context that challenges norms stemming from differentiated communicative practices based on gender.

In addition to learning how to physically fight off a mock assailant, "students explore, test, and practice combining a variety of multimodal deportments and verbal strategies that can disrupt or prevent a potential assault." With the instructors' guidance, students participate in spontaneous role-plays with a male instructor wearing a special protective suit. In these open-ended simulations, students learn to monitor and coordinate their own use of verbal, vocal and physical communication with the mock-assailant so that their communication patterns "construct coherent stances across modalities" in response to specific kinds of hypothetical situations. "Although some of these strategies are normatively linked to either men or women," says Yerian, "these courses promote a constructivist view of the body as able to engage in multiple practices and display multiple identities." By heightening students' perceptions of others' communicative repertoires, as well as giving students increased awareness, control, and agency over their own, these courses provide a foundation for enacting integrated and expanded multimodal practices of gender to other areas of these women's lives.

Moving out of doors and into the field, in "Pasture Pedagogy: Field and Classroom Reflections on Embodied Teaching," lifelong athlete and college educator Erica Tom describes embodied communication and learning in two contexts: a community-based program for teen women learning to work with horses, and

Tom's own first-year college-level reading and composition course. Adopting particular bodily and verbal stances that underscore the affordances of multimodal communication in these two divergent educational spheres, Tom uses case studies in each setting to explore what can happen when spoken language is no longer simply a default mode for teachers and learners but rather one of many possible tools in participants' communicative repertoires.

In "36 Jewish Gestures"—the title of a research project, a dance solo performed by Haft, and her chapter in this volume, theater artist, choreographer and Professor of Dance Nina Haft explores gendered and cultural dispositions of the body, asking (among other questions), whether we "embody desire and loss in culturally identifiable ways, and what our movement says about us." She describes how, in the process of creating an evening-length dance piece about Jewish gangsters in which she cast all the male roles with female dancers, most of whom had no personal experience with Jewish culture or with performing in drag, she was faced with the challenging task of "teaching them how to move like Jewish men."

As a teacher of and mentor to college-age dancers, Haft found that sharing her solo performance piece, "36 Jewish Gestures," spoke powerfully to her students, helping them critically analyze stereotypes, consider how they might embody questions of their own, and ultimately give voice to feelings about body image, gender, family, and cultural identity. By teasing apart gestures in performance, Haft inhabits, if only momentarily, "a labile space where binaries such as father/daughter, male/female, Jewish/Arab and neighbors/enemies can potentially be deconstructed and reconfigured." Finally, Haft considers what we feel when we 'speak' through culturally inflected movements. She sees dance forms as embodied literacies—types of reading and writing enacted multimodally—that use the whole body for gathering information, constructing knowledge, and transforming and disseminating ideas in specific yet varied social and historical contexts.

Whereas the first six chapters described above offer theory-to-practice examples of multimodal teaching and learning in both community and school contexts, the next three chapters, by actors Eliot Fintushel and Tori Truss, and dancer Jill Homan Randall, describe a wide array of embodied learning activities that can be integrated into college, secondary, elementary, and preschool learning environments.

In "Thinking With Your Skin: Paradoxical Concepts in Physical Theater," performance artist and educator Eliot Fintushel describes how actors in the tradition of physical theatre regularly "think with their bodies." The conceptual mind, he maintains, "is simply too slow to handle the barrage of shifting proprioceptive, social, and environmental information out of which a performer must shape not only an appropriate response but also a telling one." Although this is not easy, skilled performers routinely accomplish this by embodying a selfless "hollow flexibility" (a concept Fintushel borrows from Buddhist teacher Philip Kapleau), wherein they surrender to gravity, to inertia, to the floor, and to other performers' bodies. The student of physical theater takes herself to the edge of feeling in control in order to achieve the lightning-fast, unerring responsiveness that is the foundation of good performance.

Fintushel notes that,

> Paradoxically, the skills and appetites that physical theater invokes are not the ones most frequently rewarded in many traditional educational settings. On the contrary, these skills and talents are more likely to be used on the playground or in the streets, where imagination and play are afforded free reign, and the actors themselves get to define the rules of interaction from moment to moment.

When the physical imagination is invoked in the magic circle of an organized classroom activity, however, learning can occur in new ways for everybody—"for students who are 'good' in the traditional academic sense as well as for people who may be surprised that they are 'performing well.'" Freely and fully using all the corporeal, emotional, and cognitive resources available in physical theater "builds self-confidence and engenders respect for fellow learners by creating a social sphere in which risk-taking is rewarded and everything (even when it's 'wrong') is right." In the life of the imagination, Fintushel says, "there are no mistakes." His chapter offers educators 15 concrete activities to guide learners of varied ages toward 'thinking with their skin.'

In "Visceral Literature: Multimodal Theater Activities for Middle and High School English Language Arts," actor and educator Tori Truss describes how reading can be a full-bodied experience for college-level pre-service teachers as well as for middle schoolers.

> Just as a musician would approach a score, a basketball player the hoop, a dancer the choreography, so too, theater and English language arts students approach the words of a text from different angles and for varied purposes, finding sense and mastery within the recursivity and evolution of the task. To speak the text aloud entails playing with the sounds, rhythms and phrasing, and through such play, new meanings emerge.

As the pre-service teachers in her course begin to physically represent the text by defining place, character and action through movement qualities, gesture, posture and facial expression, they create embodied interpretations, asking and answering questions like, "What might I do if I were in circumstances similar to those of this character?" This connection to a character within a literary work invokes a personal sense of identification with the world of the text, perhaps doubly so when the process of imagining is deliberately corporeal. Holistic engagement that invites students to commit themselves physically, sensorially, emotionally, empathically, and intellectually to literature can deepen textual comprehension for students of all ages and can therefore serve as an important pedagogical tool for teachers at all levels.

Reading literature in this visceral way also connects students with imagined social, cultural, and historical worlds. "Although inspiration and creativity can have a chaotic feel that may at times seem antithetical to traditional notions of classroom order, in courses where multimodal pedagogy involves students in lifting the words off the page and into the body, students' individual and collective movements and social exchanges help them master the script on multiple levels." Such corporeal literacies create empowering opportunities to "gain not only a greater sense of expertise around texts, but also a growing sense of agency and self-efficacy."

Although there is currently increasing attention to integrating kinesthetic activities into academics (as some of the previous chapters describe), in "A Trio: Combining Language, Literacy and Movement in Preschool and Kindergarten Community-Based Dance Classes," professional dancer and educator Jill Randall integrates literacy and language activities into community-based creative dance classes. Her courses involve multiple layers of learning, not just about dance and literacy but also about collaborative social engagement; as the children cultivate relationships with peers and teacher and learn about letters, sounds, words, written language, and story, they also sharpen lifelong movement skills. Drawing from a 21-week creative dance class for 3- to 5-year-olds, the "dense physical learning" described offers classroom teachers concrete ways to connect dance, literacy, and language meaningfully, enjoyably, and coherently to reach young students from varied sociocultural and linguistic backgrounds.

While every bit as grounded in bodily experience as the first ten chapters, the final three chapters also offer rich theoretical analyses of multimodality and embodied learning that suggest where educators and scholars might focus future study and research.

Offering new perspectives on the term "transmission," musician and scholar Matt Rahaim explores how the gestures that accompany Hindustani vocal music are passed down not just from teacher to student but from one generation to the next. In "The Paramparic Body: Gestural Transmission in Indian Music," Rahaim examines "the transmission of bodily dispositions," in order to understand how vocal students come to move like their teachers.

> Whether performing in a crowded auditorium or practicing alone in a room for many hours, the body of a Hindustani vocalist is always already social; it bears the imprint of training. Gestural and vocal motions are highly disciplined, refined techniques that are nurtured through years of sitting in front of a teacher and extended daily practice.

Musicians' hand and body movements, while unique, also inflect as well as reflect the music of their particular teacher and lineage, thus transmitting the tradition while also altering it slightly through an individual's distinctive 'accent.'

And while master musicians offer plenty of clear-cut vocal instruction, gesture itself is rarely explicitly taught or mentioned. Yet such bodily dispositions are, in fact, *catching*. As Rahaim explains, "contagion of posture, gesture, and subtle facial expression (and their affiliated affective states) can occur without any conscious effort on the part of the recipient." Like the mirror neuron research mentioned throughout this Introduction and elsewhere in the volume, Rahaim, too, suggests that this "'action understanding'—the empathetic apprehension of the purpose of another's action as though it were one's own—constitutes rather a different kind of knowing than merely observing the other's hand moving in objective space (Thioux, Gazzola, & Keysers, 2008)." Particularly compelling for educators is the idea that when we observe and then imitate another person, we are actually keying into the mover or actor's intentions—a very significant and "fundamental capability of face-to-face learning," which we are capable of engaging in practically from birth (Gopnik, Meltzoff, & Kuhl, 1999). Understanding is realized in the act of perceiving others' movements and actions and that understanding is thus inscribed in our bodies. It is one of the most fundamental ways in which we learn. "Every singer," Rahaim explains, "though grounded in a tradition, moves and sings differently. Students choose what to accept and what to reject." They choose "how to constitute their own musicking bodies....The processes by which gestural dialects (and their ethical resonances) are constructed, transmitted, and modified have significance beyond music performance. No body, after all, moves in a vacuum; no body learns to be itself by itself." Thus "transmission" in this context is not about rote learning or "imitation" in a pejorative sense; it is about taking in the world, making it one's own, and exercising the modicum of agency we individuals can wield to recast our social worlds as well as our roles or positions within them.

While Rahaim's chapter explores gestural transmission from body to body within and across generations, the next chapter, "Literacies of Touch: Massage Therapy and the Body Composed," examines *literacy between bodies*, paying particular attention to the often-ignored tactile dimensions of literacy broadly conceived.

As both writing researchers and teachers, Holding and Bellwoar interrogate the extent to which tactility is systematically excluded from descriptions of writing processes.

> Although the Cartesian paradigm (where invention happens deep-mindedly) is increasingly questioned via accounts that locate inventional activity in the dynamic space between communicators...we have yet to see such an account move past what is 'visible' to what is simply felt, or touched.

This chapter considers the numerous points of contact that potentially constitute literate activity: where skin meets (reads and writes) the physical world, tracing the interface between the composition and the sensory activity of composing.

Blending an ethnographic portrait of a massage therapist with contemporary theorists of sensation (Serres, 2009; Paterson, 2007; Marks, 2002) and scholars of gesture (Goldin-Meadow, 2003; McNeill, 1996; Streeck, 2009), Holding and Bellwoar explore how touch and kinesthesia constitute learning and literacy "at the interface of bodies." Specifically, they argue that not only do massage and other body-based therapists *read* their clients' bodies through touch (e.g., pain or tightness), but that in so doing, they *compose* or *write* the body, changing the feeling of muscles through those points and patterns of contact. The degree to which reading and writing are indivisible in such tactile contexts highlights the fundamentally multimodal (and inter-subjective) nature of literacy learning—the actual feel of fingers on pencil, pen, keypad, or touch screen—which the authors suggest (following Haas & Witte, 2001) has for too long been given insufficient attention in the fields of writing and composition studies.

Affirming the body's capacity to read, write, and make meaning, scholar and educator Julie Cheville concludes this collection by reminding us that, "a primary focus on linguistic practices has often ascribed the human body a material aspect, yet denied its signifying potential. This is particularly problematic in real and virtual contexts in which the human body is a principle means of expression." Blending qualitative data from a study of embodied learning on the basketball court (Cheville, 2001) with research in social cognitive neuroscience and biosemiotics, Cheville considers the integrated sensory and spatial roles the human body can play in real and virtual contexts where verbal language is not the primary mode of communication. "For researchers and practitioners engaged in contexts of embodied and new media practice, the concept of the 'intersemiotic' is central to documenting the influence of non-linguistic modalities."

Bringing this collection full circle, Cheville considers some of the implications of recent neuroscientific discoveries for sociocultural and multimodal perspectives on teaching and learning, concluding that

> users' intense engagement with new media may have neural origins that produce the affective features we may underestimate when considered through sociocultural theoretic frames. It seems imperative that analyses of new media recognize the intersemiotic character of sign use, namely how social, spatial, sensory, and other sign systems intersect to form a broader 'semiotic ecology' (Lang, 1997).

RESOMATICIZING LEARNING

Although our bodies continually archive memories, experiences, and knowledge through gesture, posture, and corporeal dispositions (Bourdieu, 1977; Downey, 2008, 2010; Gotfrit, 1988; Iacoboni, 2008; Merleau-Ponty, 1945/2005; Noland & Ness, 2008; Sheets-Johnstone, 1998; Skinner, 2007, 2008; Wulff, 2003, 2005; Young, 2002), many conventional classrooms circumscribe what we can think and learn by insisting that we effectively check our bodies at the door. By contrast, the *embodied literacies* and *corporeal pedagogies* described in this volume reveal how multimodal learning can offer people of all ages a dynamic educational experience that promotes individual and collective knowledge construction and creates novel possibilities for agency and development.

These authors inspire not only linguistic, text-based, and multimedia conversations but also embodied dialogues and pathways that might enable teachers, teacher-educators, community-based instructors, and educational researchers to begin collaboratively re-imagining education with the body in mind. By attending to the complex multimodal dimensions of engagement across varied learning contexts for people of diverse ages and backgrounds, this group of authors hopes to spark creative educational thinking about how to enhance learners' access to knowledge, language and literacy and their sense of well-being and agency, through means they—and we—already possess, but to date, may have had too few opportunities to explicitly develop. In the chapters that follow, practitioner-scholars describe varied embodied literacies and corporeal pedagogies that bring to vivid life Elizabeth Carothers Herron's poetic claim that "the body is the text."

Notes

1. For example, in the field of somatics, see the work of Mabel Todd, 1937/2008; Thomas Hanna, 1993; Deane Juhan, 2003; Barbara Sheets-Johnstone, 1998; Caryn McHose & Kevin Frank, 2006; Sondra Fraleigh, 2004; and Bonnie Bainbridge Cohen, 1993.
2. For other accounts of embodied and multimodal learning, also see Bresler, 2004; Cahnmann-Taylor & Siegesmund, 2008; Cahnmann-Taylor & Souto-Manning, 2010; Cheville, 2001; Donahue & Stewart, 2010; Downey, 2008, 2010; Gardner, 1983; Gilbert, 1992, 2002, 2006; Goodwin, 2000; Hanna, 1979, 1999; Jewitt & Kress, 2003; Katz, 2008; Rose, 1999, 2004; Stein, 2008.
3. See, for example, Alvermann, 2010, 2011; Barton & Hamilton, 1998; Baynham, 1995; Brandt, 1990/2011; Dyson, 1997; Gee, 2012; Heath, 2000, 2012; Hull & Katz, 2006; Hull & Schultz, 2002; Cope & Kalantzis, 2000; Katz, 2008; Knobel, 1999; Knobel & Lankshear, 2007; Kress & Van Leuuwen, 2001; Lankshear & Knobel, 2006; Leander & Vasudevan, 2009; Morrell, 2004; Morrell & Duncan-Andrade, 2006; New London Group, 1996; Schultz, 2003; Street, 1985; Vasudevan, 2008.

4. See, for example, Heath, 1999, 2000; Jewitt, 2005, 2008, 2009; Kress et al., 2001; Kress et al., 2005; Jewitt & Kress, 2003; Stein, 2004, 2008, among others.

5. See Abrahamson et al., 2011, 2012; Barsalou, 1999; Bresler, 2004; Cahnmann-Taylor & Siegesmund, 2008; Cahnmann-Taylor & Souto-Manning, 2010; Cheville, 2001, 2005; Damasio, 1994, 1999; Gardner, 1983; Gazzaniga, 2008; Goldin-Meadow, 2003, 2005; Goodwin, 1994, 2000; Hannaford, 1995; Hull & Nelson, 2005; Jewitt, 2005, 2008, 2009; Kendon, 2004; Kress, Jewitt, Bourne, Franks, Hardcastle, Jones, & Reid, 2005; Kress & van Leeuwen, 2001; Lehrer, 2007, 2009; McNeill, 1996, 2005; Sacks, 1970, 1989, 1995, 2007, 2010; Stein, 2008; Trninic & Abrahamson, 2012; van Leeuwen, 2006.

6. See Damasio (1994), *Descartes' Error: Emotion, Reason and the Human Brain.*

7. See Damasio (1999), *The Feeling of What Happens: Body and Emotion in the Making of Consciousness*; Damasio (2003), *Looking for Spinoza: Joy, Sorrow and the Feeling Brain*; and Damasio (2012) *Self Comes to Mind: Constructing the Conscious Brain.*

8. See Bakhtin, 1981; Bauman & Briggs, 1990; Holland, Lachicotte, Skinner, & Cain, 1998; Hull & Katz, 2006; Katz, 2008; Kondo, 1990; Noland & Ness, 2008; Urciuoli, 1995; Vygotsky, 1978, among others.

9. Barthes, 1957; Birdwhistell, 1970; Bourdieu, 1977; Derrida, 1982; Foucault, 1977, 1981; Goffman, 1959; Hall, 1959, 1966; Ingold, 2011; Leder, 1990; Mauss, 1935/ 1973; Merleau-Ponty, 1945/2005; Scollon & Scollon, 1981.

Works Cited

Abrahamson, D., Trninic, D., Gutiérrez, J. F., Huth, J., & Lee, R. G. (2011). Hooks and shifts: A dialectical study of mediated discovery. *Technology, Knowledge, and Learning, 16*(1), 55–85.

Abrahamson, D., Gutiérrez, J. F., Charoenying, T., Negrete, A. G., & Bumbacher, E. (2012). Fostering hooks and shifts: Tutorial tactics for guided mathematical discovery. *Technology, Knowledge, and Learning, 17*(1–2), 61–86. doi: 10.1007/s10758–012–9192–7

Alvermann, D.E. (Ed.). (2010). *Adolescents' online literacies: Connecting classrooms, digital media, and popular culture.* New York: Peter Lang.

Alvermann, D.E. (2011). Popular culture and literacy practices. In M.L. Kamil, P.D. Pearson, E.B. Moje, & P.P. Afflerbach (Eds.), *Handbook of Reading Research,* Vol. 4 (pp. 541–560). New York: Routledge.

Bakhtin, M.M. (1981). Discourse in the novel (C. Emerson & M. Holquist, Trans.). In M. Holquist (Ed.), *The dialogic imagination: Four essays* (pp. 259–422). Austin: University of Texas Press.

Barsalou, L. W. (1999). Perceptual symbol systems. *Behavioral and Brain Sciences, 22,* 577–660.

Barthes, R. (1957). *Mythologies.* Paris: Editions du Seuil.

Barton, D., & Hamilton, M. (1998). *Local literacies: Reading and writing in one community.* London: Routledge.

Bauman, R., & Briggs, C. L. (1990). Poetics and performance as critical perspectives on language and social life. *Annual Review of Anthropology, 19,* 59–88.

Baynham, M. (1995). *Literacy practices: Investigating literacy in social contexts.* London: Routledge.

Baynton, D. (2008). Beyond culture, Deaf studies and the Deaf body. In H. Bauman (Ed.), *Open your eyes: Deaf studies talking.* (pp. 293–313). Minneapolis: University of Minnesota Press.

Birdwhistell, R. L. (1970). *Kinesics and context: Essays on body motion communication.* Philadelphia: University of Pennsylvania Press.

Blakeslee, S., & Blakeslee, M. (2007). *The body has a mind of its own: How body maps in your brain help you do (almost) everything better.* New York: Random House.

Bourdieu, P. (1977). *Outline of a theory of practice.* Cambridge, UK: Cambridge University Press.

Brandt, D. (1990/2011). *Literacy as involvement: The acts of writers, readers and texts.* Carbondale: Southern Illinois University Press.

Bresler, L. (Ed.). (2004). *Knowing bodies, moving minds: Towards embodied teaching and learning.* Dordrecht; Boston; London: Kluwer.

Bruner, J. (1990). *Acts of meaning.* Cambridge, MA: Harvard University Press.

Bruner, J. (1994). The remembered self. In U. Neisser & R. Fivush (Eds.), *The remembering self: Construction and agency in self narrative* (pp. 41–54). Cambridge, UK: Cambridge University Press.

Butler, J. (1993). *Bodies that matter: On the discursive limits of sex.* New York: Routledge.

Cahnmann-Taylor, M., & Siegesmund, R. (Eds.). (2008). *Arts-based research in education: Foundations for practice.* New York: Routledge.

Cahnmann-Taylor, M., & and Souto-Manning, M. (2010). *Teachers act up! Creating multicultural learning communities through theatre.* New York: Teachers College Press.

Chaiklin, S., & Lave, J. (1996). *Understanding practice: Perspectives on activity and context.* Cambridge, UK: Cambridge University Press.

Cheville, J. (2001). *Minding the body: What student athletes know about learning.* Portsmouth, NH: Boynton/Cook.

Cheville, J. (2005). Confronting the problem of embodiment. *International Journal of Qualitative Studies in Education, 18*(1), 85–107.

Cohen, B. B. (1993). *Sensing, feeling and action: The experiential anatomy of body-mind centering.* Northampton, MA: Contact Editions.

Cope, B., & Kalantzis, M. (Eds.). (2000). *Multiliteracies: Literacy learning and the design of social futures.* London: Routledge.

Cranz, G. (1998). *The chair: Rethinking culture, body and design.* New York: W. W. Norton.

Csordas, T. (1994). *Embodiment and experience: The existential ground of culture and self* (pp. 143–162). New York: Cambridge University Press.

Csordas, T. (1999). Embodiment and cultural phenomenology. In G. Weiss & H. F. Haber (Eds.). *Perspectives on embodiment: The intersections of nature and culture.* New York: Routledge.

Damasio, A. (1994). *Descartes' error: Emotion, reason and the human brain.* New York: Avon Books.

Damasio, A. (1999). *The feeling of what happens: Body and emotion in the making of consciousness.* San Diego, CA: Harcourt.

Damasio, A. (2003). *Looking for Spinoza: Joy, sorrow and the feeling brain.* Orlando, FL: Harcourt.

Damasio, A. (2012). *Self comes to mind: Constructing the conscious brain.* New York: Vintage Books.

Derrida, J., & McDonald, C. (1982). Choreographies. In N. Holland (Ed.), *Feminist Interpretations of Jacques Derrida* (pp. 23–41). University Park: Pennsylvania State University Press.

Desjarlais, R. (1992). *Body and emotion: The aesthetics of healing in the Nepal Himalayas.* Philadelphia: University of Pennsylvania Press.

Dewey, J. (1938). *Experience and education.* New York: Macmillan.

Donahue, M., & Stewart, J. (2010). *Artful teaching: Integrating the arts for understanding across the curriculum K-8.* New York: Teachers College Press.

Downey, G. (2008). Scaffolding imitation in capoeira: Physical education and enculturation in an Afro-Brazilian art. *American Anthropologist, 110*(2), 204–213.

Downey, G. (2010). 'Practice without theory': A neuroanthropological perspective on embodied learning. *Journal of the Royal Anthropological Institute,* (S22–S40).

Dyson, A. H. (1997). *Writing superheroes: Contemporary childhood, popular culture, and classroom literacy.*

New York: Teachers College Press.

Farnell, B. (Ed.). (1995). *Human action signs in cultural context: The visible and the invisible in movement and dance.* Metuchen, NJ: The Scarecrow Press.

Farnell, Brenda. (1999). Moving bodies, acting selves. *Annual Review of Anthropology, 28,* 341–373.

Finnegan, R. (2002). *Communicating: The multiple modes of human interconnection.* London: Routledge.

Foucault, M. (1977). *Discipline and punish: The birth of the prison.* New York: Vintage Books.

Foucault, M. (1981). The order of discourse. In R. Young (Ed.), *Untying the text: A poststructuralist reader* (pp. 48–78). New York: Routledge, Kegan, Paul.

Fraleigh, S. (2004). *Dancing identity: Metaphysics in motion.* Pittsburgh, PA: University of Pittsburgh Press.

Fraser, M., & Greco, M. (2005). *The body: A reader.* New York: Routledge.

Franks, A. (2003). 'Palmers' kiss: Shakespeare, school drama and semiotics. In G. Kress and C. Jewitt (Eds.), *Multimodal literacy* (pp. 155–172). New York: Peter Lang.

Gardner, H. (1983/2004/2011). *Frames of mind: The theory of multiple intelligences.* New York: Basic Books.

Gazzinaga, M.S., et al. (2008). *Learning, arts and the brain.* The Dana Consortium Report on Arts and Cognition (4th ed.). Dana Foundation. New York and Washington, DC: Dana Press.

Gee, J. P. (2012). *Social linguistics and literacies: Ideology in discourses.* Fourth edition. London: Falmer Press.

Gibson, J. (1979). *The ecological approach to visual perception.* Boston: Houghton Mifflin.

Gilbert, A. G. (1992). *Creative dance for all ages.* Reston, VA: National Dance Association/AAH-PERD.

Gilbert, A. G. (1977/2002). *Teaching the three Rs through movement.* Bethesda, MD: National Dance Education Organization/AAHPERD.

Gilbert, A. G. (2006). *Brain-compatible dance education.* Reston, VA: National Dance Association/AAH-PERD.

Goffman, E. (1959). *The presentation of self in everyday life.* New York: Anchor Books.

Goffman, E. (1977). The arrangement between the sexes. *Theory and Society 4*:(3), 301–331.

Goldin-Meadow, S. (2003). *Hearing gesture: How our hands help us think.* Cambridge, MA: Belknap Press of Harvard University Press.

Goldin-Meadow, S. (2005). What language creation in the manual modality tells us about the foundations of language. *The Linguistic Review, 22*: 199–225.

Goldin-Meadow, S., Wagner-Cook, S. & Mitchell, Z. (2009). Gesturing gives children new ideas about math. *Psychological Science, 20*(3): 267–72.

Goodwin, C. (2000). Action and embodiment within situated human interaction. *Journal of Pragmatics, 32*: 1489–1522.

Goodwin, C. (1994). Professional vision. *American Anthropologist, 96*: 3: 606–633.

Gopnik, A., Meltzoff, A., & Kuhl, P. (1999). *The scientist in the crib: What early learning tells us about the mind.* New York: William Morrow.

Gotfrit, J. (1988). Women dancing back: Disruption and the politics of pleasure. *Journal of Education, 170*(3), 122–141.

Groce, N.E. (1985). *Everyone here spoke sign language: Hereditary deafness on Martha's Vineyard.* Cambridge, MA: Harvard University Press.

Haas, C., & Witte, S. P. (2001). Writing as embodied practice: The case of engineering standards. *Journal of Business and Technical Communication, 15*, 413–457.

Hall, E. T. (1959). *The silent language.* Garden City, NY: Doubleday.

Hall, E. T. (1966). *The hidden dimension.* Garden City, NY: Doubleday.

Hanna, J. L. (1979/1987). *To dance is human: A theory of nonverbal communication.* Chicago: University of Chicago Press.

Hanna, J. L. (1999). *Partnering dance and education: Intelligent moves for changing times.* Champaign, IL: Human Kinetics.

Hanna, T. (1979/1980/1993). *The body of life: Creating new pathways for sensory awareness and fluid movement.* Rochester, VT: Healing Arts Press.

Hannaford, C. (1995). *Smart moves: Why learning is not all in your head.* Alexander, NC: Great Ocean Publishers.

Heath, S., & Roach, A. (1999). Imaginative actuality: Learning in the arts during nonschool hours. Chapter in E. Fiske (Ed.), *Champions of Change: The Impact of the Arts on Learning.* Washington DC: Arts Education Partnership and President's Committee on the Arts and Humanities, 19–34.

Heath, S.B. (2000). Seeing our way into learning. *Cambridge Journal of Education, 30*(1), 121–132.

Heath, S.B. (2012). *Words at work and play: Three decades in family and community life.* Cambridge, UK: Cambridge University Press.

Holland, D., Lachicotte, W., Skinner, D., & Cain, C. (1998/2001). *Identity and agency in cultural world*s. Cambridge, MA: Harvard University Press.

Hull, G., & Katz, M.L. (2006). Crafting an agentive self: Case studies of digital storytelling. *Research in the Teaching of English, 41*(1), 43–81.

Hull, G., & Schultz, K. (2002). *Schools out!: Bridging out-of-school literacies with classroom practice.* New York: Teachers College Press.

Hull, G., & Nelson, M. (2005). Locating the semiotic power of multimodality. *Written Communication, 22*(2): 1–38.

Iacoboni, M. (2008). *Mirroring people: The science of empathy and how we connect with others.* New York: Picador, Farrar, Straus & Giroux.

Ingold, T. (2011). *Being alive: Essays on movement, knowledge and description.* New York: Routledge.

Jang, H., Reeve, J., & Deci, E.L. (2010). Engaging students in learning activities: It is not autonomy support or structure but autonomy support and structure. *Journal of Educational Psychology, 102*(3), 588–600.

Jewitt, C. (2005). Multimodal reading and writing for the 21st century. *Discourse: Studies in the Cultural Politics of Education* 26(3), 315–332.

Jewitt, C. (2008). *Technology, literacy, learning: A multimodality approach.* London: Routledge.

Jewitt, C. (Ed.) (2009). *The Routledge handbook of multimodal analysis.* London: Routledge.

Jewitt, C. & Kress, G. (2003). *Multimodal literacy.* New York: Peter Lang.

Juhan, D. (2003). *Job's body: A handbook for bodywork.* (3rd ed.). Barrytown, NY: Station Hill Press.

Katz, M. L. (1995). Language practices in deaf education: How ideology shapes individual lives. *Open Letter: Australian Journal for Adult Literacy and Research* 6(1), 57–74.

Katz, M. L. (2008). Growth in motion: Supporting young women's identity and embodied development through dance after school. *Afterschool Matters, 7,* 12–22.

Kendon, A. (2004) *Gesture: Visible action as utterance.* Cambridge, UK: Cambridge University Press.

Klima, E., & Bellugi, U. (1979). *The signs of language.* Cambridge, MA: Harvard University Press.

Knobel, M. (1999). *Everyday literacies: Students, discourses and social practices.* New York: Peter Lang.

Knobel, M., & Lankshear, C. (Eds.). (2007). *A new literacies sampler.* New York: Peter Lang.

Kondo, D. (1990). *Crafting selves: Power, gender, and discourses of identity in a Japanese workplace.* Chicago: University of Chicago Press.

Kress, G., Jewitt, C., Bourne, J., Franks, A., Hardcastle, J., Jones, K., & Reid, E. (2005). *Urban classrooms, subject English: Multimodal perspectives on teaching and learning.* London: RoutledgeFalmer.

Kress, G., Jewitt, C., Ogborn, J., & Tsatsarelis, C. (2001). *Multimodal teaching and learning.* London: Continuum.

Kress, G., & van Leeuwen, T. (2001). *Multimodal discourse: The modes and media of contemporary communication.* New York: Oxford University Press.

Kunene, R., & Brookes, H. (2010, July 26). *Do cultural norms related to gender influence gestural behavior among South African children and adults?* Paper presented at the International Society for Gesture Studies (ISGS). European University Viadrina, Frankfurt/Oder, Germany.

Lakoff, George, & Johnson, Mark. (1980). *Metaphors we live by.* Chicago: University of Chicago Press.

Lane, Harlan. (1984). *When the mind hears: A history of the Deaf.* New York: Vintage.

Lang, A. (1997). Non-Cartesian artifacts in dwelling activities: Steps toward a semiotic ecology. In M. Cole, Y. Engeström, & O. Vasquez (Eds.), *Mind, culture, and activity: Seminal papers from the laboratory of comparative human cognition* (pp. 185–204). Cambridge, UK: Cambridge University Press.

Lankshear, C., & Knobel, M. (2006). *New literacies: Everyday practices and classroom learning* (2nd edition). Maidenhead and New York: Open University Press.

Lave, J., & Wenger, E. (1991/1993). *Situated learning: Legitimate peripheral participation.* New York: Cambridge University Press.

Leander, K., & Vasudevan, L. (2009). Multimodality and mobile culture. In C. Jewitt (Ed.), *Handbook of multimodal analysis* (pp. 127–139). London: Routledge.

Leder, D. (1990). *The absent body.* Chicago: University of Chicago Press.

Lehrer, J. (2007). *Proust was a neuroscientist.* Boston: Mariner Books.

Lehrer, J. (2009). *How we decide.* Boston: Mariner Books.

Marks, L. (2002). *Touch: Sensuous theory and multisensory media.* Minneapolis: University of Minneapolis Press.

Mauss, M., (1935/1973). Techniques of the body. *Economy and Society, 2,* 70–88.

McHose, C. & Frank, K. (2006). *How life moves: Explorations in meaning and body awareness.* Berkeley, CA: North Atlantic Books.

McNeill, D. (1996). *Hand and mind: What gestures reveal about thought.* Chicago: University of Chicago Press.

McNeill, D. (2005). *Gesture and thought.* Chicago: University of Chicago Press.

Merleau-Ponty, M. (1945/2005). *The phenomenology of perception.* London: Routledge.

Morrell, E. (2004). *Linking literacy and popular culture: Finding connections for lifelong learning.* Norwood, MA: Christopher-Gordon.

Morrell, E., & Duncan-Andrade, J. (2006). Popular culture and critical media pedagogy in secondary classrooms. *International Journal of Learning, 12,* 1–11.

Naceur, A., & Schiefele, U. (2005). Motivation and learning—The role of interest in construction of representation of text and long-term retention: Inter- and intraindividual analyses. *European Journal of Psychology of Education, 20*(2), 155–170.

National Research Council and the Institute of Medicine. (2004). *Engaging schools: Fostering high school students' motivation to learn.* Committee on Increasing High School Students' Engagement and Motivation to Learn. Board on Children, Youth, and Families, Division of Behavioral and Social Sciences and Education. Washington, DC: The National Academies Press.

New London Group, (1996). A pedagogy of multiliteracies: Designing social futures. *Harvard Educational Review, 66*(1), 60–92.

Noland, C., & Ness, S.A. (2008). *Migrations of gesture.* Minneapolis and London: University of Minnesota Press.

Padden, C., & Humphries, T. (2005). *Inside deaf culture*. Cambridge, MA: Harvard University Press.

Paterson, M. (2007). *The senses of touch: Haptics, affects and technologies*. Oxford and New York: Berg.

Robinson, K. (2006). TED Talk. http://www.ted.com/talks/ken_robinson_says_schools_kill_crea tivity.html?utm_expid=166907–14&utm_referrer=http%3A%2F%2Fwww.ted.com%2Fsearch%3F cat%3Dss_all%26q%3Dsir%2Bken%2Brobinson

Rizzolatti, G., & Arbib, M.A. (1998). Language within our grasp. *Trends in Neuroscience, 21*: 188–194.

Rizzolatti, G., & Craighero, L. (2004). The mirror neuron system. *Annual Review of Neuroscience, 27*, 169–192.

Rizzolatti, G., & Sinigaglia, C. (F. Anderson, Trans.). (2008). *Mirrors in the brain: How our minds share actions, emotions, and experience*. New York: Oxford University Press.

Rogoff, B. (1990). *Apprenticeship in thinking: Cognitive development in social context*. Oxford, UK: Oxford University Press.

Rogoff, B. (2003). *The cultural nature of human development*. Oxford and New York: Oxford University Press.

Rose, M. (1999). "Our hands will know": The development of tactile diagnostic skill—teaching, learn- ing, and situated cognition in a physical therapy program. *Anthropology and Education Quarterly, 30*(2): 133–160.

Rose, M. (2004). *The mind at work: Valuing the intelligence of the American worker*. New York: Penguin.

Sacks, O. (1970). *The man who mistook his wife for a hat and other clinical tales*. New York: Harper & Row.

Sacks, O. (1989). *Seeing voices: A journey into the world of the deaf*. New York: Vintage.

Sacks, O. (1995). *An anthropologist on Mars: Seven paradoxical tales*. New York: Vintage.

Sacks, O. (2007). *Musicophilia: Tales of music and the brain*. New York: Knopf.

Sacks, O. (2011). *The mind's eye*. New York: Vintage.

Schultz, K. (2003). *Listening: A framework for teaching across differences*. New York: Teachers College Press.

Scollon, R., & Scollon, S. (1981). *Narrative, literacy and face in interethnic communication*. Norwood, NJ: Ablex.

Serres, M. (2009). *The five senses: A philosophy of mingled bodies*. (M. Sankey & P. Cowley, Trans.). London: Continuum Publishing Group.

Sheets-Johnstone, M. (1998). *The primacy of movement*. Philadelphia: John Benjamins.

Shulman, L. (1987). Knowledge and teaching: Foundations of the new reform. *Harvard Educational Review, 57*, 1–22.

Skinner, J. (2007). The salsa class: A complexity of globalization, cosmopolitans and emotions. *Identities: Global Studies in Culture and Power, 14*, 485–506.

Skinner, J. (2008). Women dancing back—and forth: Resistance and self-regulation in Belfast salsa. *Dance Research Journal, 40*(1), 65–77.

Stein, P. (2004). Representation, rights, and resources: Multimodal pedagogies in the language and lit- eracy classroom. In B. Norton & K. Toohey (Eds.), *Critical pedagogies and language learning* (pp. 95–115). Cambridge, UK: Cambridge University Press.

Stein, P. (2008). *Multimodal pedagogies in diverse classrooms: Representation, rights and resources*. London; New York: Routledge.

Streeck, J. (2009). *Gesturecraft: The manu-facture of meaning*. Philadelphia: John Benjamins.

Street, B. (1985). *Literacy in theory and practice*. Cambridge, UK: Cambridge University Press.

Thioux, M., Gazzola, V., & Keysers, C. (2008). Action understanding: How, what and why. *Current Biology 18*(10), R431–R434.

Todd, M. (1937/2008). *The thinking body*. Gouldsboro, ME: The Gestalt Journal Press.

Trninic, D., & Abrahamson, D. (2012). Embodied artifacts and conceptual performances. In J. v.

Aalst, K. Thompson, M. J. Jacobson, & P. Reimann (Eds.), *Proceedings of the International Conference of the Learning Sciences: Future of Learning* (ICLS 2012) (Vol. 1: Full papers, pp. 283–290). Sydney: University of Sydney/ISLS.

Urciuoli, B. (1995). The indexical structure of visibility. In B. Farnell (Ed.), *Human action signs in cultural context: The visible and the invisible in movement and dance*, (pp. 189–215). Metuchen, NJ, & London: Scarecrow.

Van Leeuwen, T. (2006). Semiotic theory and semiotic practice: The case of Barnett Newman. In M. Amano (Ed.), *Multimodality: Towards the most efficient communications by humans* (pp. 17–27). Proceedings of the Sixth International Conference Studies for the Integrated Text Science. Nagoya, Japan: Graduate School of Letters, Nagoya University.

Vasudevan, L. (2008). "A picture can do things words can't": Transforming representations in literacy research. In J. Flood, D. Lapp, & S.B. Heath (Eds.), *Handbook of research on teaching literacy through the visual and communicative arts*, volume 2 (pp. 187–194). Mahwah, NJ: Lawrence Erlbaum.

Vygotsky, L. S. (1978). *Mind in society: The development of higher psychological processes.* Cambridge, MA: Harvard University Press.

Welton, D. (Ed.). (1999). *The body: Classic and contemporary readings.* London: Blackwell.

Wenger, E. (1998). *Communities of practice: Learning, meaning and identity.* Cambridge: Cambridge University Press.

Wulff, H. 2003. Moving Irish bodies: Moral politics, national identity and dance. In E. Archetti &N. Dyck, (Eds.) *Sport, dance and embodied identities* (pp. 179–196). E. Archetti and N. Dyck, eds. Oxford, UK: Berg.

Wulff, H. (2005). Memories in motion: The Irish dancing body. *Body & Society, 11*(4), 45–62.

Young, K. (2002). The memory of the flesh. The family body in somatic psychology. *Body & Society, 8*(3), 25–47.

Figure 1. Teen summer dance intensive rehearsal.

CHAPTER ONE

Growth in Motion

Supporting Young Women's Embodied Identity and Cognitive Development Through Dance After School [1]

MIRA-LISA KATZ

Dance is many things to many people. It can be a discipline, a practice, a ritual, an exercise, a form of prayer or meditation, a kind of storytelling or seduction, or a medium for artistic expression. In addition to being a powerful means of knowing oneself and communicating with others, dance can also support cognitive and developmental processes and identity formation.

In response to a friend's whimsical suggestion in 1977, I started taking classes in modern dance, ballet, and a form of classical Indian storytelling dance called Kathak. Having come to dance as an older teen, I later became intrigued with how activities outside of school can inform classroom-based learning. Given the number of choices young people have for how to spend their time outside of school, I wanted to learn more about what motivated the young women with whom I dance regularly to dedicate several days each week to their art.

As a language and literacy educator since 1991, I have worked with adolescents and adults in a variety of school, college, workplace, and community settings. Several years ago, in an effort to weave my dance and academic universes together, I began to explore the world of dance as an educational researcher, hoping to unveil the distinctive dimensions of embodied learning, that is, how we learn and know through our bodies. My forays into embodied teaching and learning fortuitously coincided with a surge of scholarship on multimodality in education. Being involved in both dance and educational research has helped me to make sense of embodied learning and development—growth in motion—at two community-based dance studios serving children, youth, and adults, ages 3 to 85.

This chapter highlights the perspectives of young women who have participated in dance for many years. Their viewpoints reveal the unique multimodal nature of embodied learning; in dance classes, teachers and learners communicate through a variety of modes: visual, auditory, kinesthetic, spatial, musical, rhythmic, tactile, gestural, and linguistic. I employed ethnographic, multimodal, and discourse analyses to investigate how dance fosters the cognitive and attitudinal benefits documented in the literature on arts learning in out-of-school-time programs.

COGNITIVE AND ATTITUDINAL BENEFITS OF ARTS AFTER SCHOOL

A substantial body of scholarship on the effects of the arts and afterschool activities has shown that when young people are allowed to determine social networks around self-defined areas of interest and when young women in particular are involved in physical activities such as sports and dance, they tend to perform better academically; build more constructive relationships with peers and adults; learn to collaborate, think critically, and solve problems; and develop more confidence and self-esteem (Deasy, 2002; Eccles & Templeton, 2002; Fiske, 1999). While critics have often suggested that popular cultural forms offer little more than shallow outlets for personal expression, there is ample evidence that popular culture and the arts can offer youth a sense of self, voice, and place in broader artistic, cultural, and communal conversations (Bresler, 2004; Eccles & Templeton, 2002; Eisner, 2002; Flood, Heath, & Lapp, 1997; McCarthy, Ondaatje, Zakaras, & Brooks, 2004; Morrell, 2004).[2] The experiences of the young women in my study confirm and expand on these findings.

EMBODIED COGNITION AND MULTIMODAL LEARNING

In Western thought, as dance anthropologist Farnell (1995) humorously writes, "[w]hen attention has been paid to a moving body it often seems to have lost its mind" (p. 8). However, as scholars from many disciplines have challenged mind-centered notions of cognition and individually based conceptions of development, theories of embodiment have increasingly begun to inform educational research (Bresler, 2004; Catterall, Chapleau, & Iwanaga, 1999; Cheville, 2001; Kress, Jewitt, Ogborn, & Tsatsarelis, 2001). Gardner's (1999) theory of "multiple intelligences" has rightly garnered significant public attention, helping a broad audience widen their notions of what it means to "be smart." Yet, helpful as this has been, Cheville

(2001) cautions that distinctions between one intelligence and another "risk reducing learners to labels without disrupting the significant philosophical divide between mind and body that has long stymied accounts of what it means to learn and know" (p. 11). Our difficulty in acknowledging the extent to which our bodies mediate cognition reflects, at least in part, our reluctance as Westerners to perceive cognition or emotion as embodied (Bresler, 2004; Damasio, 1994; Finnegan, 2002; Fraser & Greco, 2005). Some anthropological studies (Urciuoli, 1995) suggest that we convey messages and self-representations differently depending on whether we are talking, singing, writing, or dancing. In my research, I examine learning and knowing in the situated physical context of dance, where cognition, self, and emotion are consciously filtered through muscle and movement as well as through mind, language, and social interaction.

Self and Identity

In recent years, the concept of identity has come under scrutiny by scholars in many fields (Hall, 1996; Heath & McLaughlin, 1993; Holland, Lachicotte, Skinner, & Cain, 1998; Hull & Zacher, 2004; Kondo, 1990). Many of these discussions have challenged the static nature of conventional, psychologically-based notions of self—what anthropologist Kondo (1990) calls "seemingly incorrigible Western assumptions about the 'primacy' of the individual and the boundedness and fixity of personal identity" (p. 26). Following research on identity and agency (Holland et al., 1998), my study treats both in more fluid terms: Identity is ever-changing in response to social contexts. As Hull and Katz (2006) put it, "We enact the selves we want to become in relation to others—sometimes in concert with them, sometimes in opposition to them, but always in relation to them" (p. 47). Our sense of self-determination or agency at any given moment is constrained by specific social, cultural, and historical contexts, yet people can develop their agentive selves using the unique repertoire of cultural resources, relationships, and artifacts available. Afterschool programs of many different kinds seem to be especially good at helping young people gain access to such resources.

Maxine Sheets-Johnstone, author of *The Primacy of Movement* (1998), extends the notion of agency into the bodily realm. "Movement," she claims, "is at the root of our sense of agency...it is the generative source of our notions of space and time....[M]oving is a way of knowing" (p. xv). If she is correct, how might we expand our understandings of self and social connections to include our moving bodies? How are corporeal learning and knowing unique? Might such learning support development in ways that other forms of learning cannot?

STUDYING DANCE AS AN EDUCATIONAL CONTEXT

For this study, I was interested in the following questions:

- In what ways is participation in dance connected to the development of young women's identities?
- How does dance contribute to the cognitive, social, and emotional growth of the young women I studied?
- How might the nature of learning in dance help us rethink the organization of learning both in and out of school?

Methods

Combining ethnographic, multimodal, and discourse analytic strategies (Chouliaraki & Fairclough, 1999; Denzin & Lincoln, 1994; Dyson & Genishi, 2006; Kress et al., 2001), I explored a rich range of data sources: informal conversations, focus groups, interviews, student dance journals, photographs, artists' statements, field notes, and over two hundred hours of videotaped classroom observations. Together, these research methods and data provided access to how young participants viewed the self through dance, offering insights into their perceptions about potential connections between dance and everyday life.

Context

The original study, conducted from 2002 to 2005, focused on nine high school-age women who had been learning dance together at the Oakland Dance Center[3] since preschool. "The teens," as their teachers called them, welcomed opportunities to reflect on dance together. They enthusiastically engaged in informal conversations in hallways and dressing rooms, in focus groups and individual interviews, and in videotaped classes and rehearsals. They also kept dance journals (Katz, 2010), writing candidly about what dance meant to them and what it taught them about themselves and others. They explained how dance classes and rehearsals helped them negotiate multiple social worlds by creating habits of mind and body that filtered favorably—and seamlessly—into their public and academic worlds.

In 2006, with the support of a grant from the Robert Bowne Foundation, I expanded my research to include 21 young women of diverse sociocultural and socioeconomic backgrounds who participated in a Teen Summer Dance Intensive at the Berkeley Center for Dance. The Summer Intensive, then in its fifth year, hosted teens from over a dozen public and private schools in the Bay Area. Several dancers had attended every Summer Intensive since its start in 2002.

As arts education researchers have frequently pointed out, participation in the arts—while potentially beneficial to students of all backgrounds—is particularly helpful to young people considered "at risk" due to factors associated with low socioeconomic status: challenging home situations, low academic performance, dropping out, or asocial or unsafe behaviors (Catterall, 1998; Fiske, 1999; Heath, 1999; McCarthy et al., 2004). Some, though not all, of the teen participants at the Oakland and Berkeley dance studios were considered "at risk" in these ways. A number of them contended with difficult circumstances at home, such as chronically ill siblings or complex living arrangements.

The dancers at the Oakland Center came primarily from middle and working class families, and seven of the nine dancers attended public schools. Although several of the 21 dancers at the Berkeley studio's Teen Summer Dance Intensive attended private schools, the majority attended public schools serving high numbers of students from low-income neighborhoods. In 2006, one-third of these young women received partial or total scholarships to the dance program based on financial need.

How Dance Shapes Lives

The 30 young women in this study have repeatedly identified the following benefits of learning through dance:

- A chance to develop a sense of control over their bodies, emotions, intellects, and interactions
- An unusual capacity to take the long view of their own development
- An opportunity to participate in a supportive, communal learning environment
- Multiple, multimodal entry points for learning dance skills and for expanding social, physical, and intellectual repertoires
- A constructive conception of "mistakes" that underscores how strategic risk-taking fosters learning and development

Developing a Sense of Control

The young women in my study said that learning dance gave them greater control over both their bodies and minds. Not only did this control shape how they felt physically and mentally, but it also allowed them to monitor their feelings and manage their actions in other contexts. "I feel like more than anything dance has…taught me that

I can control my body…and I sort of have some control over how I feel because…dancing makes me feel so much better. It's a way of channeling my emotions and understanding them," said 15-year-old Maddy (focus group, June 18, 2003).

Jamaica, from the Berkeley studio, said that dance helped her concentrate. "It takes your mind off [problems].…You're in the moment and you're not thinking about anything else that's going on. To me dancing is my form of therapy" (focus group, August 3, 2006). Aurelia, a fellow Berkeley dancer, similarly acknowledged the power of dance to make her feel safe: "Dance to me is like an emergency exit— say, like you were in a building and it was burning, you would use an emergency exit to get out of it. It's sort of like the world is—it's like full of all these brutal realities, and dance to me is like a different world, it's safe." Aurelia also described how she learned self-confidence through dance, becoming more patient with herself. "I used to be really insecure before dance," she said. "[Now] it gives me confidence just being able to look at myself in the mirror and say, hey…if I can't do that, then I can't do it, you know, and I can work on it" (focus group, August 3, 2006).

Maddy, from Oakland, noted how the effects of dance transferred to other contexts of her life. "Like if I have to write a big paper right after I've been to dance, it's easier than if I'm just stressing out about it for a whole evening," she said. "You sort of have to be balanced and keep yourself in check a little bit. Not all the time, but you do have to have self-control.…Like, if you're all over the place inside your head…you can't focus. After dancing…I can manage [my emotions] better . . ." (focus group, June 18, 2003). The dancers' sense of control and their capacity to use dance to construct safe spaces became powerful tools for developing a sense of agency and self-efficacy outside the studio.

Taking the Long View of Their Own Development

Researchers have noted that sustained involvement in the arts leads to habits of mind and body that permeate other domains of life. For these young women, their continued involvement in dance seems to have given them an unusual capacity to take stock of their own growth across time.

For example, Jena, a teen who in 2004 had been studying at the Oakland studio since 1990, said that she appreciated the shifts she observed in herself over the years: "[Dancing] makes me feel good about myself.…And it makes me feel proud…because I know that even if I don't feel it in my body, a year ago I was different" (interview, February 1, 2004). Working hard at something over time fosters a sense of pride. A rare long view of her own development is evident in Jena's sense that significant shifts were taking place even when she was not fully aware of them. "…I think one of the effects of having done it for so long," Jena continued, "is it's like your body is home…so doing a plié feels right to me, it's like walking in my front door; I start to relax and get centered....And so when it feels that good inside your body it starts to make the rest of you feel good. . . ." Echoing Aurelia's claim that "dance is like an emergency exit," Jena's metaphor of "body as home" implies that through dance the body itself can become a safe haven—a rare notion for women, young or old, in present times.

While Jena viewed beauty as something one is "born with," she saw dance as a powerful medium for instigating beauty: "Just making pretty shapes makes me feel beautiful....And it's not even me that's gorgeous—I'm making something gorgeous which is even more rewarding because you have no role in being gorgeous—that's how you were born, but to make something gorgeous is your creation" (interview, February 1, 2004). Redefining beauty through participation in dance allowed Jena to construct it in ways that fell outside of societally sanctioned norms, and, in so doing, to consciously shape a sense of self that embodied beauty of her own design.

The young women also claimed that dance helped them develop patience with themselves. Jena explained, "I've come to be patient when I'm dancing in a long-term sense of the word...patient in the sense that important change can come over time. Just because you don't see it doesn't mean [you're] not growing and changing" (interview, February 1, 2004). Physical or intellectual development and self-crafting are simultaneous processes; as we learn to dance or paint or play music, we also begin to define ourselves as artists. Over time, involvement in dance and other embodied activities can allow young people to build nuanced and changing portraits of themselves as movers, learners, thinkers, actors, and human beings.

Such an understanding of one's own development requires opportunities for reflection, which students in many traditional learning environments rarely have. Perhaps learning time could be more meaningful and effective if students were given more opportunities to reflect on their own development as well as their embodied experience.

A Supportive, Communal Learning Environment

Unlike many formal instructional contexts where students privately receive grades based on individual performance, learning to dance is a highly communal activity. During a dance class, each dancer's performance is visible to anyone interested in assessing it; students witness the corrections and feedback their classmates receive. Even dancers who are not the direct recipients of a teacher's comment often physically try out corrections intended for others. Receiving feedback involves not only listening and making mental notes but also incorporating the new information; internalizing it through the body's senses, intellect, and musculature; and then externalizing the gestalt—the newly reorganized understanding of the whole—as

Figure 2. Teen summer dance intensive technique class.

strategic motion through space. Feedback is also frequently offered to the class as a whole. A teacher might say, "As I look around the room, I'm getting the sense that you're not sure where your arms should be; in this particular movement the path of the arms looks like this," accompanying her words with gestures, movements and often with metaphors and images, to demonstrate the trajectory and its quality.

Aurelia, Livy, and Hannah, who attended a large public high school in San Francisco and commuted each day by train to participate in the Summer Intensive, shared their insights about the camaraderie that builds through dancing with others. Having been involved in dance for several years, they described the advantages of shared learning spaces. Hannah described how, when dancing with other people, "In case you're insecure about it, you can just work off their movement and trade information. I think in dance class you can make better bonds and relationships with people…because you automatically have something to share…[so] you can, like, learn and vibe off them" (focus group, August 10, 2006). Embodied learning allowed these young dancers to support one another's learning and growth by sharing information not only through language but also through their bodies.

Dance also helped Livy to trust others. "In partnering…what really makes the bond is that you have to trust that person…to hold your body, so then you automatically kind of trust them emotionally and mentally," she said (focus group, August 10, 2006). Though it is impossible to trace the precise path along which trust travels between the dance floor and other parts of the girls' lives, they put forward a convincing case for its journey between fields and domains (Csikszentmihalyi, 1991, 1996).

In 2005, three years into the study and approximately 15 years into her dance experience, Jena thoughtfully described how safety grows from the vulnerability of learning dance in a group:

> I think in dancing there's a comfort in watching other people learn…and a safety in [seeing] another person's uncertainty….You know, you learn something with someone when you dance in a way that you can't really learn something with someone in an academic way….The gears and the whole mechanism is exposed in a way that it's not when you're learning something academically—you both start at the starting line and you end at the finish line together but you don't run together. In dancing, you get to go together, which is great….It makes you feel confident in your ability, you have camaraderie, you can help someone in the learning process….And I think it's sort of community or relationship building also…and that demands a certain amount of safety in the room, you know, otherwise no one would ever go in. (interview, October 23, 2005)

In contrast to Jena's metaphor for academic learning, evoking an image of individual runners moving toward a finish line, her vision of learning dance is rooted in community, where "you get to go together." The young women in this study clearly benefited from regular participation in the complex social and kinesthetic practices of dance classes, in which youth and adults jointly crafted a community. For these young women, the social organization of learning dance not only promoted physical skills but also broadened their social, emotional, and intellectual repertoires for engaging with others in the many social worlds they encountered outside the studio.

MULTIMODAL TEACHING AND LEARNING

Teacher feedback in dance tends to be highly imagistic, metaphorical, and, above all, multimodal. The verbal cues, metaphors, and vocalizations that indicate movement quality are accompanied by gestures and demonstrations of the movement phrase or transition in question. Similarly, "taking feedback"—whether offered to oneself, a peer, or the whole class—involves not only listening and making mental notes but also incorporating new information, internalizing and digesting it in the body through the senses and muscles. Dancers are then able, for example, to more competently execute a revised version of a movement; they externalize the whole of what they have learned as organized expressive movement. Such structures of interaction between teachers and learners in dance classes can support young women in developing skills, forming their identities, and cultivating agency.

The following exchange, transcribed from approximately one minute of video, took place during an intermediate-level modern dance class during the 2006 Teen Summer Dance Intensive. As is typical of student-teacher interactions in dance classes, the process of guidance was also one of negotiation, clarification, and discovery for both teacher and learner. The teacher, Nadia, was helping a student named Angela perform a turn initiated by a *rond de jambe* (a circular sweep of the extended leg), followed by a circular sweep of the head. As they worked together in front of the mirrors and the class, Nadia demonstrated and explained, while Angela watched, listened, and attempted the movement phrase several more times. Fellow dancers looked on, some listening and observing intently, others trying out the movement in their own bodies. (In the excerpt below, a double asterisk ** indicates times when other students can be seen in the video emulating the demonstration.) Still others moved their bodies almost imperceptibly in sub-gestural response as they too absorbed Nadia's feedback and demonstrations and studied Angela's repeated attempts at the movement phrase.

As one group of dancers completed a combination across the floor, Nadia shouted words of encouragement over the music, first to Angela, and then to the group:

Nadia:	{to Angela} YES, Angela. {to the group as a whole} All right! Good. Good. Hey Angela, {walking toward the girls} you can drop your head more on this place. I know that you don't wanna kick somebody but {begins demonstration of turn and continues talking} once your leg is around, you're home free. {makes an auditory gesture[4]—"foooosh"—as she turns, suggesting the lyrical quality the movement should embody} Yeah? Let me see you do that. Come on out. {Nadia gestures with her hand, inviting Angela to come toward the center of the dance floor.}
Angela:	{steps tentatively out without saying anything}
Nadia:	Really drop your head. {notices Angela's reluctance and speaks in a high voice} You can do it!
Angela:	{laughs nervously}
Nadia:	{in a high voice} We love you! {As Nadia demonstrates the movement again to help Angela get started, she simultaneously talks Angela through it.} Alright, so you're here.** {Nadia begins the movement.} You're gonna do that rond de jambe…
Angela:	{emulates Nadia doing the movement}
Nadia:	{While Angela is moving, Nadia continues to vocalize.} Um hm, uh huh.
Angela:	{completes movement and turns expectantly to Nadia}
Nadia:	Okay. So you got to about here…{places her body in the approximate position of Angela's body during the turn}

Angela: Uh huh.

Nadia: And I want you to get to {vocalizes "fooosh" as she demonstrates the turn
               again} get your head down below right around your knees.

PORTION OF TRANSCRIPT OMITTED

Nadia: Like hug a big beach ball between your knees. {gestures as she speaks,
               mimicking holding a giant beach ball}

Angela: {As Nadia is demonstrating, Angela experiments some more with the
               movement.}

Nadia: Try it one more time.

Angela: {steps into position next to Nadia and attempts the turn again}

Nadia: {As Angela is finishing the turn, Nadia begins to talk.} Better. Yeah!
               {addresses the class} See now you can really see that Angela's initiating
               the movement with her head.

Angela: {tries the movement again}

Nadia: {to Angela as she completes the turn} Did you feel the difference?

Angela: {says something inaudible as she presses her hands around her lower back,
               curving it as Nadia had instructed, then laughs lightly}

Nadia: Yeah. Yeah. {moves into place for another demonstration of the movement
               as she talks} You know where it starts is here.** {stays in position, allowing
               time for the body image to register} The head movement starts here.

Angela: {initiates the turn again after revising the beginning position in her own
               body}

Nadia: There ya go!! {addressing the whole class with both gaze and voice} See
               what a difference that makes? {demonstrates the movement again, break-
               ing it down even more} So the head doesn't start HERE, {Nadia demon-
               strates what the movement is not, and then what it is. Angela tries it
               again.} the head starts HERE. To the side.** {Nadia continues talking and
               demonstrating. As she finishes, she turns to see Angela finishing her most
               recent attempt.} THAT is GORGEOUS.**

This episode illustrates the multiple modes of communication regularly used
in teaching and learning dance. Nadia switched from physical demonstration to verbal instruction, which included the beach ball metaphor. She added vocal intonation that suggested the quality of the movement she was teaching as well as verbal
content and physical gestures.

Meanwhile, Angela was connecting new information to her existing base of
knowledge and integrating her physical and mental understanding multimodally—
watching and listening but also embodying her learning through her own move-

ments. Using several modalities simultaneously increased Angela's capacity to take in new information. Angela was also monitoring her own learning process and responding intellectually and corporeally to moment-by-moment feedback. As she was absorbing the movement, she was also "learning how to learn"—which is, according to some, "perhaps the most important instrumental benefit of arts education" (McCarthy et al., 2004, p. 27).

Finally, in this supportive environment, peers and teacher are intimate witnesses to the learning process. As Jena said earlier, "The whole mechanism is exposed." Angela was learning to challenge as well as to trust herself. The episode not only demonstrates how multimodal entry points can enhance learning but also highlights the importance of feeling safe enough to take risks.

TAKING CHANCES

In a focus group exchange (August 4, 2006), Berkeley teens Angela and Mara took turns comparing learning at school versus learning dance.

Angela: Although it's not as much memorization [in school] as it used to be, it's a lot of, like, just having information being thrown at you…and I think there's a lot less risk…a lot less putting yourself out there and going with it even if you're wrong in school. And in dancing there's still a lot being thrown at you, but it's more about your confidence and…

Mara: how far you're willing to go…

Angela: yeah, and what risks you're willing to take because you're not going to be right 100 percent of the time, where on a test, that's your goal.

Mara: Generally in dance if you make a mistake it just brings you closer to what you're actually trying to get…whereas if you make a mistake in school it's considered to be bad, and people who make a lot of mistakes get bad grades—that's not what you want. In dance it's more about feeling it and understanding how to get to the right place, and getting there is really important, but it's not the ultimate goal.

Angela and Mara emphasized the "one-time-chance" nature of assessment tools such as grades and exams, where the consequences of "messing up" are sometimes brutal. By comparison, in the context of their community-based dance program, they understood that taking risks (and feeling safe enough to take them) was fundamental to developing new levels of expertise and gaining confidence in their developing abilities.

How can we realistically ask young people to become intellectual risk takers—to play with ideas, images, language, movement—if the consequences for doing so put them at such obvious disadvantage? What might learning look like—both in and outside of school—if, instead of measuring what learners have yet to master, we used multiple modes to support students in constructing knowledge? Although Angela and Mara clearly understood that discovery and growth require working at the edge of one's current capacity, risk taking in school often feels too dangerous. As Mara pointed out, "Generally in dance if you make a mistake it just brings you closer to what you're actually trying to get…whereas if you make a mistake in school…that's not what you want."

What would it take for young people to feel that they have permission to experiment and play? For youth to learn and grow and change, they need spaces that are emotionally and psychologically safe, where they can work at the edges of their evolving abilities. Working at the edge means making mistakes. In school, mistakes are frequently punished with reprimands or low scores, rather than serving as rich launching points for learning and growth as in the case of Nadia's instructions to Angela. Rather than interpreting mistakes as measures of a student's inadequacies, why not approach them as road maps for teaching and learning? Such an orientation toward development raises the bar by simultaneously balancing work at the edge with rigor. It communicates to young people that we have faith in their abilities to exceed expectations—their own and others'—and rewards rather than punishes risk-taking and vulnerability, which are arguably both needed for growth to occur.

Mara and Angela wisely suggested that end products—one-time shots demonstrating what students know—should not be our only goals. The high-stakes tests and other assessment measures so prevalent these days stunt the very capacities education in our democratic society aims to promote: independence, reflection, critical thinking, innovation, respect for others, negotiation, and confidence. By rewarding end performance almost exclusively, the design of most formal education and the measures of student success on which we currently rely are at cross-purposes with some of our most deeply held convictions about the development of young people. It is striking that dance, a performing art, should turn out to accord these young women more occasions than their schools did to take the intellectual risks and exploratory chances necessary to achieve real growth. Such daring work also helps young people develop a durable sense of identity—one that is not fixed but that shifts in nuanced and thoughtful ways, responding spontaneously to the inevitably unpredictable nature of life.

MULTIPLE MODES, TRUST, AND EDUCATION

Strategically designed afterschool programs can support youth with interactional and multimodal opportunities for positive identity formation and cognitive growth. Out-of-school multimodal learning contexts like those I investigated provide space for a powerful kind of learning that we know far too little about. As school-based and out-of-school curricula are being narrowed in the current age of testing and account-ability, I fear that we are failing to pay adequate attention to the promise of multi-modal learning. In doing so, we are forfeiting significant resources for constructing positive educational experiences.

Educators, both in and out of schools, can cultivate environments where young people are encouraged to use their minds and their bodies to experiment and explore. Respectful, self-reflective learning spaces can help young people develop self-awareness, confidence, and a sense of control over their physical, intellectual, emotional and social lives. Learners of all ages, but especially youth, deserve such spaces where, if they lose their sense of balance or perspective from time to time, there are no negative consequences.

Such havens are no small accomplishment. They can broaden our understand-ings of cognitive and developmental processes as well as identity formation. Combining use of multiple modes of communication with supportive social rela-tionships and varied opportunities for participation can offer young people potent environments for cultivating agency. If selves have their roots "not in words but in corporeal consciousness," as Sheets-Johnstone (1998, p. xx) suggests, then oppor-tunities to enact a self through dance after school may help us imagine educational practices that could more successfully support youth development both on and off the dance floor.

For the young women I worked with, dance enabled them to become the peo-ple they aspired to be. Hall (1996) suggests that identities are about reinvention: We utilize "the resources of history, language, and culture in the process of becoming" (p. 4). As these women suggested, the "resources of history, language, and culture" are experienced through our bodies as well as our minds. If identity is indeed about reinvention, and education is, broadly speaking, about nurturing our changing (moving) selves, we would do well to broaden our notions of learning and develop-ment, treating all communicative modes and educational spaces—in the classroom or garden, on the dance floor or basketball court—as places to invite one another to engage more fully in the multiple and multimodal processes of becoming.[5]

Notes

1. The research reported in this chapter was funded by the Robert Bowne Foundation and was orig-inally published in the journal *Afterschool Matters* in 2008. It is reprinted here with permission.
2. In keeping with the research of these educators, in particular the work of Bresler (2004) and her colleagues, I believe the arts and popular media provide unusually rich opportunities "to explore what embodiment means for educational researchers and practitioners" (p. 9).
3. All names of organizations and individuals in this chapter are pseudonyms.
4. The term "auditory gesture" is borrowed from UC Berkeley Linguistics Professor Eve Sweetser (personal communication).

5. I am grateful to fellow dancers and educators Jill Randall, Nina Haft, Marlena Oden, Julie Kane, Rebecca Johnson, Randee Paufve, Victor Anderson, Frank Shawl, Beth Hoge, Ernesta Corvino, Andra Corvino, Glynda Hull, and Anne H. Dyson, and to the young dancers who so openly shared their experiences.

Works Cited

Bresler, L. (Ed.). (2004). *Knowing bodies, moving minds: Towards embodied teaching and learning.* Boston: Dordrecht; London: Kluwer.

Catterall, J. (1998). Risk and resilience in student transitions to high school. *American Journal of Education, 106,* 302–333.

Catterall, J., Chapleau, R., & Iwanaga, J. (1999). Involvement in the arts and human development. In E. Fiske (Ed.), *Champions of change: The impact of the arts on learning* (pp. 1–18). Washington, DC: The Arts Education Partnership and The President's Committee on the Arts and the Humanities.

Cheville, J. (2001). *Minding the body: What student athletes know about learning.* Portsmouth, NH: Boynton/Cook.

Chouliaraki, L., & Fairclough, N. (1999). Discourse in late modernity. Edinburgh, UK: Edinburgh University Press.

Csikszentmihalyi, M. (1991). *Flow: The psychology of optimal experience.* New York: Harper Collins.

Csikszentmihalyi, M. (1996). *Creativity: Flow and the psychology of discovery and invention.* New York: Harper Collins.

Damasio, A. (1994). *Descartes' error: Emotion, reason and the human brain.* New York: Avon Books.

Deasy, R. (2002). *Critical links: Learning in the arts and student academic and social development.* Washington, DC: Arts Education Partnership.

Denzin, N., & Lincoln, Y. (1994). *Handbook of qualitative research.* Thousand Oaks, CA: Sage.

Dyson, A., & Genishi, C. (2006). *On the case.* New York: Teachers College Press.

Eccles, J., & Templeton, J. (2002). Extracurricular and other after-school activities for youth. In W. Secada (Ed.), *Review of Research in Education, 26,* 113–180. Washington, DC: American Educational Research Association.

Eisner, E. (2002). What can education learn from the arts about the practice of education? *The encyclopedia of informal education.* Retrieved on November 30, 2007, from http://www.infed.org/biblio/eisner_arts_and_the_practice_of_education.htm

Farnell, B. (Ed.). (1995). *Human action signs in cultural context: The visible and the invisible in movement and dance.* Metuchen, NJ: Scarecrow Press.

Finnegan, R. (2002). *Communicating: The multiple modes of human interconnection.* London: Routledge.

Fiske, E. (Ed.). (1999). *Champions of change: The impact of the arts on learning.* Washington, DC: The Arts Education Partnership and The President's Committee on the Arts and Humanities.

Flood, J., Heath, S. B., & Lapp, D. (1997). *Handbook of teaching and research on literacy through the communicative and visual arts.* London: Prentice Hall International.

Fraser, M., & Greco, M. (2005). *The body: A reader.* London: Routledge.

Gardner, H. (1999). *Intelligence reframed: Multiple intelligences for the 21st century.* New York: Basic Books.

Hall, S. (1996). Who needs identity? In S. Hall & P. du Gay (Eds.), *Questions of cultural identity* (pp. 1–17). Thousand Oaks, CA: Sage.

Heath, S. B. (1999). Imaginative actuality: Learning in the arts during the nonschool hours. In E. Fiske (Ed.), *Champions of change: The impact of the arts on learning.* Washington, DC: The Arts Education Partnership and The President's Committee on the Arts and the Humanities.

Heath, S. B., & McLaughlin, M. (Eds.). (1993). *Identity and inner-city youth: Beyond ethnicity and gender*. New York: Teachers College Press.

Holland, D., Lachicotte, W., Skinner, D., & Cain, C. (1998). *Identity and agency in cultural worlds*. Cambridge, MA: Harvard University Press.

Hull, G., & Katz, M. L. (2006). Crafting an agentive self: Case studies of digital storytelling. *Research in the Teaching of English, 41*(1), 43–81.

Hull, G., & Zacher, J. (2004, Winter/Spring). What is after-school worth? Developing literacies and identities out-of-school. *Voices in Urban Education, 3*, 36–44.

Katz, M.L. (2010). Dance journal prompts: Reflecting on dance, cognition, culture and identity: How dancing shapes thinking and experience on and off the dance floor. In Wendy Oliver (Ed.), *Writing about dance* (pp. 38–39). Champaign, IL: Human Kinetics.

Kondo, D. (1990). *Crafting selves: Power, gender and discourses of identity in a Japanese workplace*. Chicago: University of Chicago Press.

Kress, G., Jewitt, C., Ogborn, J., & Tsatsarelis, C. (2001). *Multimodal teaching and learning*. London: Continuum.

McCarthy, C., Ondaatje, E., Zakaras, L., & Brooks, A. (2004). *Gifts of the muse: Reframing the debate about the benefits of the arts*. Santa Monica, CA: The RAND Corporation.

Morrell, E. (2004). *Linking literacy and popular culture: Finding connections for lifelong learning*. Norwood, MA: Christopher Gordon.

Sheets-Johnstone, M. (1998). *The primacy of movement*. Philadelphia: John Benjamins.

Urciuoli, B. (1995). The indexical structure of visibility. In B. Farnell (Ed.), *Human action signs in cultural context: The visible and the invisible in movement and dance* (pp. 189–215). Metuchen, NJ: Scarecrow Press.

CHAPTER TWO

Chroma Harmonia

Multimodal Pedagogy Through Universal Design for Learning

CATHERINE KROLL

> We think by feeling. What is there to know?
> I hear my being dance from ear to ear.
>
> —THEODORE ROETHKE

INTRODUCTION [1]

Too often, we have to "check our bodies at the door" when we enter classrooms and embark upon formal learning (see Katz, Introduction to this volume). This idea provokes for me the question of how to teach students in ways that deeply engage who they are. In my general education courses, I have come to know students who are musicians, artists, future nurses, sports therapists, and business people. In my courses for future English teachers, I have students whose very identities are defined by their involvement with drama, poetry, and a whole range of athletic pursuits: in other words, their very sense of self is dependent upon their involvement in activities that are "total body experiences." I think of the competitive swimmer who visited me in office hours five times near the end of the term to work on her literature review on the role of mental preparation for swim meets. Then there was the ceramic artist who found a way to incorporate chocolate into every essay he wrote and whose trademark gesture was to turn in his papers stuck together with silver duct tape.

My quest to find memorable, whole-body ways to teach writing and grammar is born out of coming to know such students and out of my compulsion to help them sustain their focus beyond that ten-minute interval when, as we know, attention begins to flag. As a lifelong athlete, I have felt a particular kinship with these students. And, as a writer who must physically write in order to find form within the writing (rather than working from the abstraction of an outline), I have felt their impatience with overly didactic, mono-modal instruction.

Taking my turn at teaching my department's Pedagogical Grammar course recently, I predicted that many students would struggle to learn grammar, which can be so technical that it is sometimes referred to as "the math of English." This course is required of all English majors on the secondary teaching preparation track and is taken in students' junior or senior year of college (although many students so fear the course that they postpone taking it until the spring of their senior year).

During the same semester in which I taught Pedagogical Grammar for the first time, I continued to participate in the EnACT Faculty Learning Community (FLC) at Sonoma State University. Over the previous three semesters, this small group of faculty had been working on redesigning its courses according to principles of Universal Design for Learning (UDL). Our discussions centered on pedagogical concerns and strategies to mitigate the struggles that college students face, particularly those students with learning challenges. At one of our meetings, my colleague, Brian Wilson, a music theory professor, described his experiments using color and movement to help his students code the score of Stravinsky's "Rite of Spring." As he spoke, I immediately envisioned the possibilities of such a strategy for the grammar course. For many years, I had encouraged students to use heuristics such as doodling, drawing, and charting their ideas in order to stimulate the "hand-eye-brain connection" (Emig, 1978), and I suspected that color-coding sentence elements could help reinforce the grammatical concepts students were learning in the course. I decided to incorporate exercises with color and shapes to help students learn about clauses and other major sentence elements.

In the pages that follow, I present the core principles of UDL and then describe how I redesigned my Pedagogical Grammar course so that it became more multimodal, hands-on, and accessible. I show how using UDL principles in the classroom enhances learning for all students, and I suggest that an awareness of the neural basis of learning, particularly the new research on mirror neuron theory, can help us understand the reasons multimodal teaching benefits all learners.

In brief, mirror neuron theory suggests that the traditional model of learning—commonly believed to consist of the separate stages of visual observation followed by imitation (activities long thought to be controlled by distinct areas of the brain)—should be replaced by the understanding that learning actually takes place in a combined visual-motor neural sensing that *precedes* concept-formation, linguistic mediation, and imitation. We learn through grasping intentions, not analyzing actions into pieces and then imitating them. Maurice Merleau-Ponty (1945/2002), the inspiration for so much of mirror neuron research, puts it this way: "...I do not understand the gestures of others by some act of intellectual interpretation...I join [the act I perceive] in a kind of blind recognition which precedes the intellectual working out and clarification of meaning" (p. 216). We know the world and its meanings through our grasping of the intention-suffused actions of others: "It is as if the other person's intention inhabited my body and mine his" (p. 215).

Looking at the neural basis of learning another way, we can use the mirror neuron researchers' favorite example: the same neurons fire in the brain whether a person witnesses another individual drinking from a coffee cup or whether the person herself drinks from it. Later in this chapter, I will look specifically at the implications of mirror neuron research for human learning and will suggest that the commonplace notion of teaching as a one-way transmission of knowledge and skills needs to be replaced by an understanding of the brain's creative, empathic, and predictive capabilities that, in fact, shape the way we read the world and function in it.

THE CONTEXT AND THE NEED FOR UNIVERSAL DESIGN FOR LEARNING

To judge from certain well-publicized studies of student learning in higher education, it is tempting to conclude that we are in the midst of a distinctly downward trend in students' educational achievement. Gerald Graff's *Clueless in Academe: How Schooling Obscures the Life of the Mind* (2003) and Richard Arun and Josipa Roksa's recently published *Academically Adrift: Limited Learning on College Campuses* (2011) both point to students' and professors' mismatched expectations about education and conclude that college students are learning far below their given potential. Sensing more and more student disengagement in the classroom, my colleagues at the university frequently blame the policies of No Child Left Behind (NCLB) in K-12 education, including scripted instruction and mind-numbingly narrow student learning outcomes. College students, they argue, increasingly lack self-direction, creativity, and the confidence to think critically. Add to NCLB mandates the economic pressures students face as they cope with rising college tuition rates as well as the increased levels of psychological stress that hinders many students' progress, and you can grasp some of the new challenges in university education today.

Our students candidly discuss the sometimes overwhelming pressures that they feel in college: including balancing school, work, and family, and approaching challenging course content while adapting to multiple instructors' varied pedagogies. Whatever the particular combination of external stressors and individual cognitive factors, the struggles students endure often manifest in their class work. But there is a further reason for the often-cited "mismatch" between professors' expectations and students' actual work in their courses. According to recent student surveys conducted throughout the California State University system, somewhere between one-third to over one-half of all students struggle to learn what their college professors are trying to teach them.[2]

Even as students, professors, and administrators encounter increasing challenges within higher education, the positive news is that there have been notable advances in what we know about student learning, with the result that increasing numbers of professors have altered how they teach. As a result of the passage of the Americans with Disabilities Act of 1990 and its further amendments, educators and institutions have become committed to ensuring that students with physical, cognitive, or psychological disabilities have the same access to educational materials, course content, and learning experiences as other students in a given course. The need is clearly there: the percentage of college students who report having a disability is 11% based on 2003–2004 statistics (U.S. Department of Education, 2006), while the percentage taking medication for psychological conditions has grown from 9% in 1994 to 24.5% in 2004 (Gallagher, 2004 qtd. in Souma and Casey, 2008, p. 98). The percentage of students with disabilities on college campuses is likely much higher, as college support staff and professors acknowledge that students with disabilities often choose not to disclose them, and frequently students cannot afford the costs of the private testing necessary to obtain educational accommodations and other campus services. Although certainly part of the college experience should be to learn to adapt to a wide variety of learning contexts (Durre et al., 2008, p. 90), a number of research-based pedagogical practices can be used to help create the best possible conditions for student learning.

For example, over the past decade, insights from Universal Design for Learning (UDL)—inclusive educational practices sometimes referred to as "pedagogical curb cuts"—have enabled professors to rethink their courses and to reconfigure their teaching multimodally. Student surveys also indicate that when the course content, presentation of the material, and the means of expressing comprehension of that material are designed multimodally, *all* students benefit, not only those who need instructional accommodations or who learn in non-traditional ways.

The California State University's EnACT grant, funded by the U.S. Department of Education, is designed to encourage faculty to design multimodal instruction so that it allows for multiple means of representation of course content, multiple means of student engagement, and multiple means of expression of the material learned.[3] Rather than tailoring instruction to an individual student's particular disability after the course is already underway, instructors use principles of

Universal Design for Learning to plan for accessibility as they design their courses. Borrowing a metaphor from its architectural forebearer, Universal Design, we might say that UDL principles help instructors build the ramp up front, rather than adding it on later.

By highlighting the benefits of multimodal instructional design, I by no means wish to advance a binary model of an instructor-designed learning environment in which students are the more or less passive recipients of instruction. On the contrary, as I will discuss below, qualitative data suggest that we ought to conceive of instructional relationships as fluid in time and space on both "ends": the teacher engaged in a lesson-designing process teaching students who are engaged in a collaborative learning-creating process. The "shared space of action" (Rizzolatti & Sinigaglia, 2008, p. 131) created by these mutual teaching-learning relationships is what I would emphasize as definitive here. Students' action-understanding and purposeful imitation of their instructor's lesson design may be far more important to their learning than any one particular multimodal strategy the instructor uses in the classroom. I hypothesize that it is the very experience of observing an active teacher/learner investigating the course material with her students that produces, in turn, *a shared space of active learning* in which students are stimulated to create their own self-instructional strategies. I will take up the implications of this hypothesis in more detail in the concluding section of this chapter.

HEART-TO-HEARTS AND HANDS-ON GRAMMAR

From the very beginning of the first Pedagogical Grammar course I taught, I wanted to know who my students were: where they'd come from, what their attitudes were toward grammar, and what their technical knowledge consisted of. So, in addition to a multiple intelligences survey, I gave students a half-sheet of paper on which to write or draw the answer to this question: "This is your brain on grammar: what does it look like? Where has it been?" What students revealed about their "brains on grammar" ranged between solid confidence born of daily grammar work in elementary school to characterizations of a brain that is "a mob of mass confusion," a brain with "some holes, a little rusty," to a brain stuffed with "a bunch of random words and definitions that no matter how hard I try never make it correctly onto my papers."

In our class discussion of these responses, some students disclosed fears of not knowing anything about grammar, and they shuddered at the prospect of having to teach grammar to their own students in the near future. As one student put it, "I'm taking this course so I'll know what I'm teaching." Others recalled having absorbed their own past instructors' anxieties and uncertainties about grammar, so that it became a subject that was frequently ignored in their schooling.

Students' confusion about using grammar showed up in the brief punctuation pre-test I gave them as well, with approximately half of the group being unable to locate dependent and independent clauses or to punctuate sentences accurately. Now that I have taught the course multiple times, I have continued to probe my students' metacognitive awareness of themselves as learners. Because I want to know more about what truly motivates people to learn (and because this is a pedagogy class that considers such affective and cognitive questions), I ask students what would be most likely to stimulate their motivation to learn grammar and its practical applications. We talk about the way grammar is typically presented in schools, as being "something you'll need to know for the future," or "something you'll need to know in order to write a cover letter that will get you an interview." We also discuss teachers' own reasons for teaching it: often, to be able to spend more time working on Higher Order Concerns such as rhetorical strategies and style rather than devoting essay-marking time to Lower Order Concerns such as incorrect grammar. Perhaps predictably, students state that *none* of these three reasons for learning grammar would motivate them to want to learn it.

I then offer a fourth reason, which is actually an audacious claim: that I had taken 60 pages of grammar rules and condensed them into a single handout which, with the knowledge of a few simple grammatical terms, students could use to handle 95% of their sentence construction and punctuation issues. At this point, the majority of the class agreed that they would be motivated to learn the fundamentals of grammar (or at least they were intrigued by my claim).

In order to help students solidify the material in our textbook of common sentence patterns, types of clauses, and the rhetorical effects generated by various grammatical structures, I vary the presentation techniques and use sentences from pieces of realia as vivid examples of the grammatical structures we are studying. I take sentences off of the backs of tea boxes, bags of chips, and restaurant menus. I also bring into class whimsical sentences in different verb tenses about weasels (extensions of those used by textbook authors Martha Kolln and Loretta Gray), and, hamming it up a bit, I use an exaggerated voice and facial expressions to elongate the syllables of the word "weasel" so it becomes "weeeeeeasel." Arm gestures that accentuate the word "weasel" further keep students focused on what can otherwise be a tedious catalog of verb tenses. The multimodal approach here—acoustic, textual, expressive, and gestural representations of verb tenses—is an example of UDL brain-based learning in action.

The role of gesture in communication (both from the speaker's as well as the listener's perspective) has been studied extensively. Marco Iacoboni, one of the original University of Parma scientists working on mirror neuron theory, has suggested that "gestures accompanying speech have a dual role of helping the speakers to express their thoughts and helping the listeners/viewers understand what is being said" (p. 81). These scientists, drawing on Susan Goldin-Meadow's *Hearing Gesture: How Our Hands Help Us Think*, confirm that "for math problems, children are more likely to correctly repeat a procedure when the teacher's speech is matched with an appropriate gesture, compared with no gesture at all" (ibid.). In addition to aiding the speaker as she searches for, processes, or emphasizes thoughts and language, gestures offer the *listeners* a means of grasping the intentions embedded in the speaker's actions, thus prompting the listeners to adopt a similar embodied stance. Using gestures "reduces the cognitive load of explanation" for the speaker and enhances learning for the listener (Goldin-Meadow, p.157).

Further, the expressive devices I use in my teaching of grammar—vocal intonation, facial expressions, gestures, all laced with wry humor—go a long way toward lowering the affective filter and helping students feel receptive to learning, encouraging their attention on the lesson, and serving as mnemonic devices when they are studying outside of class. Because multimodal instruction causes neurons to fire in different parts of the brain simultaneously, there is a greater likelihood of students remembering the lesson, due to this physical stimulation across different sensory receptors.[4]

One anecdote from the first semester that I taught the course will illustrate the flow between lesson design and students' own learning. Early on, I was determined to make grammar relevant and alive by helping students see the place of grammar in daily life—whether used correctly or intentionally or unintentionally altered. I copied onto the whiteboard sentences taken from pretzel bags and Starbucks muffin wrappers. My intention was to help students learn to identify the difference between independent and dependent clauses (and between complete sentences and sentence fragments), so I marked each type in a different color—a darker color for independent clauses and a lighter color for dependent clauses. To give students hands-on practice with such identifications, I gave them bundles of colored pencils so that they could color-code their own handouts on clauses.

Students' response to this exercise was enthusiastic: there was a ripple of gaiety and animated gestures as they set to work. Although not every student identified clauses correctly during this first exercise, the class as a whole expressed a positive attitude about continuing to work with color. In the classes that followed, I observed that many students began turning in homework in which they had color-coded grammatical elements, and all students chose to use color to explicate sentence grammar on their midterms. So as not to confuse students who were possibly color blind, concurrently with the grammar lessons on color, I also used a drawing program to code grammatical elements according to shapes: circles for subjects and subject complements, arrows for verbs, lozenge shapes for prepositional phrases. I projected these shape-coded sentences onto the LCD projector as part of the day's activities.[5]

The most striking result of the introduction of color into the curriculum was that a number of students evolved their own unique symbol and color systems: some used an elaborate color-coordinated key, while others devised their own means of marking sentence parts, drawing wavy lines under dependent clauses and straight lines under independent clauses. This development prompted me to ask *why* students' learning processes progressed beyond mere imitation of the grammar lessons they observed in class. There may be an answer from the mirror neuron experiments that Parma scientists Iacoboni, Rizzolatti, and Sinigaglia conducted. In particular, the answer may lie in their finding that mirror neurons fire in the human brain not only when one performs an action but also when one merely *observes* that action: "[mirror neurons] allow you to grasp the minds of others, not through conceptual reasoning, but by modeling their actions, intentions, and emotions in the matrix of your own body mandala" (Blakeslee & Blakeslee, 2008, p. 166). We possess a wide repertoire of goal-oriented actions. Echoing Merleau-Ponty, Iacoboni (2009) has even gone so far as to maintain that we code objects in our immediate world in terms of intention, such that our perception of a physical apple involves such intentions as grasping and eating it (p. 14).

Accordingly, it seems likely that, built into students' observation of a lesson in which the instructor uses color- or shape-coding, is a shared understanding of the goal of that lesson. Students can readily develop their own personal coding systems because they possess an action-chain of understanding about the teacher's intentionality in the lesson. As Rizzolatti and Sinigaglia explain,

> The mirror neuron system and the selectivity of the responses of the neurons that compose it, produce a *shared space of action*, within which each act and chain of acts, whether ours or 'theirs,' are immediately registered and understood without the need of any explicit or deliberate 'cognitive operation.' (p. 131)

Thus, in a classroom lesson, as in every other social encounter, the mirror neuron system operates through an exquisitely attuned understanding of the motor possibilities and goal-orientations of both objects and people. Our students observe our goal-orientations by reading the motor possibilities of our actions, which enable them, in "a shared space of action," to create their own creative learning and study processes. Wohlschläger and Bekkering (2002) hypothesize on the basis of mirror neuron experiments that

> *Because* action understanding precedes imitation the observer can decide whether or not he wants to imitate the goals and intentions of the model. In addition, a goal-directed theory of imitation also gives room to creativity in imitation, because the way the goal is achieved is left to the imitator....(p. 111)

Similarly, Knoblich and Jordan (2002) highlight the observer's grasp of the essential goal of the action, which the observer can then act upon: "…it is not the observed movement per se that is matched with the observer's own action. Rather, it is the perceived effect the action exerts on the object that is matched to a possible effect that could be also exerted by one of the observer's own actions" (p. 116).

These insights from neuroscience should offer us an enhanced appreciation for the role of creativity in our students' learning as we observe the wide variety of instantiations of what we are teaching that come back to us stamped with individual students' creativity and understanding. I will not go so far as to claim that color- and shape-coding enabled students to produce error-free grammar identifications and analyses, but the coding did become part of their repertoire of learning strategies, and it enhanced students' motivation, confidence, and pride in their work. Considering the negativity with which many students approach grammar, these results are notable. Further, because there was an element of improvisation in my first-time efforts to try out multimodal approaches to grammar, students (future teachers themselves) could witness their teacher's efforts to *learn* which grammar teaching methods were most effective. The importance of the teacher putting herself in the role of learner here ought not to be overlooked, as the teacher's own receptivity to the surprises and experiments of learning was no doubt more engaging than the resolute authority of the grammar sage.

What also seems remarkable about the mirror neuron theory is that it replaces the "theory theory": the idea that, in learning how to act in the world, human beings first visually observe actions, formulate a theory about what they mean, and then replicate them in motor movement (Iacoboni, 2009, p. 71). The mirror neuron theory, by contrast, suggests that contained within the observation itself is an understanding (present in the firing of mirror neurons) of motor action and intention, so there is no fixed sequence of observation followed by action. The shared awareness of meaningful action is so automatic and so fast that it obviates the brain's need for any preliminary "theory-building" or analysis: "the mirror neuron system mechanism embodies that modality of understanding which, prior to any form of conceptual or linguistic mediation, gives substance to our experience of others" (Rizzolatti & Sinigaglia, 2008, p. 192). This means that our students read our movements as goal-intentions, and they experience these movements not just through the visual sensory system, but through the mirror neuron system, which enables an understanding of the movements' meanings or goals on an immediate physical level.

For creative writing and literature majors, learning to think about grammar as a working linguistic system with—usually—exact answers (based on specific sets of conventions) is a new dimension of their studies. English majors who have spent many years learning how to read literature in *expansive* terms, to explore ambiguity and polysemy (multiple meanings), and to read for the social and historical context of a work are now asked to learn precise, technical definitions of grammatical elements. Seeing the furrowed brows and perplexed expressions of 40 students during the first couple of weeks of the term, I know that I am taking them into new terrain. At first, when we try to discuss the grammar of a sentence, students point to a metaphor or other trope, instead of to the sentence's basic structural elements such as clauses or subjects and predicates. By referencing a chart showing the differences between literary analysis and grammatical analysis (and the overlap), students gradually learn to focus more on the grammar of the sentence. The color-coding of grammar functions as a "focusing force" that helps English majors learn a new way of analyzing sentences, and all of the multimodal approaches to grammar help solidify this new way of seeing.

Working with manipulatives, colors, and shapes (using sentence strips, color-coding, and drawing sentences as shapes) is not a matter of mere sensory or motor imitation. Understanding how mirror neurons make possible our encounter with the

world reveals how sophisticated and meaningful our motor activities are. When we see an object, we see it as *"graspable in this* or *that manner,* with *this or that grip,* etc., endowing it with a 'meaning' that it otherwise would not have had" (Gallese, cited in Rizzolatti & Sinigaglia, 2008, p. 50). In other words, these neurons appear to respond not to the mere sensory aspect of an action in time and space but to the meaning the stimulus conveys to the

Pre-service teachers collaborate in small groups to create multi-modal 'grammar four-square' posters.

individual, and, further, "reacting to a meaning is precisely what one means by *understanding*" (Petit, cited in Rizzolatti & Sinigaglia, 2008, p. 50). So, when students are using embodied exercises to work on a grammar concept, they are unconsciously making decisions about the clause as "usable in this or that manner," "in this or that position," or as an object movable in the space of an English sentence: to the front, to the middle, to the end. And through this process, we can glimpse our students' understanding of the principle of clause movability in English.

The written surveys I received from students confirmed that embodied, multimodal approaches to grammar—such as color- and shape-coding, vocalized slogans ("He doesn't know 'X'" or "He doesn't know BEANS" that help students conceptualize nominals as direct objects), and the manipulation of sentence strips—work to reinforce their new grammatical knowledge. Many students found the color-coding of grammatical elements to be a useful way of marking their function within sentences. Some suggested that multimodal grammar activities using colors, shapes, and manipulatives not only made learning easier and more fun but also provided "a clear visual aid that [one] can take away from the exercise to refer to later." From students' perspectives, these activities shaped present as well as future learning.

End-of-course survey responses emphasized students' belief that the modality of color-coding helped them visualize and retain grammar concepts. Students pointed to an enhanced metacognitive awareness as well: color enabled them to "realize…grammar strengths and weaknesses" and to create an aid "to refer to later." Two students commented in particular on the use of sentence strips to manipulate phrases within sentences: "It was useful and fun as it allowed us to see how certain elements can get changed around to create different grammatical effects, and how some can't be switched at all." Another student agreed that it was "very useful [because] it allowed us to physically take words apart and rearrange, emphasizing the movability of words and phrasings."

For one student, color-coding and sentence strips were less useful learning reinforcements than were vocal intonation and movement:

> FANBOYS [a mnemonic tool for recalling the list of coordinating conjunctions: for, and, nor, but, or, yet, so] and rhythmic emphasis helped. It mattered, too, because you always changed your vocal tone, for example, when you were teaching that 'X' trick for locating a direct object (described above). Your vocal variety and moving around helped me not get bored and remember key points. I think your humor might have helped, too, but I can't explain why.

Interestingly, the students' responses as a whole suggest that using color and shapes are but *one* type of effective learning modality. In fact, students pointed to a whole range of learning activities that they found helpful, including hands-on work with worksheets (used for individual, paired, and whole-class work). These responses suggest that what may be most important about multimodal instruction is the very fact of its *flexibility within and across multimodalities* rather than any one particular type of instruction through visual, aural, or kinesthetic means. Students' observation of their instructor's engagement and play with the material seems to be a crucially important modeling device that stimulates the students' own creative learning strategies.

It is important to emphasize that future teachers in particular benefit from experiencing multimodal learning strategies. Through embodied learning and through discussion of their own metacognitive responses to these strategies, these teachers in training gain new skills to help them teach grammar to their own students. My students have noted the "fun" and "motivating" power of learning through color and shapes: responses that highlight the way hands-on activities seem to lower the affective filter, to reduce anxiety about grammar, and thus to help students enter "the zone" of learning. Now that students have experienced these multimodal strategies (which, it appears, help them learn more deeply), they will be better equipped to teach in more engaging ways when they enter middle and high school classrooms of their own.

Conclusion: Toward an Embodied Grammar

Here it becomes possible to draw together several strands of analysis supporting multimodal learning. This chapter began by recognizing the need for teachers to redesign their courses for maximum accessibility using principles of Universal Design for Learning (UDL) or other multimodal approaches. Students explain that when teaching and learning are actively multimodal—when learning is experienced in the body—they learn more easily, with more confidence, and with the result that learning is sustained over longer periods of time. Far from being merely an acute observer of the elements of an action, the brain is actually well-equipped to grasp the action-intentions of others and to create its own parallel action-intentions: the representation—and embodiment—of new learning.

The brain's ability to grasp intention is akin to the kind of predictive functions that structure the reading process. We know that, in reading, the brain races ahead in prediction, hypothesis, and inference, "filling in" the sense of the sentences, paragraphs, and pages to come based on the "intentions" of the author gleaned thus far from the text. Reading is a search for meaning that takes shape through prediction and through asking and answering questions. Thus, whether reading a text or grasping the action-intentions of others, we are astute readers of the intentions embedded in the movements and events that unfold around us. As Blakeslee and Blakeslee (2008) put it, "one function is now clear: Your mind operates via prediction. Perception is not a process of passive absorption, but of active construction" (p. 41). Prediction entails hypothesizing about the meanings of others, whether those meanings are expressed in print or via the body.

What are the implications for learning, once we understand the brain's predicting and grasping processes? What can teachers do to support learning and minimize our future students' struggle with the way we teach them? Concretely, we can teach via multiple modalities, creating opportunities for students to learn across them. We ought also to be aware that how our students learn and represent their learning back to us may not look exactly like what we've taught them. This is because learners understand the action-intentions of others and generate their own purposeful, creative instantiations of their instructor's lessons. Finally, as a guiding principle, we can understand the teacher-as-learner and learner-as-teacher relationship as unfolding in the vibrant space that Caribbean poet and cultural critic Édouard Glissant (1990) refers to as "Relation." Here the poles of teacher and learner dissolve, and we inhabit the space between, that shared space of action, since "in Relation, every subject is an object and every object a subject" (p. xx).

Notes

1. I am grateful for research support from the Ensuring Access through Collaboration and Technology (EnACT): Partnerships, Technology & Dissemination grant, 2009–2011, from the U.S. Department of Education. Special thanks are due to the EnACT Project Director, Dr. Emiliano Ayala, to my early collaborator Dr. Brian Wilson, and to the EnACT Faculty Learning Community at Sonoma State University for their probing questions.
2. Unpublished data from EnACT grant student surveys, 2009–2010.
3. For more information about the EnACT grant and about these three UDL principles, see http://enact.sonoma.edu/.
4. New research into optimal study habits suggests that dividing study time into short segments and studying in different physical locations enhances subject matter retention. See Benedict Carey, "Mind: Forget What You Know About Good Study Habits." *The New York Times*. Sept. 6, 2010. Available at: http://www.nytimes.com/2010/09/07/health/views/07mind.html?emc=eta1.
5. In one of our discussions in class on designing multimodal strategies for teaching, a student proposed that creating manipulatives with these sentence elements would help make grammar literally tangible. So, using old file folders, I created "sentence strips" made up of dependent and independent clauses which students used to build a variety of sentences. In this exercise, they could arrange clauses in various ways and compare the differences in rhetorical effects generated by clause placement.

Works Cited

Arun, R., & J. Roksa. (2011). *Academically adrift: Limited learning on college campuses*. Chicago: University of Chicago Press.

Blakeslee, S., & M. Blakeslee. (2008). *The body has a mind of its own: How body maps in your brain help your body do (almost) everything better*. New York: Random House.

Burgstahler, S. E., & R. C. Cory, eds. (2008). *Universal design in higher education: From principles to practice*. Cambridge, MA: Harvard University Press.

Carey, B. (2010). Mind: Forget what you know about good study habits. *The New York Times*. September 6. Available at: http://www.nytimes.com/2010/09/07/health/views/07mind.html?emc=eta1.

Durre, I., et al. (2008). Universal design of instruction: Reflections of students. In S. E. Burgstahler & R. C. Cory, eds. *Universal design in higher education: From principles to practice.* (pp. 83–96). Cambridge, MA: Harvard University Press.

Emig, J. (1978). Hand, eye, brain: Some 'basics' in the writing process. In C. R. Cooper & L. Odell. *Research on composing: Points of departure.* (pp. 59–72). Urbana, IL: NCTE.

Glissant, É. (1990/1997). *Poetics of relation.* Trans. B. Wing. Ann Arbor: University of Michigan Press.

Goldin-Meadow, S. (2003). *Hearing gesture: How our hands help us think.* Cambridge, MA: Harvard University Press.

Graff, G. (2003). *Clueless in academe: How schooling obscures the life of the mind.* New Haven, CT: Yale University Press.

Gruber, O. (2002). The co-evolution of language and working memory capacity in the human brain. In M. I. Stamenov & V. Gallese, eds. *Mirror neurons and the evolution of brain and language.* Amsterdam: John Benjamins.

Iacoboni, M. (2009). *Mirroring people: The science of empathy and how we connect with others.* New York: Picador.

Knoblich, G., & J. S. Jordan. (2002). The mirror system and joint action. In M. I. Stamenov & V. Gallese, eds. *Mirror neurons and the evolution of brain and language* (pp. 115–124). Amsterdam: John Benjamins.

McNeill, D. (2005). *Gesture and thought.* Chicago: University of Chicago Press.

Merleau-Ponty, M. (1945/2002). *Phenomenology of perception.* Trans. C. Smith. London: Routledge.

Profile of undergraduates in U.S. postsecondary education institutions: 2003–04. (2006). (NCES 2006–184). U.S. Department of Education, National Center for Education Statistics. Available at: http://nces.ed.gov/pubsearch/pubsinfo.asp?pubid=2006184.

Rizzolatti, G., & C. Sinigaglia. (2006/2008). Trans. F. Anderson. *Mirrors in the brain: How our minds share actions and emotions.* New York: Oxford University Press.

Souma, A., & D. Casey. (2008). The benefits of universal design for students with psychiatric disabilities. In S. E. Burgstahler & R. C. Cory, eds. *Universal design in higher education: From principles to practice,* (pp. 97–104). Cambridge, MA: Harvard University Press.

Stamenov, M. I., & V. Gallese, eds. (2002). *Mirror neurons and the evolution of brain and language* (pp. 77–86). Amsterdam: John Benjamins.

Wolhlschläger, A., & H. Bekkering. (2002). The role of objects in imitation. In M. I. Stamenov & V. Gallese, eds. *Mirror neurons and the evolution of brain and language* (pp. 101–113). Amsterdam: John Benjamins.

CHAPTER THREE

"All the World's a Stage"

Musings on Teaching Dance to People With Parkinson's

DAVID LEVENTHAL

Sometimes, in the middle of a grocery store, Herb Heinz, a musician and composer in his mid-40s, finds it difficult to move. For almost ten years, he's had Parkinson's disease (PD), a degenerative neurological disorder that can affect muscle control, balance, and coordination, among other things. In 2007, he started taking dance classes specially designed for people with Parkinson's. A few months into the sessions, he found that he had absorbed elements of the dance class so completely that when he experienced difficulty initiating movement at the local supermarket, he was able to choreograph a sequence in his mind to help him move again with graceful flow. By thinking like a dancer, Heinz leap-frogged over his body's physical condition and started moving gracefully again. Just as dancers have been doing for thousands of years, he created vital movement out of stillness and forged a road where there had once been an impasse. He experienced dancing as a particularly profound type of embodied learning that activates the mind, body, and spirit in service of movement.

Professional dancers and people with Parkinson's disease share a similar challenge: to execute difficult movement with ease and natural grace. For dancers, choreography or technical objectives establish the level of difficulty. For people with PD, the disorder's effects complicate the act of moving. Both populations must use learned strategies to fill time and space with fluid, fluent action. To approach this imposing task and to reach a point at which awareness and imagination guide their actions, both populations need embodied tools—tools that dancers consider second nature and rarely analyze.

In the summer of 2001, Olie Westheimer, executive director of the Brooklyn Parkinson Group in New York City, approached the Mark Morris Dance Group (MMDG) with the idea that the dance company, which had recently opened a new studio in Brooklyn, offer a class for people with Parkinson's disease. Nancy Umanoff, MMDG's executive director, supported the plan, offering studio space, a musician, and two teachers, and a few months later, John Heginbotham and I began teaching "Dance for PD" at the company's headquarters at 3 Lafayette Avenue. Neither Heginbotham nor I had ever worked with this population before, and neither of us had any training in dance therapy. Despite our inexperience, the monthly class succeeded almost immediately in helping the participants approach movement as dance students rather than as patients. By 2003, the weekly Dance for PD class had grown in size from eight to twenty and had added a third teacher, Misty Owens, a professional tap dancer who was on the faculty at the Mark Morris Dance Center.

Westheimer had danced as a younger person and had trained with a graduate of the Royal Ballet School in London. She understood the mental, physical, and emotional effects that dance could have, and she wondered if some sort of dance training might be helpful for the members of her Parkinson's group, many of whom experienced difficulty initiating and controlling movement. The class' success vindicated Westheimer's theory and helps explain Heinz's experience in the grocery store.

She knew that as part of their training, dancers absorb a complex set of learning tools that allow them to naturalize complicated movement concepts and make technically difficult feats, like turning and balancing, consistently successful. "What well-trained dancers know how to do very, very well is control their movements with cognitive strategies and conscious use of all sensory input," Westheimer wrote (Westheimer, 2008, p. 128). By welcoming people with Parkinson's into a specialized dance class taught by professional dancers and accompanied by an accomplished musician (the wonderful musical theater composer and Broadway accompanist William Wade), Westheimer hoped that the participants would step inside a dancer's brain and begin to understand movement in a dancerly way. These classes, she suspected, would represent a confluence of artistic expression, physical training, social interaction, and mental focus.

This chapter explores how the strategic tools dancers use to refine their expressive powers, and the contexts and situations in which dancing takes place, can support a population for whom movement is a daily struggle. Understanding that movement is largely a mental activity, I will look at the ways in which dancing, with its emphasis on verbal and visual cues, imagery, and music, alters the relationship people with Parkinson's have with movement and their bodies. I'll suggest that dance training helps people internalize an aesthetic awareness that allows them to guide themselves. Finally, I'll propose that by dancing for each other, people with Parkinson's reject their medical classification as "patients" and learn to embody states of physical flow, confidence, and power. As Carroll Neesemann, an attorney with Parkinson's who's been attending classes since Dance for PD's launch, says of his dancing experience: "It's nice not to be clumsy. It's wonderful to be in control and be somewhat graceful again" (Fallik, 2007, p. 31).

A DANCE CLASS GROWS IN BROOKLYN

Westheimer assured the teachers when we started that although we weren't experts on Parkinson's disease, the knowledge we passed on to the Parkinson's participants would be immediately useful. It was reassuring to believe that we could take what we already knew—tricks of the trade—and apply that knowledge within new contexts that would serve new populations. But what were the tricks that Westheimer was referring to? What was the essence of our specialized knowledge, passed on through centuries of dance pedagogy? Which pieces of it would be most helpful to participants, who seemed to have such a wide range of challenges? Would our participants be able to embody the information we passed on to them? How could they dance, we wondered, if even basic movement created such frustration?

In light of these doubts, Westheimer's confidence was inspiring. "I don't have a medical background at all," she said. "But I knew that dancers use all the tricks in the book to get their bodies to do difficult things. That was my gamble—that it would be beneficial" (Fallik, 2007, p. 31). In fact, Westheimer insisted at first that we shield ourselves from clinical facts about the disease. Westheimer asked us to develop the class through trial and error, using our powers of observation, and using the feedback from her and members of the Parkinson's group to guide our teaching.

What Westheimer specifically did not want, she explained to us, was a therapy class. Dance therapy, as we understand it, uses movement to address specific symptoms, conditions, and emotional concerns. It can be extremely effective for a variety of conditions, but the therapist often begins by focusing on the symptoms themselves, using movement as a treatment. Westheimer envisioned a class in which the emphasis would always be on dancing. She trusted that the physical, cognitive, and emotional benefits dancing held for participants would be implicit in the art form itself.

As dancers, we trusted this too—and knew it firsthand from our own experiences. With this in mind, we decided we wanted our participants to feel the way we felt when we took dance class, which we figured was as far from life with Parkinson's as one could get. After all, as Westheimer wrote, "The support group attendees needed to do something enjoyable, together—just plain fun, unrelated to PD" (Westheimer, 2008, p. 127). So as the class progressed, we paid specific attention to the building blocks of our own training and artistic development to understand how the "DNA of dance"—of ballet, tap, modern, and jazz instruction—might provide useful techniques that we could pass on to our students. Approaching the class as a mutual collaboration, we watched and listened to what the participants did and said in response to our exercises. From this two-way process, we began to understand the elements that would help our Parkinson's participants use mind, body, and spirit to embark on a journey away from disease via artistic exploration.

THE IMPORTANCE OF PLACE

As professional dancers, John and I knew about the power of how specific surroundings could affect mood and motivation. We experienced first hand what it was like to walk into a theater and feel a sense of purpose and anticipation. We knew what it felt like to be on stage and sense the rush of energy: a heightened awareness of space and sensory input, and a separation from quotidian existence. We also understood that our participants spent a lot of time in medical and clinical settings. So from the very first Dance for PD class at the Mark Morris Dance Center, we assumed we had a serious advantage over clinical settings. The studio setting encouraged class participants to approach the experience as dancers rather than as patients. Misty Owens, who joined our teaching team in the third year and since then has gone on to be one of the program's most innovative and inspiring teachers, explained in an interview: "Therapy means you're getting dressed to go to the doctor's office. It's more of a doctor's prescription, whereas when you're getting dressed to go to a dance class, it's more of an opportunity" (Gehris, 2008). The simple act of entering our Brooklyn studios changes participants' outlook and enthusiasm, even their posture. As they cross the threshold, their identities shift; they move from seeing themselves as medical patients to feeling like active participants in a world-class performing arts organization.

Joy Esterberg, a teacher and writer whose doctor diagnosed her with PD in 2003, explains how she feels empowered to imagine and embrace possibility and change her identity, even if that change is temporary. "The fact that our condition is acknowledged but not the focus of the class allows us the dignity of managing that ourselves and frees us to maintain the illusion that we are dancers," Esterberg told me. "This creative pretending is as powerful for adults as it is for children and contributes to the joy of the class." By approaching the class as dancers rather than as patients, Esterberg and her fellow participants embody an important distinction between taking part in group therapy and attending a Dance for PD class.

But it wasn't enough to let the setting do the transformative work. Architecture has powerful effects on the psyche, and we wanted to thread this sense of empowerment through the structure of the session itself, which we felt needed to reflect that of a traditional dance class as closely as possible. We hoped that structuring the class like other dance classes would enable participants to identify themselves as dancers, temporarily allowing them to shed their medicalized identities, to think and solve problems like dancers, and approach movement with the same combination of strategic awareness and joyful passion that dancers do in class. So although we start seated in a circle to build a sense of community among all the participants and to take away any concerns about balance, the structure of the class closely and intentionally follows that of other dance classes.

We start every class by progressively warming up the torso, arms, feet and legs, just as we do in any ballet or modern class. During the warm-up, we integrate repetition and variation, encouraging mastery but keeping the dancers alert. Throughout the class, we create longer sequences of movement (choreography) just as we do in other dance classes, and these progressions, which contain individual components (steps or moves) of contrasting qualities, dynamics, shapes and directions, challenge participants to learn, execute, and find logic in complex phrasing, a process that is one of the hallmarks of dance training not found in other movement modalities, except perhaps Tai Chi. Midway through the class we stand up and work on *pliés* and *tendus* at ballet *barres* (at the participants' request, we use ballet terms in the class). Later, we move gracefully across the floor, often culminating in the reconstruction of a piece of choreography. We always end in a circle, as we began, reconfirming our unity and sense of mutual support as we pass a pulse from hand to hand, and then a bow, one at a time, around the group. The "pass the pulse" activity, which takes place in some form in the more than forty Dance for PD classes offered around the world, stems from our model and is one of the highlights of the class, but any ballet student would recognize it as a form of *reverence*, or ritualized bowing exercise at the end of a ballet class so that students can thank their teacher and musician (and practice bowing for the audience that may appear later in their professional lives).

The traditional elements of the class clearly resonate with the participants. Neesemann observes, "They teach us as if we were any students, and that makes me feel good" (Sulcas, 2007). When they are treated as dancers, they tell us, they feel empowered to leave the burdens of medical categories and perceived limitations behind and focus on being dance students.

That effective learning occurs in an arts setting rather than a clinic has a lot to do with a single word: fun. A dance studio filled with space, light and music invites opportunity, challenge, and hard work, but it is also a space for highly enjoyable structured play, which is the basis for so many human artistic endeavors. Yet that doesn't mean that our class isn't serious. To borrow from Seneca the younger, "true pleasure is a serious business" (*Mihi crede, verum gaudium res severa est*). The class is structured with the understanding that dance is essentially joyful and playful in spirit, and the importance of fun—something perhaps missing in other aspects of our participants' lives—should not be underestimated. When asked what impact the class had on their lives, one participant reported anonymously in a survey: "Well, for one thing it's fabulous fun—like stepping into a totally loving, kind and beautiful universe" (Westheimer, 2008, pp. 139–140). A joyful atmosphere relaxes and reassures students in any learning environment, and this class is no exception. Fear and hesitation slip away in the spirit of play. Participants open their minds and bodies to learn and absorb everything that a dance class has to offer through multiple modalities.

SWANS ON A RED CARPET

When people learn to dance as beginners, they generally start with the basic craft of movement, focusing primarily on the mechanics of the steps. They learn what to do, where to do it, and when it happens in relation to (or in opposition to) the music. These are some of the basic tools of the form. Over time, much as violinists hone their awareness of phrasing and dynamics or actors learn to vary the rhythm and tone of a line to add nuance and depth to a role, dancers learn what specific qualities and textures they need to color and shade each movement, making it expressive and interesting to watch. Much of this information is already embedded in the language of technique. For example, ballet steps themselves are linked to specific images—a *fondu* is a melting action, while a *pas de chat* imitates the movement and quality of a cat. But the training builds on this vocabulary by engaging the world of imagination and metaphor—in short, the world of art and poetry. Dancers gradually add more and more layers of qualitative information to their technical training and to the movements they create, so that they can execute choreography with full artistic range and command (see Hagendoorn, 2003, for the implications of this training on the viewer). By the time they are professional artists, most dancers work primarily in the realm of qualitative exploration and refinement as choreographers, artistic directors, and rehearsal coaches demand ever-increasing specificity and nuance.

This same process occurs in an accelerated way when professional dancers learn new choreography: steps, then color, then complete internalization. As Diane Solway writes:

> That dancers can remember such a wide range of steps, roles and styles is sometimes forgotten in the awe produced by a great performance [....] But in getting to that point, most

dancers share a relatively similar path, first learning the choreography and then adding layers of detail and color. Finally, they absorb the work so completely that its elements literally
become automatic, leaving the dancer's brain free to focus on the moment-to-moment
nuances of the performance. (Solway, 2007, AR19)

Advanced training aims to give the professional dancer multiple strategies to
overcome the inevitable challenges that choreography presents. Eventually, dancers
must internalize these strategies completely, allowing them to achieve a high level
of ingrained neurological patterning (which dancers call 'muscle memory') and
turn-on-a-dime physical control. Indeed, dancers practice for years so that their *ability* to control movement in space becomes automatic without causing them to
resemble automatons (unless they are pretending to be windup dolls in *The
Nutcracker*). Like great musicians, when they finally get up on stage, well-trained
dancers can execute and express exactly what and how they want to, moment to
moment. The moves themselves, like the notes, are practiced—embodied—so the
performance is spontaneous and immediate. A performer who takes your breath
away is no longer thinking technically; although she's using the hundreds of concrete and imaginative tools at her disposal, all we see is articulate, expressive grace.
This quality, with its inherent sense of flow and inevitability, is what starts to disappear in people with Parkinson's disease.

As a result, Dance for PD classes try to incorporate all of the strategies dancers
acquire throughout their training. But instead of focusing at first only on steps and
mechanics, as we might do with other novices, with the PD dancers we emphasize
imagery, imagination, qualitative direction, and dynamics right away. For people with
Parkinson's, imagery seems to motivate the body in ways that purely technical craft
does not. So by using concrete, vivid images, we make arbitrary, technical movements—like curving an arm or pointing a foot—appear more natural or approach-
able. Bending over becomes "diving into a pool." Wrapping our arms around
ourselves becomes "taking off a sweater." Standing up to walk forward becomes
"accepting the Academy Award" (which works wonders for posture and confidence). In many cases, the image is complex and contains a discernable narrative.
The dive, for example, helps people trace the path of descending from one point to
another while evoking the sensorial memories associated with water—enveloping
softness, resistance, coolness. Such tactile and kinesthetic memories affect how that
story of the descent occurs and help us remember the mechanics and quality of the
movement. In our class, it doesn't matter if participants can do twelve leg lifts; we want
them to do one leg lift with an explorative mind. Whether the imagery is something
that the teachers evoke through words or through the quality of their movement
(which then spurs the participant to construct her own motivating image), the
image-based approach seems to pay off immediately for Neesemann and others:

"When the dancers move their arms, they look like swans," he told a reporter. "And you try to do the same. In the beginning, people would just stumble around. Now they are actually trying to be graceful" (Gehris, 2005). Here, Neesemann seems struck by the quality of the teachers movements, and he translates this into a specific and personal image (swans) that he then uses to initiate his own movement.

Neesemann's comment reveals the crux of image-based instruction: when people have an image, memory, or mimetic imitation to strive for (do it like the teacher, who is evoking a bird), they're able to tap into their own imaginations to initiate movement. They are able to achieve recognizable goals with impressive results. Scientists are just beginning to explore this phenomenon which we see so clearly with our PD dancers to try to understand how and why our brains are wired to respond this way and how something like dance could help people transcend some of the limitations of Parkinson's disease (Brown & Parsons, 2008; Calvo-Merino et al., 2008).

Perhaps it is something like the "shared space of action" to which Kroll refers (see Chapter 2 in this volume). The narrative evoked by specific imagery (diving into a pool, for example) enables those with Parkinson's to 'grasp' an idea through visual and kinesthetic means and subsequently execute previously unavailable movement trajectories. Through multimodal engagement, their bodies can bypass the mind's neurological trouble spots and literally forge new pathways into and through the world. Put another way, the use of imagery harnesses the power of our minds to control our bodies and the ability of our bodies to re-envision the present moment in more accessible ways. Using the mind's eye to initiate movement is an invaluable "way in" for people who feel their bodies are failing them. It gets at the heart of what Olie Westheimer's husband, Dr. Ivan Bodis-Wollner, a neurologist, thinks is valuable about the class. Bodis-Wollner, the Director of the Parkinson's Disease and Related Disorders Clinic Center of Excellence at Kings County Hospital and SUNY Downstate Medical Center, sees enormous motivating power behind the gentle pressure of aesthetics. The set of images in our minds informs and guides our bodies, helping us strategize corporeal ways to achieve a desired aesthetic goal.

In one of our standard class exercises, for example, we ask participants to imagine they are painting shapes, lines, and dots in space. We specify the brush and color and encourage the students to imagine that they are actually applying paint to a canvas. Drawing huge shapes that go far beyond their usual range, their brains seem to push their bodies to fulfill the imagined task; the imagination drives the body and creates a satisfying sense of kinesthetic pleasure. This seems in some way to echo Dutch choreographer and neuroscience researcher Ivar Hagendoorn's proposition, made in reference to the process of watching dancing, that "if the movement trajectory predicted by the brain coincides with the actual movement, we are filled with pleasure, which we ascribe to the movement that gave rise to it by calling the movement beautiful or graceful" (Hagendoorn, 2003). Although Hagendoorn is referring specifically to the relationship between the viewers' brains and the movement on stage, mirror neuron research (also cited in Kroll's chapter) suggests that there is a similar connection between the expectation set up by the dancer's imagination and the resulting embodiment of the movement—either by one's own body or by another.

I know this process first hand as I struggle with my own *arabesque*, a ballet line with a lifted straight leg that extends behind the pelvis while the torso stays relatively vertical. It isn't my forte. The late Marjorie Mussman, a genius teacher with whom I trained for more than a decade, coached me on it for years. She used two types of cues to try to improve my arabesque. Sometimes, she focused on the mechanics—the three lines of frontal eye focus, front arm and back leg separate but parallel to one another. Other times, she relied on imagery to make her point: "The arabesque," she used to say, "is about flight. It's designed to mimic a bird taking to the air." The more technical, anatomical explanation rarely worked for me. But the image of a bird in flight kept my leg and foot stretching back like a long tail feather, curved my chest like a bird's breast, and lifted my focus like an eagle about to take off. The gentle pressure of aesthetics, as Bodis-Wollner puts it, creates a motivating and beautiful image (I happen to love birds) and helps me overcome things my back and leg wouldn't necessarily do if I were simply thinking of mechanics. The idea of flying—something humans have long aspired to—turns out to be an intensely motivating, if fantastical, image. When I achieve it, which is more rarely than I'd like, I feel a sense of reward and satisfaction.

There's something else that helps me with challenging movements—music. For many dancers, rhythm and music are the teachers, directors, choreographers, and prompters that continue to coach and coax even when the actual director is no longer standing around shouting reminders. That's probably because, as some scientists speculate, dance and music developed together in human cultures and support each other. As Steven Brown and Lawrence Parsons write,

> So natural is our capacity for rhythm that most of us take it for granted: when we hear music, we tap our feet to the beat or rock and sway, often unaware that we are even moving. But this instinct is, for all intents and purposes, an evolutionary novelty among humans." (Brown & Parsons, 2008, p. 78)

So today, even with the advent of post-modern, post-musical dance, many dancers still feel lost without some kind of music. Even for dancers who don't use rhythmic or melodic music, like members of the Merce Cunningham Dance Company, the idea of an internal physical rhythm is important, and anyone who has seen Cunningham's company knows how silently 'musical' his dancers are, even as the choreography is designed to obviate the idea that dance and music are related.

In our Parkinson's class, we've come to refer to music as the red carpet: it rolls out seamlessly before us to support, remind, and guide participants out of uneasiness or rigidity and into a state of flowing grace. We are certainly not the first to remark on the incredible effects music can have on people with Parkinson's, and it would be impossible to do the subject justice in this short chapter. In *Awakenings*, Dr. Oliver Sacks writes at length about the power of music "to integrate and cure, to liberate the Parkinsonian and give him freedom while it lasts" (1980, p. 60). In both *Awakenings* and in his more recent book, *Musicophilia*, Sacks speaks of one patient, Edith T, a former music teacher who felt that her movements were "wooden" and "mechanical—like a robot or a doll." She told Sacks: "…as I am unmusicked [by Parkinsonism], I must be remusicked" (1980, p. 60). Sacks concludes in *Musicophilia*:

> It is music that the Parkinsonian needs, for only music, which is rigorous yet spacious, sinuous and alive, can evoke responses that are equally so. And he needs not only the metrical structure of rhythm and the free movement of melody…but the 'will' and intentionality of music. (2007, p. 258)

Since dancing is the physical embodiment of music and rhythm, the swaying branches of music's solid trunk, it makes sense that moving rigorously, spaciously, sinuously, and intentionally to music would be particularly important and rewarding to people with Parkinson's as it is for most people in most dancing cultures around the world.

Rhythm is the most obvious guide for dancers—with or without Parkinson's—because it unifies different perceptions of time under a single, kinesthetic, and audible metric order. This element of music seems especially helpful for people with Parkinson's, which in many cases affects a person's organic physical rhythm and swing. Parkinson's symptoms can cause a festinating walk that speeds up seemingly without control or bradykinesia, a slowness in the execution of movement. We see both effects in our class, and both appear to the eye to occur in opposition to any steady, internalized rhythm. Because music organizes time so clearly and in essence commands the body and our brains to move to it, audible rhythm seems to have the power to bypass some of these symptoms and bring order and unified duration of movement to the body. As noted Harvard neurologist Gottfried Schlaug suggests in reference to other disorders, music may provide "an alternative entry point" (Healy, 2010) to the brain that allows our participants to find in class a natural rhythm they had trouble finding as they walked to the dance center.

But music does more than tell us when to do a step; it tells us how to do those steps and, if we have an emotional connection to the music we're hearing, helps us keep track of sequences of steps and consecutive movement, something that is particularly difficult for people with PD yet is an essential component of dance training (Sacks & Tomaino, 1991, p. 11). Rhythm shows us which road we're on, but melody, harmony, and emotional tone show us the scenery along the way, what color it is and suggests how one feels about it and what might be around the corner. In our class, music becomes another source of transformational imagery that motivates our participants. Just as a visual image supports dancers trying to achieve a solid arabesque, music adds a layer of aesthetic motivation and lays out a clear qualitative objective that participants can achieve. More importantly, it feels satisfying and rewarding to move to music. In its evocation of a certain quality, mood, or place, music informs and directs our Parkinson's dancers like nothing else. Music is the key to creating what Carroll Neesemann calls "magic moments"—times when symptoms seem to dissolve, artistry takes over, and students enter a state of flow. Their bodies are moving because their brains are dancing.

AESTHETICS, CHOREOGRAPHY, AND THE REALM OF THE POSSIBLE

Mark Morris' choreography embodies the perfect synthesis of musical sensitivity and visual representation. Morris understands the structural and emotional nuances of music and uses his vivid imagination to translate those nuances into movement. His choreography always emphasizes quality (how movement is initiated) over quantity (how many times you can kick your leg high up in the air). In this way, he creates unique aesthetic worlds that require his dancers to take an imaginative approach to the work. Because of his work's innate musicality and because we enjoy sharing his work with others, we regularly introduce phrases from Morris' repertory to our Dance for PD classes. For us, the inclusion of Morris' choreography in the class represents the ultimate shedding of disease and the embrace of aesthetic, a place where the pathology of PD dissolves and participants can develop an artistic sensibility. When participants learn the same dances they see the Mark Morris Dance Group performing down the street at the Brooklyn Academy of Music or at Lincoln Center, they feel included in a creative, artistic, and educational community that values them as vital members. More specifically, when participants execute movement that they know has a particular aesthetic context—either because they've seen it on stage or heard teachers describe the dance from which it derives—they have another motivating layer of information at their fingertips. This information stimulates their imaginations and memories in the service of dancing in the same way that it does for professional dancers charged with putting a choreographer's vision on stage.

In *Dido and Aeneas*,[1] Morris' choreographed version of Henry Purcell's opera, the corps of dancers represents a Greek chorus. In our Dance for PD class, participants learn a section of the dance called "Oft She Visits," which tells the story of Diana and Actaeon through specific arm and hand gestures, and torso bends. The movement itself is a terrific coordination exercise because it demands the use of different qualities and a series of rather complicated moves that develop range and attack. In addressing range, we encourage participants to imagine they are projecting their movement to the back of an ancient amphitheater so that they are thinking about 'shouting' their movements and making them as large and clear as possible. The dance also poses an initial cognitive challenge because it is made up of a series of seemingly distinct, consecutive gestures. But the fact that the dance is completely image based and tells a recognizable, linear narrative means that participants can engage, internalize, and remember it relatively easily and develop mastery over it so that they become confident physical storytellers. Just as they do for the Mark Morris dancers, the demands of narrative—the need to physically describe a series of important events—imbue participants' movements with specificity and dynamic control.

In *L'Allegro, il Penseroso ed il Moderato*,[2] to an eponymous pastoral oratorio by Handel, Morris transforms images from William Blake's paintings and John Milton's words into fluid physical poetry through which dancers embody, among other things, birds, shepherds, city dwellers, and the four elements. We teach our participants a section we call "Each Action," which allows them to explore the starkly contrasting movement qualities inherent in earth, air, fire, and water. Once again, there are very specific challenges that come with each movement: the earth move requires a soft rising and lowering of the back and ripple of the hands; the water move demands a specific controlled tremolo in the hands as they pass across the chest; and the air move involves a small explosion of fingers while the cheeks exhale air in a percussive blow. But vibrant poetic imagery supports the mechanics of each of these moves. Here, the imagery is less word based than the bathing and wild dogs in the Diana and Actaeon story from *Dido and Aeneas*, and for that reason it requires more imaginative effort. No one could say how earth dances, but once we explain that the earth move represents the tilling of the soil, the participants understand it and can interpret it in their own way. The fire move seems relatively abstract until we say that the heels of the hands are like flint and rock that strike each other to create a spark. So with these descriptions—the same descriptions Mark Morris uses to help his dancers embody the movement—the imagination adds a layer to the steps, creating logic and impetus for the body.

When we teach this material to our participants, their imaginations freely enter the worlds of each dance. They embrace and embody the qualitative ideas of Morris' choreography. They know what to strive for. "I've come to realize that unlike other physical endeavors, dance is about the 'how,' not just the 'what' of an action," Neesemann told me in an interview. "You really have to think about how you are doing a movement for it to work as a dance." Enriching this process is the fact that many of the participants have seen Morris' dances on stage or on video, and they remember the artistic context of the piece when they do it in the studio. Many of them carry an aesthetic model in their minds that informs a deeper approach to the movement they're learning. They understand the context of the phrase, or the story they are trying to tell through the movement, and the experience becomes richer as a result. Neesemann, for example, has been asking us for months to teach a section of Morris' *Mozart Dances* (2006) because he feels that it embodies the kind of communal grace he'd like the class to achieve, a state he'd like to hold out for himself as a challenge and inspiration. By engaging in repertory that they can see and know, Neesemann and others experience an active loop of observation, awareness, and engaged execution. This process, Bodis-Wollner surmises, creates "an enormous internal reward" (Fallik, 2007, p. 34). It is crucial to note that the elements of the repertory phrases that make them easier to learn—the fact that they are image based, engage the imagination, tell stories, and are set to beautiful music—are the same things that make them immensely satisfying to do. The strategy and reward are one and the same. It feels good to achieve something physically that you have imagined, remembered, or desired. The rewarding act of embodying and manifesting the poetic beauty of these pieces seems to provide participants with a physical, emotional, and cognitive satisfaction that may be difficult for them to find in other parts of their lives. This may be a unique pleasure, in fact, that people from all backgrounds—with or without PD—experience when they learn and meaningfully execute dances together.

Through such a concentrated focus on aesthetic objectives, the Parkinson's dancers are able to use their minds to unlock ways of moving that are otherwise inaccessible. There seems to be a dramatic difference between telling someone to shake his hands while dragging them across the front of his body and telling someone to create the shimmering ripples on a beautiful blue lake (as they do in "Each Action" from *L'Allegro*). "One thing that's changed for me," says Neesemann, "is that I'm able to get into movement that seems out of character for me. I'm not a wiggler," Neesemann says in reference to some salsa moves we did recently across the floor. "By picking up some of the qualitative things we work on, I find myself trying to put a wiggle into things, which is much more fun." Heinz agrees: "We had a class in which the teacher talked about three kinds of movement: resisted, flowing, and sparky." The teacher's approach to the class, Heinz says, "helps me think about a certain kind of movement, and explore movement that I might not otherwise have encountered just walking around." The aesthetic goal is key, concurs Heginbotham:

> Often there is such an emphasis on what you can't do; our class is about what you can do. Any conscious version of a movement is a beautiful version. As opposed to a very specific

goal of doing ten repetitions of one movement, you have an aesthetic goal for yourself and set out to achieve it. (Gehris, 2008)

Both Neesemann and Heinz speak to the dramatic power of aesthetics and imagery in the service of movement, about how dance's ability to represent the physical manifestation of visual, imaginative, and musical ideas allows them to initiate and execute movement that isn't necessarily accessible to them when they're just walking down the street. However, their statements point to an important secondary effect of the class. Like most of the participants, these men know what they need in order to feel better. The reward of doing certain kinds of movement is so strong that it empowers participants like Neesemann and Heinz to ask for more of what they need in the class (like Neesemann requesting *Mozart Dances*). Instead of a medicalized environment, which can often feel diminishing and silencing, the dance studio emboldens, and some even say empowers, learners.

THE EMPOWERING GAZE

The act of being watched also changes us. Dancing in the living room brings personal joys that are private and often wonderful, and many of us are content to stay there. But doing something for an audience brings a heightened state of concentration and commitment to any activity. This is a basic condition of the performing arts. The context and framing of aesthetic material—whether it is eventually enjoyed by a few viewers or a thousand—affect the parameters of its production. An audience changes a random assortment of choices and movements into a conscious aesthetic statement that says "We are doing this for you as well as for us."

As active professional performers, Heginbotham, Owens, and I aim to translate the essential qualities of performance—clarity, confidence, focus, expansiveness, projection and spontaneity—into the exercises we design for our participants. We know that the act of stepping out on stage in front of people, under the lights and before the audience's gaze, forces us to be hyperconscious about every part of our bodies—where we are in space, what each limb is doing, how our eyes are engaged, what our faces look like. Being watched gives us the tingling awareness of being fully present in every cell, which can be joyful, exhilarating, and sometimes frightening. We're also particularly interested in the way an audience affects the range and power of a dancer's movements. Just as an actor or singer has to project her voice in a large hall (or an ancient amphitheater), a dancer must learn to make her movements larger and fuller in front of an audience. For a person with Parkinson's, whose movements often shrink to a sliver of what they once were and lack a sense of full presence, the way the stage affects the range of movements is particularly relevant. We believe that if we can adapt the transformational effect of the stage to the studio and pass it on to our Parkinson's dancers, they will be able to embody those anti-Parkinsonian performance qualities themselves. But how do we do this?

To begin with, the experience of dancing in a dance studio is itself performative. Dance classes, like all social gatherings, are more than just a place to meet other dancers—they are places to observe, imitate, impress, judge, analyze, compete, and compare. In dance classes, there are always other people in the room who are watching you whether you like it or not. For professionals-in-training, this can be a constructive dynamic because it means that by the time you reach the performance stage, you've performed for hundreds if not thousands of tough but empathic peers. But we weren't sure whether any of these elements would be healthy for, or supportive of, our Parkinson's participants. And in early surveys of our class, being on display was not mentioned as something that brought people back each week. In fact, several participants mentioned that they enjoyed "performing movements relatively free of embarrassment and inhibition" (Westheimer, 2008, pp. 139–140) and appreciated "the comfortable, anxiety-free company of this group" (Westheimer, 2008, pp. 139–140). Knowing all of this, we were ambivalent about highlighting a performance component. As professionals, we knew that performing—intentionally on stage or more subtly in a studio setting—could have negative effects as well. It could place an enormous stress on dancers. We wanted our participants to feel the way we felt on stage on a good night but without any performance anxiety.

Carroll Neesemann was the first to admit that he actually liked the pressure of having to move with someone else watching. He told us it gave him an added incentive to try to achieve the aesthetic goals we laid out in our combinations. It helped him focus on doing it well, not just muddling through. Surprisingly to us, Neesemann even adopted the philosophy that company dancers feel when they're dancing as a group: "I try to do the moves well so that the whole ensemble will look good to you guys," he told me in an interview. Herb Heinz agreed, expanding the idea of audience to the entire class. "There's a strong element of human connection in the class. By the end, when we're standing in a circle holding hands, we've been through the experience together and offer ourselves to each other. I sometimes have trouble dancing on my own, but in the class, I'm just there." Heinz explained that his choreography in the grocery store was also an attempt, in the face of feeling clumsy, to impress an unwitting supermarket audience with his grace. Reflecting further on the class he said, "There's something about being with other people that makes moving feel like performing. It's incredibly motivating because being in a situation in which people are observing me gives everything I do weight and meaning. I really appreciate that kind of motivation." As it turns out, many participants rely on the gentle pressure an audience provides to help them focus on moving with power and grace. The gaze of the audience—even if it's a group of supportive classmates who are all "in it together"—becomes another important tool, like music, imagery, or narrative that some—not all—participants have come to value. We see this very clearly when we play the "Name Game," in which one by one, each participant says his or her name and does a gesture. In effect, the dancers do a five-second solo in front of everyone else; amazingly, even people who have trouble initiating movement on their own rise to the occasion and choreograph on the spot, in front of 35 others. The group's eyes and the power of the group's expectation—"now it's your turn"—create a strong motivating cue. In some cases, we see participants' resting tremors disappear during their turn at the "Name Game." We don't know how much of this is simply because the person is fully focused on his or her own movement or whether it has to do with being watched—or a combination of the two.

As a result of participants' responses, we now integrate an intentional audience/performer dynamic into every class. Sometimes we give participants the opportunity to do a short solo at the end, but more often we encourage the audience/performer dynamic to enter the class in the form of a structured mirroring improvisation. In this exercise, which developed collaboratively among participants, teachers, the musician, and Westheimer, dancers break into seated couples and face each other. In each couple, one person leads—invents movement on the spot—for the other person to follow. Sometimes, we add layers of specific narrative ("Jekyll and Hyde" or "The Four Seasons"), but often we leave the improvisation open. In fact, Owens notices that during this part of the class, the teachers are "not in control of it. It is the dancers totally overcoming their movement difficulties" on their own (Gehris, 2005). This is important because it once again highlights the empowering structure of the class. Participants enjoy the opportunity to lead themselves, to return to a state in which they have full agency and control over what they do with their bodies (and what their partners do with theirs). In this part of class, they choreograph their own paths out of resistance.

A few months after we introduced the mirroring exercise to the class, Heginbotham made a surprising announcement. One half of the class was to do the improvisation in pairs while the other half watched. One of his rationales was simply that the movement was very beautiful: "The way PD manifests itself means that everyone's approach to moving is different, and obviously PD dancers do not all look the same as they might in a classical ballet company. You get the same movements in thirty different ways. How often do you see that? It's very inspiring" (Fogg, 2010). But Heginbotham had other motives, too. He wanted to test Neesemann's postulation that the pressure of an audience would actually help movement, not hinder it. By creating an audience, Heginbotham designed a house of mirrors in which there are several layers of viewer and participant. We've come to realize that few activities better incorporate the ideas of embodied learning—a confident self-guided navigation through challenges—than the mirroring dance.

The participants who are cast into the leadership positions become choreographers on the spot. They must hear the music, use the tools of their imagination, and express themselves through movement to their partners, as well as to the audience across the room. The situation demands clarity, confidence, and a split yet intensified focus. Even more, it encourages the leaders to control and project their movement fluently, a particularly constructive challenge for people with Parkinson's. In the PD class, this exercise becomes a transformational artistic event that is as political as it is beautiful. Multiple simultaneous activities—creating a dance, participating in a spontaneous *pas de deux*, and watching fellow participants perform—appear to empower leaders, followers, and viewers alike. In this heightened state, which echoes what happens in a theater, participants' movement undergoes a visible change: movements become smoother, tremors diminish, posture lengthens, faces become expressive and engaged. Playfulness, humor, drama and joy abound as participants dance for one other. Thinking on the fly, the Parkinson's dancers call on every embodied tool and instinct to move with confidence and grace. In defiance of a disease that disjoints or freezes, they dance.

A COMMUNITY OF LEARNERS

At its core, Dance for PD reflects one of the primary objectives of all arts education: to change the way we understand, experience and engage with the world around us. Learning to dance helps people with Parkinson's see movement in an entirely new, positive way—as a creative, joyful path to agency rather than as a frustrating problem. Dancing gives our participants access to grace and control. For a disease in which people gradually lose fluidity and basic actions become difficult—tying a shoe for example—learning to dance provides a new paradigm for engaging with the world. By training with professional dancers, people with Parkinson's start to think like professional dancers, and by doing so, they discover ways to make life imitate art.

From the very first day, our classes have emphasized collaboration over hierarchy. In some ways, this emphasis reflects the communal spirit on which the Mark Morris Dance Group was founded, a belief that dance and music are not elite, rarified, inaccessible art forms but rather the joyous, meaningful glue that keeps us together as a species. As Joan Acocella wrote in her biography of Morris, "The one love that Morris has concentrated on more than any other does have a name: community. The idea of the group as the fundamental unit of meaning in the dance was there in his work from the beginning" (Acocella, 1993, pp. 112–113). This spirit of unity means that in our PD class, everyone is welcome and everyone dances together. But this emphasis is also a reflection of our teaching philosophy: that the best kind of class is one in which participants learn how to guide themselves in newly conscious ways. The best class creates teachers out of learners, helping people lead themselves to action. This type of embodied training is an underlying principle of all good dance training and arts education in general. Aesthetic, creative encounters aim to inform, coax, and foster independence in those who engage in them. By developing and maintaining a toolkit of strategies and techniques that help them move, by leading each other in spontaneous improvisations, and by asking to do specific choreography, our participants regain confidence and agency that may be difficult to draw upon outside of the dance studio.

But the collaborative model goes even further. The Dance for PD class has become a mutually beneficial learning community in which people with Parkinson's teach the professional dancers as much about their own art as the dancers teach the participants. Amanda Fogg, who teaches a dance class for her community in Weymouth, England, says that the focus of the class has reminded her of how important it is to approach dance from the inside: "Having minor physical difficulties myself, and working with people who have considerable challenges, has really emphasized to me that dance lives within—and that there is always a way of bringing it to light."

For me, the class has completely refocused my perspective on dance. The isolated, somewhat cloistered reality that most full-time professional dancers experience to some degree is far removed from the way most people experience dance, and the way people have experienced dance for thousands of years. The Dance for PD classes have helped me rediscover the transformative power that people of all body types and abilities create when they dance together in a connected community, with a common purpose. I've come to appreciate how important and beautiful the simple activity of learning and dancing together in a diverse, collective group can be. Once you open your eyes to this, one person with PD putting all of her intent into lifting an arm with a certain quality can be as stimulating to watch as a highly trained ballerina doing *"Swan Lake"* because it's completely honest, committed, and unique—no one else moves like that.

The class also makes those who lead it clearer dancers and stronger teachers. Participants demand—whether implicitly or explicitly—that we demonstrate more clearly, project movement more emphatically, and explain our images more colorfully in words and action. We must revisit our assumptions about what we do, thinking deeply and searching for purity in the movement. To do this, we must embody what we want to express with more commitment and clarity. And in this way, the participants demand from us exactly what we ask from them. It's a perfect, nourishing loop of continuous investigation, a loop represented during every class by the communal circle that starts and ends our sessions together. In this nurturing community, everybody learns from everybody.

Notes

1. Mark Morris choreographed *Dido and Aeneas* during his time as the artistic director and resident choreographer of the Théâtre Royal de la Monnaie in Brussels, Belgium. It premiered in March of 1989. Morris choreographed Henry Purcell's 1688 opera with himself playing the lead parts of Dido and the Sorceress while company members played courtiers, witches, sailors, and spirits. All of the musicians and soloists are in the orchestra pit, while the dancers tell the story on stage. A film of the production was produced in 1995.
2. Mark Morris choreographed *L'Allegro, il Penseroso ed il Moderato* in 1988. It was the first dance that he premiered during his tenure at the Théâtre Royal de la Monnaie.

Works Cited

Acocella, J. (1993). *Mark Morris.* New York: Farrar Straus Giroux.

Bodis-Wollner, I. Personal conversations with David Leventhal, 2007–2011.

Brown, S., & Parsons, L. M. (July 2008). The neuroscience of dance. *Scientific American* (http://www.sci-amdigital.com/index.cfm?fa=Products.ViewIssue&ISSUEID_CHAR=5F26785B-3048–8A5E-105CB11D7B06A2D6), 78–83.

Calvo-Merino, B, C. Jola, D.E. Glaser, & P. Haggard. (2008). Towards a sensorimotor aesthetics of performing art. *Consciousness and Cognition, 17*, 911–922.

Esterberg, J. (2010). Email Interview. 13 July.

Fallik, D. (January/February 2007). Finding new life through movement. *Neurology Now, 3*(1), 30–33.

Fallik, D. (January/February 2007). Why exercise helps people with movement disorders. *Neurology Now, 3*(1), 34.

Fogg, A. (Spring 2008). We are all dancers: Dance and Parkinson's disease. *Animated* (Foundation for Community Dance UK), 32–35.

Fogg, A. Email Interview. 12 July 2010.

Gehris, A. (2008). *Brooklyn Parkinson Group newsletter*, pp. 2–3.

Gehris, A. (2005). Parkinson's sufferers get their groove back through dance. *The Tuscaloosa News,* 3 Nov., p. 2D.

Hagendoorn, I. (Spring 2003). The dancing brain. *Cerebrum: The Dana Forum on Brain Science, 5* (2). http://www.ivarhagendoorn.com/files/articles/Hagendoorn-Cerebrum-03.pdf)

Healy, M. (2010). The hope of music's healing powers. *Los Angeles Times,* 1 Mar. http://articles.latimes.com/2010/mar/01/health/la-he-0301-brain-music-therapy-20100301

Heinz, H. (2009). Personal Interview. 1 June.

Neesemann, C. (2009). Personal Interview. 16 July.

Sacks, O. (1980). *Awakenings.* New York: Vintage.

Sacks, O. (2007). *Musicophilia: Tales of music and the brain.* New York: Alfred A. Knopf.

Sacks, O., & C. M. Tomaino. (1991). Music and neurological disorder. *International Journal of Arts Medicine, 1* (1), 10–12.

Seneca the younger. *Epistulae morales*. 23, 4. (Translation by Richard M. Gummere). New York: G.P. Putnam's Sons, 1925, p. 161.

Solway, D. (2007). Learning to dance, one chunk at a time. *New York Times*, 27 May, p. AR19.

Sulcas, R. (2007). Getting their groove back, with help from the magic of dance. *New York Times,* 25 Aug. http://www.nytimes.com/2007/08/25/arts/dance/25park.html?_r=2&oref=slogin&)

Westheimer, O. (2008). Why dance for Parkinson's disease. *Topics in Geriatric Rehabilitation, 24* (2): 127–140.

CHAPTER FOUR

The Communicative Body in Women's Self-Defense Courses

KELI YERIAN

INTRODUCTION

The classroom is[1] a large space covered with blue mats and full-length mirrors along one side. In one corner are two strangely dressed figures. Both have bulky clothes on with special padding underneath. One is wearing a large padded helmet with holes cut out for the eyes and mouth, while the other has put his helmet down to the side on the mat. Along the opposite side of the room is a line of women—the students—in gym clothes. Another woman in the role of a coach leads the first student in the line out to one end of the room. She signals to the man in the helmet that they are ready, and the student jogs out onto the mat as the man steps out towards her in the opposite direction.

The woman is pretending to be a jogger out on the trails where she habitually runs, and she has requested that the helmeted man play the role of a person she passes on the path. As the two approach each other, the woman hesitates and starts to veer around the man. The helmeted man raises his hand casually, says "Hi" and continues to walk past. As the jogging woman pulls up at the other side of the room, the rest of the class laughs. The coach calls out, "That's usually what's going to happen!"

They begin the scenario again. This time the man holds up his hand with his palm facing the woman, appearing to be both greeting and attempting to stop her.

The student greets him in turn but does not slow up until he physically steps into her path. She stops and faces him, assessing the full range of his behavior as she decides how to respond.

This scenario is a common one in courses offered by a full-force self-defense program on the West Coast of the U.S. These courses stand apart from the martial arts, in that they give students practice using a variety of vocal and physical self-defense techniques in role-play scenarios and full-force 'fights' with mock assailants in specially padded suits. Although some of these courses are designed for men or children, the majority of them are designed for women. The courses are taught by both female and male instructors who undergo a year or more of instructor training. The female instructors act as coaches to the students while the male instructors double as mock assailants.

This chapter explores the importance of the body as a source of knowledge, perception, and communication for participants in these courses. Students of full-force self-defense learn to pay attention to a wide range of both physical and vocal behavior in others and to monitor their own range of behaviors across contexts as well. They are encouraged to assess situations that may involve danger and 'test' these situations, through their own words and actions, to determine whether they really may be dangerous. Finally, they are encouraged to expand the range of responses they may have physical familiarity with, including speaking firmly, yelling, gesturing, fighting physically, and even acquiescing or reassuring in certain cases for strategic purposes. These practices allow the students to experience their bodies as capable of various forms of symbolic and 'real' actions and to become aware of the ways that the body and voice can be integrated to affect others' perceptions and actions. When considered against the backdrop of social expectations related to gender, these courses represent an educational context that, unlike most such contexts these women have likely encountered, challenges and disrupts the way gender is often managed through the body.

The following analysis draws from over 100 hours of videotaped data from five intensive courses for women taught in 1999. I use Goffman's (1974) frame analysis approach to consider how students learn to resist the framing of an activity as 'normal' or 'safe' by the mock assailant and re-frame it as 'unacceptable' or 'potentially dangerous' by using an expanded range of communicative strategies that are clearly grounded in bodily practices. Although some of these strategies are normatively linked to either men or women, these courses promote a constructivist view of the body as able to engage in multiple practices and display multiple identities. These courses provide students with an unusual opportunity to be mindful of expanding rather than restricting the body's resourcefulness in interaction. Multimodal learning thus leads to greater potential for empowerment and agency at personal, interactional, and societal levels.

EMBODIMENT AND GENDER IN INTERACTION

Bodies are powerful communicative resources, as they allow us to perceive and perform, through gesture and other physical means, various meanings and interactional functions. Work in gesture studies, for example, has revealed ways in which the face, head, and hands may all help a speaker to relate propositional information, such as how something moves, its shape, its size or direction (e.g., see McNeill 1992, Sherzer, 1972). In an educational context, Goldin-Meadow (2004) identifies how the hand gestures of students and teachers can reveal and effect conceptual understandings (or misunderstandings) of equations in math and science, even when these concepts are not expressed verbally. Pragmatic meaning can also be demonstrated through the body; gesture and posture can highlight the relative importance of elements in discourse, indicate the type of speech act intended (such as requesting or scolding), or display one's attitude towards the topics or interlocutors (Kendon, 2004; Müller & Posner, 2002; Goodwin, 2007). The body is not limited to individually produced meanings; however, people also mutually manage multi-party face-to-face interaction through bodily practices, such as the regulation of turn-taking and the organization of mutual attention and perception within the physical environment (Goodwin, 1994; Streeck, 1993, 2009).

Despite its rich potential in communication, however, the body is not a neutral resource. It is visibly shaped and restricted by norms of social practice. In the words of Foucault (1975), it is 'disciplined' through social processes in ways that are tied to social identities and roles, including gender identities. In his book, *Gender Advertisements*, sociologist Erving Goffman (1976) described early on what he called "the arrangement between the sexes." He shows that in images of women and men in western media, femininity is associated with poses and gestures of dependency and deference, such as might be found among children or other socially subordinate people. The cocked head, the inwardly bent knee, delicate gestures, smiling, and averted eye contact of feminine displays are contrasted in his analysis with the upright, square, serious and protective postures of masculine displays. "These expressions," he writes, "turn out to be illustrations of ritual-like bits of behavior which portray an ideal conception of the two sexes and their structural relationship to each other, accomplishing this in part by indicating, again ideally, the alignment of the actor in the social situation" (p. 84). Henley's (1975, 1977) feminist review of early psychological, sociological and linguistic research on non-verbal sex differences in interaction resulted in similar conclusions for women in the U.S. Her review found that women tend to be touched more by others, be more restricted in posture, gesture, and motion than men, smile more often, take up less space, and make less eye contact with men than men do with women. Although later research found that such patterns vary widely by function and context (see Epstein, 1986; Tannen, 1996, for discussion), no researcher has argued that gender as a social construct is not a powerful organizing force behind differences that do occur.

In recent decades, scholars interested in gender and identity have emphasized the socially constructed nature of gender to explain how differences are produced and resisted (e.g., Butler, 1990, 1993, 2004; Bucholtz, 1999). This approach is consistent with Goffman's (1974, 1977) and Tannen's (1996, 1999) work in frame analysis. Goffman argues that differences in gendered behavior in social interaction are not "sex-linked," or true of each individual woman or man, but "sex-class linked"— linked to the class of women or the class of men (1977, p. 305). He writes:

> An interactional field…provides a considerable expressive resource, and it is, of course, upon this field that there is projected the training and beliefs of the participants. It is here that sex-class makes itself felt, here in the organization of face-to-face interaction, for here understandings about sex-based dominance can be employed as a means of deciding who decides, who leads and who follows. Again, these scenes do not so much allow for the expression of natural differences between the sexes as for the production of that difference itself. (1977, p. 324)

Here, gender is a matter of 'display' rather than (fixed) 'identity' and as such requires the performance of many everyday behaviors and rituals, verbal and physical alike, to produce it. In this way, social norms linked to gender produce specific interactional rituals, and specific interactional rituals (re)produce social norms linked to gender.

Work on gender and non-verbal practices has provided insight into the early socialization processes inherent in interaction. Both Martin (1998) and McMurrey (1998) describe how preschool children attend to and develop gendered non-verbal practices through daily interactions with peers and teachers. Nayak and Kehily (2006) show how British adolescent girls and boys monitor one another's speech and physical behavior along gendered, heterosexual lines. In South Africa, Kunene and Brookes (2010) show how the physical and gestural repertoires of Zulu-speaking men and women differ in accordance with local expectations for gendered behavior. Specifically, young men who use expansive combinations of gesture and movement while retelling stories and bragging gain a certain level of social capital, while women who engage in similar behavior are considered decidedly transgressive.

Gendered practices are embedded within specific institutional practices for much of a child's life. As Ross (2004) argues, school systems strongly regulate how all students are allowed to use and experience their bodies. In her words, "the body has been a hidden student in America's classrooms" (p. 169). Even arts education programs that focus on music, dance, and drama are often too constrained by time,

resources, and space to allow students to deeply or creatively engage in physical practices (Davidson, 2004). Martin (1998) argues that when educational contexts regulate the bodies of children they do so in ways that also help produce differences
among girls and boys. For example, in the preschool classrooms she studied, boys
engaged in 80% of the "relaxed" behaviors observed (e.g., crawling on the floor,
yelling, lying down while listening to the teacher), while 82% of the more formal
behaviors (e.g., sitting up, raising one's hand, speaking quietly, covering one's mouth
when coughing) were observed in girls (p. 501). Moreover, teachers in these classes
were more likely to reprimand girls for relaxed behaviors than boys. Sadker and
Sadker (1994) found a similar pattern in teachers' responses to hand-raising: girls
who did not raise their hands were more likely to be reprimanded. Thus, within an
already disciplined school environment, girls appear to be expected to monitor
their own physical comportment and expression even more carefully than boys.

These socially produced bodily practices are considered by women's self-
defense instructors to disadvantage women in contexts of psychological or sexual
assault later in life. Women accustomed to gender-appropriate ways of using their
voices and bodies are less likely, they believe, to have familiarity with embodied practices that would help them resist assault. They cite research on sexual assault which
shows that when women actively resist assault, either verbally or physically, they tend
to be more successful in avoiding or breaking off the assault, and do so with no more
risk of bodily injury (Queen's Bench Foundation, 1976; Kleck & Sayles, 1990;
Ullman & Knight, 1992, 1993).

For these reasons, the self-defense organization discussed in this chapter has created an educational context that challenges the social norms that produce differentiated ranges of physical and communicative practices for women and men. Students
are encouraged to explore, test, and practice a variety of embodied practices that could
disrupt or prevent a potential assault. Course curricula include physical training in
the kinds of strikes and kicks that are most effective for women resisting assault as
well as frequent role-play scenarios that may or may not involve physical contact. In
these open-ended simulations, students are urged to monitor their own use of verbal, vocal and physical strategies with the mock assailant but not with the goal of
restricting or subduing them. Rather, the students are encouraged to use these various strategies to construct coherent 'stances' across modalities in a way that is
responsive to the specific situation. Sometimes these stances require using the voice
and body in ways that are less familiar to some of the women in the class, for example, using a firm tone, direct eye contact, and a clear 'stop' gesture; sometimes the
stances may feel more familiar but are being strategically re-purposed for resistance,
for example, when a woman acts compliant if trapped in order to escape as soon as
she sees a chance. The students also practice perceiving mismatches in how other peo-

ples' words and bodies are communicating, such as when a stranger is saying "I'll leave you alone" but continues to approach or when a date says "I do care about you" but continues to touch the woman who has asked him to stop. All of these topics are raised and, more importantly, experienced through explicit attention to the multimodal self as a means of perceiving, responding, and initiating action in the world.

MATCHING WORDS AND BODY CONSCIOUSLY: CONSTRUCTING COHERENT STANCES

Instructors of these self-defense courses are very aware of how the small details of interaction become crucial to the outcome of a potential assault. They note that would-be assailants will often pay close attention to such subtle details as how a prospective victim carries herself and how she responds to him in interaction. It is common, for example, for assailants to 'test' a woman, whether she is a stranger or not, by acting more demanding or aggressive and seeing if she responds in a compliant or non-compliant manner (Queen's Bench Foundation, 1976). Often 'compliant' responses, such as a ducked head, a shrinking posture, a nervous laugh, or a polite vocal response, are among the same strategies that form the building blocks for the construction of normative displays of femininity (McCaughey, 1997). As a result, rather than only practicing the physical aspects of fighting back, a large part of the course is devoted to raising students' awareness about their own ways of talking and behaving. Students begin to 'deconstruct' the vocal and non-vocal elements of complex interactional stances and behaviors and then 'reconstruct' them in various ways, first during group drills and then in the improvised role-plays.

Both vocal and non-vocal means of displaying the self are presented in the course as essential channels of communication and action in the deterrence of an assault. Students learn that vocal and physical strategies can reinforce each other in the construction of a coherent stance, or, alternatively, they can contradict each other, creating dissonance within a stance. Often, one of the most challenging aspects of the course for students is learning how to project stances that do not display contradictory meanings. For example, a student may firmly tell the mock assailant to leave her alone, contributing to a stance of authority, yet turn her body away and avert her gaze, simultaneously communicating a possible lack of assurance. These contradictions, of course, could also be present within as well as across vocal and non-vocal strategies such as when a student's voice wavers and fades while delivering a directive, or when a student smiles while holding up her hands in a 'stop' gesture.

In the first example below (see Appendix for transcription conventions), the instructor is introducing the idea of constructing stances deliberately. She pretends to be a person walking down a street and invites the students to critique her physical demeanor and break it down into smaller components of physical stance and action, including use of space, orientation, posture, gaze, and gesture:

Example 1 (FI = female instructor, MI = male instructor, S = a student)

1 FI: [speaking to the whole class] So…what we're gonna do is we're gonna start talking about how you can use your stance. . just the way you stand and walk through the world. . and how you can use your voice to help protect you and keep you safe…Okay?…

                 [walks over to MI]

2   So if this is a menacing person. [indicates him with hand] who is looking for someone to victimize I want you all to help me be less likely to be that person, okay? So I want you all to help change my [starts walking] my walk and how I'm just walking down the street

3   [walking slowly with head down, shoulders rounded, arms stiffly at sides, gaze down. MI with helmet on walking closely behind her]

4 S1:   Look up

               [

5 S2:   Look up. .

6 FI: [brings gaze up slightly]

7 S3:   Look up higher. . higher!. .

8 FI: [brings gaze up so she is looking straight ahead as she continues to walk]

9 S2:   Straighten your shoulders

               [

10 S1:   Bring your shoulders back. .

                       [

11 FI: [straightens shoulders]

12 S4:   Walk faster!. .

13 FI: [walks slightly faster]

14 S1:   Look both si:des!

               [

15 S3:		Swing your a:rms. . when you walk. .
16 FI:	[swings arms a little more]	
		[
17 S1:		Look around
		[
18 S3:		Look around!. .
19 S1:	Look arou:nd…	
		[
20 FI		[turns her head from side to side]
21 S3:	Turn around!	
22 FI:	[turns around quickly to face the MI behind her, going into what they call 'protective stance': body square, knees slightly bent in readiness to move, hands up and palm out in 'stop' gesture, looking directly at MI]	

In the excerpt above, the instructor lets the students recognize for themselves the elements of her body and movement that could be adjusted in order for her to project a person who is aware, confident, and prepared to face potential conflict. She first adopts a stooped posture with arms and body stiff and tense and gaze averted toward the floor. These physical elements are easily recognizable to observers in this context as displaying a stance of fear, nervousness, or denial of the environment. The students then engage in collectively coaching her in how to change these aspects of her demeanor to project solidity, confidence, and awareness, instead. At this point, she turns to the students and explains:

Example 2:

1 FI:	Okay. . my self-defense was this [walks with head down, MI walks behind her again] "Okay nothing can happen to me nothing can happen to me" [turns around and faces MI with hands up]…Okay so stop and take a look, okay?. . And you know hopefully he'll just walk by….But so you want the upright body stance [pats chest]. . If you're looking at the ground, looking up [looks up at ceiling] and not looking around….You exude someone who doesn't know where they are…Then you can easily be approached. . [starts walking looking down again] 'Cause if I'm walking like this…I can easily have someone in my space before I know it [MI walks up to pass closely behind her]….Okay?…

This interactive demonstration between the instructors and students lays the groundwork for the notion that how one carries oneself can be a matter of strategic choice rather than one of habitual default. It gives the students the opportunity to see how a complex physical arrangement of the body can unwittingly project a socially meaningful stance. It also allows them to deconstruct the stance the instructor is embodying into smaller, specific elements that can then be adjusted more consciously in their own bodies. This is the first step to understanding stances as mutable and constructed through interaction. With conscious attention to these aspects of the body in interaction, the women are more likely to influence the moment-to-moment unfolding of a potentially dangerous situation.

INTONATION WITHIN A MULTIMODAL STANCE

In a similar dramatization, a female and a male instructor pinpoint the issue of rising intonation. They warn students to be aware of any tendency to 'go up at the end' of their directives when telling the mock assailant to leave them alone, as this would be a conflict in messages. Rather than isolate and define rising intonation, however, the instructors present it as a part of an embodied, multimodal demonstration that includes many other physical and verbal elements:

Example 3:

1 FI: You- you guys did a great job with this. . but it's just the option of. um. [turns to face MI with hands raised in protective stance position as he approaches]...[voice is high pitched] Go- go away?....Go away?. .

2 MI: [Stands in front of her, cocks his head to one side, and looks at her quizzically]

Are you asking me to go away?

3 FI: [high pitched] Go- go...go- go awa:y?. . [keeps body very still as she remains facing him]

4 Sts: [laughing audibly]

5 MI: Soun—

6 FI: [loud, pitched lower, sentence-final intonation] GO AWAY!

[remains in protective stance, but raises and re-settles her whole body firmly, feet planted on the floor, including reestablishing her arms and hands in front of her and raising and lowering one foot on the floor]

7 MI: [Backs away]…

8 S: Mm hm…

9 FI: 'Kay [turns to students].. It's that inflection- that 'Go awa:y?' [curves
             hand upward] .. It doesn't sound like you're certain. [turns again to MI,
             hunches shoulders, tips head to side] [high-pitched] I'm sorry but can you
             please go awa:y. I really-.. I- I don't mean to offend you but I

                                        [

10 MI: No:: [rolls eyes up]

11 FI: want you to go away. .

12 MI: [taking female role] Go. away.

13 FI: [loud, low] Go. away…[assumes protective stance again]

In the above example, the female instructor dramatizes the feature of rising intonation within an assembly of other features associated with politeness or sub-
servience, such as holding her head to the side and cringing slightly as she says
"please," "I'm sorry," and "I don't mean to offend you." As is often the case in these
classes, enactments of these stances are used to illustrate these points more than
explain them.

INTEGRATING AWARENESS AND ACTION IN THE ROLE-PLAYS

Instructors spend relatively little time presenting these concepts in order to maxi-
mize the time students can physically practice them. The process of constructing
coherent stances in this unsettling context is far from straightforward for most students. Occasionally students need a significant level of coaching to merely organize
their bodies to 'set a boundary' as the instructors did in the examples above.

This is the case in the following example. Here Maria (all proper names are
pseudonyms), who is doing a role-play for the first time in the class, has suggested
a scenario in which a man approaches her in a parking lot when she is opening her
car door. As shown in the excerpt below, she has difficulty making her vocal and
physical strategies 'match' the content of her words, thus most of the female instructor's coaching is directed not at what Maria is saying to the mock assailant but at
how she is saying it.

Example 4:

[Maria pretends to be unlocking her car. The mock assailant comes up behind her. She turns
to face him as he gets close, and he stops]

1 MI: Hey…go ahead and open it

              [

2 Maria: [speaking quickly] Hey. . get away!. . get away!. . get away!

3 MI: Open your car…

4 Maria: [high pitched, speaking quickly] Get away. . I don't know you get away!

5 FI: [Female instructor moves next to Maria, slightly behind her, and lays the flat of her hand against the small of Maria's back] Strong stance. don't look fearful. put your hands like this nice and solid. [holds hands up, elbows bent]

6 MI: (I'd like to) get to know you better. I want to get to know you rea::l good

7 Maria: [high, fast] Get away. . get away!. . you're too close!

8 MI: C'mon. let's get to know each other huh?. . hh hh hh! [moves towards Maria with hands together close to his body as if mock-pleading. Maria moves back with each of his steps.]

9 FI: [coaching Maria] Lower voice

10 Maria: Xx- [still backing up, FI backs up to stay behind her]

11 FI: Don't back up!

12 Maria: Oh that's right [glances in direction of FI, flashes smile]

13 FI: Don't back up

              [

14 MI: HU:H?. .

15 Maria: [quickly] Get away. . get away

              [

16 FI: So ni:ce and x.

17 Maria: [lower] Get away.

18 MI: Do you think xx xx?

19 FI: [coaching Maria to not hold her arms stiff and straight] I- I want you to bend your hands. . [reaches over to take hold of Maria's arms, bends them more at the elbows] and I want you to stand- in a lo:w voice really strong voice. [moves around close behind Maria, puts hands briefly on her shoulders, facing MI who is still pacing in front of them] [low, loud] GO. AWAY!

20 Maria: [low, loud] GO. AWAY!

21 FI: [coaching] That's it.

22 Maria: [quickly] Go. away! [3 seconds pass as MI paces in silence in front of her]

23 MI: I'm not afraid of you!...

24 Maria: [quickly] Go away!. . that's too close. go away. . keep your distance [arms
              are extended straight again]

25 FI: [coaching] He can grab that ha:nd [reaches from behind Maria and pulls
              her arms in again]

26 Maria: Oh okay

                        [

27 FI: It's too far out

                              [

28 Maria: Sorry

                                    [

29 FI: Good. that's it, that's it

                                        [

30 Maria: [loud] Go away. . [high,
              loud, almost a squeal] Go away!. . no [shakes head at her high voice]

                                    [

31 MI: [softly] You shut up

                                        [

32 Maria: [very loud] GO AWAY!

33 MI: [MI jumps back]

34: FI: Goo:d

35: S: Tha:t's it

36 Maria: hh hh [smiles]

              [Many students are clapping. Maria continues to pivot to face the man as
              he continues to pace farther out.

37 FI: Try not to walk

                    [

38 Maria: Okay

                                [

39: FI: [leans forward to place hand briefly on Maria's back.] try just to stand really solid. . good

                            [

40 Maria: [loudly, quickly] Go away. . [loudly] Go away I said!

               [

41 MI: xx really xx…xx xx! [lunges forward to grab her arm]

42 Maria: [strikes him on the chin of his helmet (a specific technique) and a self-defense fight begins]

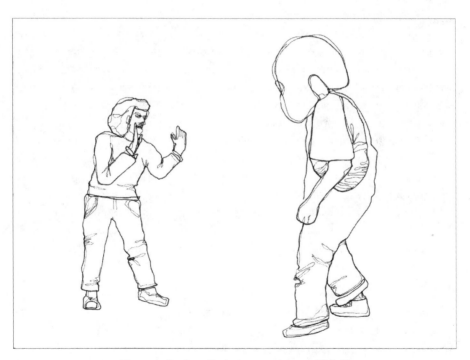

Figure 1. Student displaying a multimodal "No!"

In the excerpt above, Maria initially uses many vocal and non-vocal features that unintentionally display anxiety and nervousness. For example, although she is telling him to go away, she is repeating it over and over at an accelerated pace and high pitch, with her body leaning stiffly and arms outstretched toward the man. As the female coach intervenes, Maria attempts to change these multimodal features, but the coherence of her strategies wavers in the face of the intimidating mock assailant, causing her arms to extend stiffly out again as she sidles backwards, and her voice returns to its initial strident pitch. The male instructor maintains a generally threatening stance as he waits for Maria to feel more solid. In a moment of frustration in line 30, Maria squeals, "Go away!" but then rolls her eyes at herself and corrects herself, emphatically bellowing, "GO AWAY!" The contrast in the delivery of these two directives is so striking that the male instructor jumps back (he is deliberately providing observable, positive feedback to her) and the other students erupt, cheering and laughing.

This activity, though unrealistic in its initial stages, encourages the student to become more aware of her display of self through the smallest of bodily cues and encourages an integrated awareness of both body and voice. Most importantly, it encourages this awareness in bodily practice rather than just in the abstract. Faced with a mock assailant who may grab her at any moment, Maria is placed in an adrenalized situation that, the instructors hope, will allow the newly practiced stances to become engrained in bodily memory.

Despite the focus on women's self-defense in these courses, the instructors I observed did not use the notion of 'gender' as a central organizing principle in their discussions of such communicative strategies. They did not label some ways of speaking or behaving as 'the way women speak/act' or 'the way men speak/act,' nor did they describe some ways of speaking or acting as inherently better or worse. Rather, they presented the strategies in terms of how they construct different stances or alignments (such as 'confident' or 'uncertain'), and how effective these stances may be in certain contexts.

CONSTRUCTING COHERENT STANCES OF COMPLIANCE

Although stances that display confidence and assertiveness are considered preferable in most assault situations, passive or compliant stances are not dismissed as weak or useless if they are used mindfully in cases where the intended victim is unable to resist or retreat to safety, such as when she is physically pinned. In these cases, strategies that may calm and mollify the assailant or otherwise trick him into believing she will remain acquiescent are highly valued. Such strategies are, in fact, considered to be only superficially passive, for they have been actively chosen as a prelude to other defensive efforts whenever possible. This constructivist approach to self-defense highlights the importance of being able to choose a range of alignments that have been previously experienced and practiced through the body.

Example 5 illustrates a scenario from one of the last days of a course. Unlike Maria in the previous example, this student, Benta, has practiced a number of scenarios already and is now choosing to do a scenario in which she is pinned by the mock assailant (a situation for which she has been taught various strategies for resisting). She is pretending she has been surprised in her bed by a stranger who has entered her house and has pinned her by holding her legs between his knees and holding her wrists above her head as he crouches over her. She does not know what kind of character he will assume. For the first 15 seconds of this scenario (not included here), only the mock assailant speaks. He plays a character that is mentally unstable and paranoid. Benta eventually tries to soothe him by initiating a conversation with him:

Example 5:

1 MI:	I've seen them…I've fucking seen them they know all about Area 51 and Oswald and UFOs and everything man—
	[
2 Benta:	You're safe with me..
3 MI:	(No but xx xx) know me
	[
4 Benta:	You are..
5 MI:	I don't know if I'm safe
	[
6 Benta:	You're safe here you are you're safe.
7 Other S:	Goo:d
8 MI:	What makes you think I'm safe here?
9 Benta:	I know you're safe here
	[
10 MI:	They've found me over and over and over again […] I don't

think I'm safe, and you know what?. . I don't think you're safe either. .
because if they find me. . they're gonna find you. . and if they're gonna kill
me?. . [quickly, loudly] they're gonna have to kill you too!. . you know
what I'm saying?

[

11 Benta: (Hold on) xx

[

12 MI: No I think it's too late!. . I
think it's too fucking late! [puts his weight on her] I think x xx xx xx!

[

13 Benta: NO! [heaves him off
with a leverage technique taught in the class, spins into a side position
away from him and begins to kick as the other students cheer and yell
with her 'NO! NO!']

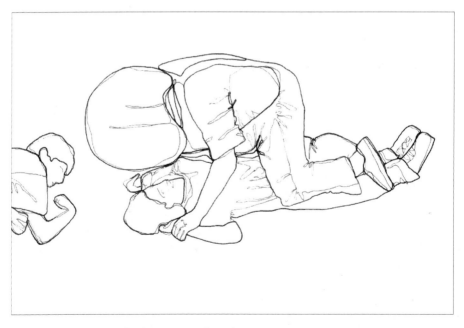

Figure 2. Student waiting for a chance to surprise mock assailant.

In this example, Benta takes advantage of the way the mock assailant is framing himself in order to try to trick him into calming down and possibly letting go of her. She supports the needy aspect of his character by framing herself as 'safe,' as someone who can help him. She aligns herself with him against an external threat. She uses a low-pitched, soft, soothing voice, as if she were comforting her own son, and lets her body remain limp to project a lack of intent or ability to take physical action. Both nurturing and submissive displays are sex-class linked in mainstream United States, a nurturer being associated with motherhood specifically (Ochs, 1992). Although often the male instructor will 'reward' this type of coherent student performance by pretending to be fooled, in this case he rejects her attempts and proceeds with the assault. This gives her the opportunity, however, to take physical advantage of his sudden weight to flip him to the side and break his grip, at which point she becomes a screaming, kicking woman who is anything but passive.

Students are thus encouraged to understand interactional strategies not as predetermined or fixed aspects of themselves or of others but as fluid displays of a partial self, one that may or may not reflect what kind of person each woman considers herself to be. Rather than being seen as limitations for women, the associations that some strategies have with gender are in fact used to the women's advantage in these courses. Students learn to see the potential vulnerability of an assailant who hopes for them to be compliant based on his expectations of women or femininity. An assailant who expects submission will be surprised and, one hopes, repelled by defensive strategies that do not match his expectations. This same assailant may likewise be more inclined to trust that a compliant victim will remain passive if he lets go of one of her hands for a moment, turns his back, or leaves the room.

CONFLICTS ACROSS MODALITIES: NOTICING INTERACTIONAL 'DISSONANCE' IN OTHERS

Another key aspect of these self-defense classes is learning not only how to manage one's own body and voice coherently in potential assault situations and choose stances that are most likely to be effective according to the opportunities afforded in the situation but also how to make accurate judgments about the behavior of others (namely, those suspected of being potential assailants). Instructors of these courses do not want to produce paranoid or overly reactive women who inappropriately hold everyone at bay. For this reason, male instructors will occasionally choose to play the part of a friendly, unthreatening person, one who quickly moves away if the student asks him to do so. This reminds the students that in real life, threatening characters are the exception rather than the rule. Students note carefully how the male instructors react to the subtle (or not so subtle) boundaries students set before assuming bad intentions. If the boundaries are not respected, however, students are urged to hold their ground. In the following example a female and male instructor demonstrate this point:

Example 6:

1 FI: I don't mind telling someone what time it is but. . beware of the question-asker trying to get their foot in the door…Okay so [looks over at MI]…it's the foot-in-the-door person…[MI starts walking over]. I'm waiting at the bus stop…[stands facing students as the MI approaches from the side]

2 MI: Hey do you know what time it is?. . [standing next to FI, body angled towards her]

3 FI: [glances at imaginary clock on wall] It's four-twenty. .

4 MI: Thanks….. You live around here? [looking at FI, body still angled towards her]

5 FI: I'm waiting for the bus…I told you what time it is. I'm just gonna sit here and wait for the bus [looks forward, not at him]

6 MI: What's- where are you going? Which bus you going on?. . [shifts weight, remains turned to her]

7 FI: It's none of your business. I'm sitting here waiting for the bus. and I'd just like to xx xx—

            [

8 MI: I'm just. . making conversation. . what's your problem?

            ]

9 FI: I don't want [shaking head] I don't want to make a conversation.…

10 MI: Jesus! [starts to turn away] You've got a real attitude problem you know that? [slowly walks away].….

11 FI: [to students] So I don't want to engage. . How many times do people […] ask one question, and it leads- it leads to another…It's important to- to head it off there…

Here, despite the female instructor's simulated efforts to discourage interaction, the male instructor continues to engage her. His claim to friendliness is contradicted by his pressing questions, even in the face of her physical and verbal withdrawal. He also suddenly becomes offended when she refuses to answer him, a deliberate move on his part as an instructor to 'inoculate' students against being made to feel mean or guilty for setting a boundary. His character is playing upon the sex-class linked expectation that the woman he is talking to should be polite and accommodating, even to the point of revealing where she lives to a stranger. Both instructors follow up this demonstration, however, by repeating that not all strangers who initiate conversation deserve suspicion; students should simply be aware of how behavior unfolds in the interaction.

Below, in Example 7, a student is given the chance to gauge the behavior of the mock assailant and respond as she feels is appropriate. In this scenario (the same one that was previewed at the beginning of this chapter), Katia has requested to pretend she is running along the forest trails she often frequents in real life. Although the male instructor only greeted her casually as she passed him the first time, causing the other students to laugh at this 'normal' moment, when they enact the scenario a second time he behaves differently:

Example 7:

[Katia is jogging towards the middle of the mat; the mock assailant is walking in the opposite direction. She stops to swerve around him, then stops as he stops and moves in front of her]

1 MI:	[hands up, palms facing Katia] Hey. . hey wait. . wait…Th- there's cops down there?. . [points around behind him] Apparently some woman got attacked down there. .
2 Katia:	Uh huh . . Well I'm going to run this way [turns around to run in other direction]
3 MI:	I don't think it's really safe to be going down—
4 Students:	[some laughter at how quickly Katia turned around]
5 MI:	Hey hey wait wait…wait [runs after Katia. She looks behind her, then turns and moves to side as if to let him pass. He stops and they face each other about 5–6 feet apart]
6 FI:	[coaching] So: set your boundary. . [FI circles around so she is behind Katia.
Katia:	[Katia bends her knees and puts her hands up with palms facing the MI]
7 MI:	Look if you don't know what's going on. . [hands out to sides, palms up] I think you're in danger (see Figure 3)
8 Katia:	Thank you very much for the information. . bye-bye now. . [Katia starts to move away from him sideways. The MI also moves to the side and slightly closer to her] I'm going to go now.

[

9 FI: [coaching] s- st- stay stay he's blocking you breathe stay still
                [moves up behind Katia, places one hand on Katia's back momentarily to
                stop her from moving]

10 MI: Hey…look…whoever she was…he ran up on her from behind. . and

                                                        [

11 Katia: I- I'm sorry I

12 MI: tackled her

                [

13 Katia: Leave

14 FI: [coaching] Good

                [

15 MI: I don't think you should be- [taking half-step towards her]

                [

16 Katia: I want you to leave NOW [emphasizes words with hands ges-
                turing down]

17 MI: I think you should be jogging that way [points in direction Katia came
                from]   [

18 Katia: I want you to leave NOW

19 MI: [takes step back]

20 FI: [coaching] Good

                [three seconds pass as MI's posture shifts: he drops his hands to sides,
                shifts weight to one foot, cocks head, and looks briefly from side to side]

21 MI: You know- [shakes finger at her]

22 Katia: I want you to leave NOW. I don't care what you have to say!

                                [

23 MI: It's women like you [points at her] that's
                the reason other women [points in direction he came from] get
                attacked…because of women with an [sudden large rapid gesture towards
                her—his whole body shifts with the gesture] attitude!

                                [

24 Katia: Leave now!

25 MI: [moves slightly away in response to her 'Leave now!']

26 FI: [coaching] Goo:d Katia

27 MI: I'm only fuckin' trying to help! [stalks away]

28 FI: (Nice job) [other students cheering and clapping]

Figure 3. Student assessing mock assailant's dissonant stance.

Throughout this encounter, the mock instructor's character presents himself as aligned with her in solidarity against something or someone else. With his breathless pleas for her to stop and his palms-up gestures to his sides, he constructs a stance of concern, yet his spatial positioning relative to Katia is potentially threatening, for it functions to control her movements and prevent her from running back the way she came. Here we see dissonance between meanings created through talk and gesture, and meanings created through the manipulation of space.

It is when Katia's second attempt to leave (line 5) is blocked by the man that the female instructor insists that Katia treat him unambiguously as a threat. She moves behind Katia and prevents her from moving away by placing her hand on Katia's back, telling her "S- st- stay stay he's blocking you breathe stay still" (line 9). Here the female instructor physically insists that Katia feel her body hold its place rather than cede to the physical presence of the man.

When the female instructor tells Katia to stay still, she is also encouraging Katia to challenge how the man is framing what is going on in the interaction. Although the man is offering a scenario in which he can protect Katia from danger, Katia is encouraged to focus on the aspects of his behavior that do not appear protective or friendly and to reject his version of the situation. Here Katia refuses to be positioned as a defenseless woman, vulnerable to attack either from the alleged assailant down the path or from this man who is claiming to be protecting her. She rejects the expectation that she should be polite and thankful to this stranger and by doing so undermines his possible attempt to assault her by surprise.

As she repeatedly tells him to leave, drowning out his efforts to alarm her, the man becomes angry and finally turns to go, leaving open the possible interpretation that he really never did intend to assault her. Was he planning a physical attack? Was she really in danger? The 'truth' of this dramatized encounter is not as important as Katia's ability to perceive and react to the contradictions in the behavior of the man on the path, and to use her own body and voice coherently to reframe the encounter as unacceptable.

WHEN IT'S SOMEONE YOU KNOW: RECOGNIZING MULTIMODAL DISSONANCE IN FAMILIARS

The examples thus far have involved scenarios in which the mock assailant is a stranger, yet many assaults on women involve people they know (National Institute of Justice, 1996). Students are also given the opportunity, if they choose to, to practice ways of handling acquaintances, dates, co-workers, and family members, among others. Students can choose to re-enact situations from their past or construct ones they think could occur in the future.

Interactions with people the women have dated are a common choice. In these cases, a certain level of trust between the characters is usually assumed, and expectations about being nice and not hurting feelings tend to be stronger. Thus recognizing and responding to moments of dissonance in the character's talk or actions are often balanced with explicit attempts to give him the benefit of the doubt, and the ambiguity of such moves as hand-holding and other touches is often heightened in circumstances where conflict over intimacy is taking place.

In Example 8 below, a student named Nancy has chosen to re-enact a situation in which she is alone with a man she has been dating for some time but has not been sexually involved with yet. She wants the character to try to push sexual intimacy on her by acting caring and concerned and saying specific things that a man had said to her in the past. Her goal is to resist his framing of the situation as 'normal.'

Example 8:

[Nancy is sitting cross-legged on the mat. Her 'date' kneels next to her and puts his hand on her back]

1 MI:	Xx. . we'll have a good time together xx xx…come on…
2 Nancy:	Um…(no) I- I like being close to you?. I like, you know, hugging you and stuff?. . But we talked about this before. . I'm not. . ready. . to have a sexual relationship
	[
3 MI:	Come on this is what people do: [touches her leg] xx that's what they do. .
4 Nancy:	[leans back from him and puts hand up between them, holding it there] [speaking slowly] I know that's what. . a lot of people do. I'm not ready. .
5 MI:	Now listen. you know you want to do it. . hey, no one else is going to want to do it if xx x.…come on…come on I love you. Don't you want to do this (with me)?
	[
6 Nancy:	If you love me, then respect what I say.
7 Other Sts:	[supporting her] Yeah!
8 MI:	I do respect what you say. . you know that. . you know I do…It's just xx xx xx xx xx it's what people do!. . That's all!. . That's what people do…[shifts towards her and touches her again. Nancy leans back farther] Come on. .
9 Student 1:	He's not hearing you
	[
10 Student 2:	xx xx back up
	[
11 Nancy:	I know that's what people do. . [shifts away from him]
12 MI:	Come o:n [leans forward and rubs his hand along her ankle]
13 Nancy:	But. . let's wait…just WAIT [puts her hand against his chest at arm's

length]

14 MI: We don't have to wait. . What are we waiting for [caressing her ankles with one hand]

15 Nancy: I want to wait until I'm ready. I want to wait until I feel good about this. .

16 FI: [very softly coaching her] xx xx xx xx…

17 Nancy: [looks at female instructor while her hand remains against date's chest]

18 FI: xx xx xx…

19 Nancy: [looks at date again] I don't want to do this now…If you feel you must. do this now. . then I want you. . to leave. . you can come back when you're in control. .

20 MI: [shifts away from her so they are no longer touching]

21 Students: Yeah! [some clapping]

22 MI: Nobody else is going to want to do this…[reaches out and laces his fingers with the fingers of the hand Nancy is holding up between them] nobody else is going to (touch you you know that)….Nobody else is going to

[four seconds pass; Nancy seems at a loss for words as he touches her fingers]

23 Student: Tell him what you want…Tell him what you want.

[

24 Student: Tell him!

25 MI: [caressing her fingers] Come on. . don't you want to? (come on)…

26 FI: [coaching] (You already told him)…

27 Nancy: [loudly] I already told you. . that I don't want to do this now. . And you're making me feel like I don't want to do this with you. EVER

[

28 MI: [releases her hand]

29 Students: Yeah! [lots of clapping]

30 MI: Nobody else is going to want you…xx—

[

31 Nancy: That doesn't matter…I want to be with someone who respects me and if I can't find anyone who

RESPECTS ME....then it doesn't matter. Please go home now

32 Students: Yeah!.. Yes! [clapping]
[MI stands up with hands held up palms out, as if in capitulation, and slowly turns and walks away. Students and FI cheer]

Above, the male instructor combines the phrases Nancy has specified with some of his own interactional strategies to create the character she has requested. With his soft and soothing voice and gentle touches, he frames himself as a caring boyfriend. Yet despite Nancy's initial polite attempts to refuse his advances, his strategies become increasingly discontinuous with his claims of respect for her. Even as she leans away and holds up her hand to stop him, he continues to lean in and touch her. Here the female instructor encourages Nancy to stop explaining herself, and Nancy eventually tells him directly to leave.

Her date, at this point, strategically reframes her 'stop' gesture into a gesture of intimacy by intertwining his fingers with hers. Nancy appears to be rendered momentarily speechless, as four long seconds pass in silence. It is only when the female instructor quietly prompts her that she comes to life again, stating loudly and in measured words that she wants him to leave, which he does soon thereafter.

Scenarios such as this one allow students like Nancy the opportunity to refuse the mock assailant's embodiment of a script that normalizes sexual coercion as well as reject their own internalization of the script. Nancy is able to talk back to and physically resist the role that her body and mind together have internalized, first by consciously recognizing the contradictions in the framing of the situation by her date and then by reframing the situation as non-consensual.

CONCLUSION

If indeed many girls and women are socialized into monitoring and restricting the range of expression and experiences of their bodies, then the context of sexual assault makes clear just how harmful the effects of this socialization can be. The 'knowledge' that one's voice is capable of unequivocally yelling 'NO!' or that one's body will react swiftly to an attack is one that comes with the experience of trusting in one's body rather than disassociating from it. Women are shown how to notice specific features of their voices and bodies as part of an integrated system and are led step by step through the process of consciously feeling the possibilities their bodies offer them at every moment, even moments of stress. These courses allow women to connect with their bodies through repeated physical practice and interactional role-plays and to integrate their bodies into their conceptions of themselves in ways that, for some, may have been inaccessible since early childhood. These courses also encourage women to trust in their bodies' perceptions of others, as they learn to acknowledge and be mindful of that 'funny feeling' they may have about someone else or their actions. Whether that 'funny feeling' is indicative of real danger can be determined by consciously noticing as well as influencing how an interaction unfolds through words, intonation, gesture, and stance, Thus all aspects of one's communicative repertoire, including the body, are seen as resources in learning about and understanding the self, others, and the interactional environment. One can learn about danger or discomfort by paying attention to 'gut' reactions in the body; one can learn about the possible intentions of others from their vocal and bodily stances (and from how coherent or dissonant these may appear to be); one can learn how sincere others may be from how they react to one's own use of stance to 'set a boundary.' In essence, one can learn that the body is wholly part of the self, that it can know about aspects of the world just as the mind can, and in fact is only superficially separable from the mind. Far from being a neutral appendage to the self that one uses to inhabit the world or a fixed set of physical attributes that cannot be changed, the body is a fluid, dynamic, inhabited self that offers a wealth of possibilities for perception, knowledge, and personal as well as social transformation.

As more women learn to credit what their bodies can know and do, societal perceptions of what 'women' can know and do may follow suit. As McCaughey puts it in her book, *Real Knockouts*, "Self-defense at its core challenges what it means to have a female body, what it means to be a man or a woman. Self-defense thus offers a critique of the way gender is written into our bodies" (1997, p. 18). Although the immediate goal of these courses is to reduce the likelihood of assault for women, they contribute in a more fundamental way to positive social change. Those who learn through such multimodal means are more likely to acquire a deep-seated, literally visceral, sense of agency in the world, one that will, with time, become increasingly visible on a societal scale.

Appendix: Transcription Conventions

: indicates a lengthened vowel.

, indicates a pause of less than one-half second

.. indicates a pause of about a half second. Each additional . represents another half second.

text in parentheses ( ) indicates speech that was difficult to hear.

(xx) indicates inaudible speech. Each x represents a perceived syllable.

CAPS indicates relatively loud volume.

material in brackets [ ] represents non-verbal or contextual information, including the time of a pause length over one second.

ellipses in brackets […] indicates that significant elements of the spoken text were edited for concision.

A bracket [in a blank line indicates overlap or latching between the spoken text or action in the line above the bracket and the spoken text or action in the line below.

Note

1. In keeping with ethnomethodological conventions I use the present tense throughout this chapter.

Acknowledgments

I would like to thank all those who supported this research in both words and action. These supporters include most directly my dissertation advisor, Deborah Tannen, the dedicated instructors at the self-defense organization, and the women who allowed me to document their experiences in the course.

Works Cited

Bucholtz, M. (1999). Bad examples: Transgression and progress in language and gender studies. In M. Bucholtz, A. C. Liang, & L. A. Sutton (Eds.), *Reinventing identities: The gendered self in discourse* (pp. 3–24). New York: Oxford University Press.

Butler, J. (1990). *Gender trouble: Feminism and the subversion of identity.* New York: Routledge.

Butler, J. (1993). *Bodies that matter: On the discursive limits of "sex."* New York: Routledge.

Butler, J. (2004). *Undoing gender.* New York: Routledge.

Davidson, J. (2004). Embodied knowledge: Possibilities and constraints in arts education and curriculum. In L. Bresler (Ed.), *Knowing bodies, moving minds: Towards embodied teaching and learning* (pp. 197–212). Boston: Kluwer.

Epstein, C. F. (1986). Symbolic segregation: Similarities and difference in the language and non-verbal communication of women and men. *Sociological Forum, 1*(1), 27–49.

Foucault, M. (1975). *Discipline & punish: The birth of the prison.* New York: Vintage.

Goffman, E. (1974). *Frame analysis: An essay on the organization of experience.* Cambridge, MA: Harvard University Press.

Goffman, E. (1976). *Gender advertisements.* New York: Harper & Row.

Goffman, E. (1977). The arrangement between the sexes. *Theory and Society, 4*(3), 301–331.

Goldin-Meadow, S. (2004). Gesture's role in the learning process. *Theory into Practice, 43,* 314–321.

Goldin-Meadow, Cook, S., S. W., & Mitchell, Z. A. (2009). Gesturing gives children new ideas about math. *Psychological Science, 20*(3), 267–272.

Goodwin, C. (1994). Professional vision. *American Anthropologist, 96*(3), 606–633.

Goodwin, C. (2007). Environmentally coupled gestures. In S. Duncan, J. Cassell, & E. Levy (Eds.), *Gesture and the dynamic dimensions of language* (pp. 195–212). Amsterdam/Philadelphia: John Benjamins.

Henley, N. M. (1975). Power, sex, and nonverbal communication. In B. Thorne & N. Henley (Eds.), *Language and sex: Difference and dominance* (pp. 184–202). Rowley, MA: Newbury House.

Henley, N. M. (1977). *Body politics: Power, sex, and nonverbal communication.* Englewood Cliffs, NJ: Prentice-Hall.

Kendon, A. (2004). *Gesture. visible action as utterance.* Cambridge, UK: Cambridge University Press.

Kleck, G., & Sayles, S. (1990). Rape and resistance. *Social Problems, 37*(2), 149–162.

Kunene, R., & Brookes, H. (2010). *Do cultural norms related to gender influence gestural behavior among South African children and adults?* Paper presented at the International Society for Gesture Studies (ISGS), July 26. Viadrina European University, Frankfurt/Oder, Germany.

Martin, K. (1998). Becoming a gendered body: Practices of preschools. *American Sociological Review, 63*(4), 494–511.

McCaughey, M. (1997). *Real knockouts: The physical feminism of women's self-defense.* New York: New York University Press.

McMurrey, P. (1998). Gender behaviors in an early childhood classroom through an ethnographic lens. *Qualitative Studies in Education, 11*(2), 271–290.

McNeill, D. (1992). *Hand and mind: What gestures reveal about thought.* Chicago: University of Chicago Press.

Müller, C. & Posner, R. (Eds.). (2002). *The semantics and pragmatics of everyday gestures.* The Berlin Conference. Berlin: Weidler.

National Institute of Justice [NIJ]. (January 1996). *The extent and cost of crime Vvictimization: A new look.* United States Department of Justice, Office of Justice Programs.

Nayak, A., & Kehily, M. J. (2006). Gender undone: Subversion, regulation, and embodiment in the work of Judith Butler. *British Journal of Sociology of Education, 27*(4): 459–472.

Ochs, E. (1992). "Indexing gender." A. Duranti, & C. Goodwin (Eds.), Rethinking context: language as an interactive phenomenon (pp.335–358). Cambridge, UK: Cambridge University Press.

Queen's Bench Foundation. (1976). *Rape: Prevention and resistance.* San Francisco: Queen's Bench Foundation.

Ross, J. (2004). The inscrutable body: Student bodies from classrooms to prisons. In L. Bresler (Ed.), *Knowing bodies, Moving minds: Towards embodied teaching and learning* (pp. 169–181). Boston: Kluwer.

Sadker, M., & Sadker, D. (1994). *Failing at fairness: How America's schools cheat girls.* New York: Scribner and Sons.

Sherzer, J. (1972). Verbal and nonverbal deixis: the pointed lip gesture among the San Blas Kuna. *Language in Society, 21,* 117–131.

Streeck, J. (1993). Gesture as communication I: Its coordination with gaze and speech. *Communication Monographs, 60*(4), 275–299.

Streeck, J. (2009). *Gesturecraft. the manu-facture of meaning.* Amsterdam: John Benjamins.

Tannen, D. (1996 [1994]). *Gender & discourse.* New York: Oxford University Press.

Tannen, D. (1999). The display of (gendered) identities in talk at work. In M. Bucholtz, A. C. Liang, & L. A. Sutton (Eds.), *Reinventing identities: The gendered self in discourse* (pp. 221–240). New York: Oxford University Press.

Ullman, S., & Knight, R. (1992). Fighting back: Women's resistance to rape. *Journal of Interpersonal Medicine, 7*(1), 31–43.

Ullman, S., & Knight, R. (1993). The efficacy of women's resistance strategies in rape situations. *Psychology of Women Quarterly, 17*(1), 23–38.

CHAPTER FIVE

Pasture Pedagogy

Field and Classroom Reflections on Embodied Teaching

ERICA TOM WITH MIRA-LISA KATZ

CROSS-TALK IN THE CLASSROOM

Sometimes I find myself clucking. When people texting madly veer across the walkways on campus. When a driver, irritatingly cautious, takes too long changing lanes, blinker flashing. When my students, slow as molasses, move their desks after I have asked them to get into groups: chk, chk, chk, chk! It's a bad habit. And a hard one to break when more often than not, people respond, quickening their pace (though not without some quizzical facial expressions) to an encouraging cluck.

In my first year teaching college English, I began to realize how deeply embedded my habits of working with horses were in all of my communication. As I tried to stop clucking and gesturing with an invisible crop at my students, there were other elements from my equine background that I consciously used to enhance my approach to teaching. In horsemanship, the basic assumptions of human communication go by the wayside. In the earliest known treatise on human-horse communication, Xenophon wrote, "The gods have bestowed upon man the gift of teaching his brother man what he ought to do by word of mouth; but it is evident that by word of mouth you can teach a horse nothing" (Morgan, 1894, p. 49). While verbal communication through intonation and rhythm is possible with a horse, it is rather kindred to the experience of those who immerse themselves in communities where they do not share a language. In horsemanship, humans must work beyond what is said in words, re-evaluating and exploring other communicative pathways.

The use of spoken language, the "gift bestowed upon man," has its limitations. Humans tend to view spoken language as the primary means of communication, often overlooking our inherently multimodal nature. As an equine student of thirteen years, I have witnessed people who learn to communicate successfully with their bodies, and who experience a sense of empowerment and possibility through that embodiment. Although body language (paralinguistic communication, gesture) has long been acknowledged as an essential part of communicative practice (Kendon, 2004; McNeill, 2005; Goldin-Meadow, 2003; Hall, 1966; Birdwhistell, 1952), the significance and power of speaking through the body is ripe for further inquiry specifically regarding effects in educational interactions.

In this chapter, I explore opportunities for embodied learning experiences in both equine and academic contexts.[1] Beginning with my personal experience working at a non-profit horse rescue program, I then share a case study of a young girl in an educational horsemanship program that I helped to develop and run. Following case studies of students in English 100 classrooms, I conclude with reflections on how experiences in these varied educational contexts resonated in my academic life as a graduate student teaching a lower division English class at Sonoma State University.

Below is a brief introduction to horsemanship's expansive approaches to communication.

THE NATURE OF THE HORSE: DEEPENING AN AWARENESS OF BODY LANGUAGE

Once a necessity, then a seemingly superfluous pet or an expensive pasture ornament, the horse is currently coming to occupy new niches as companion, teacher, and even therapist.[2] The potential for communication with the horse—a thousand gentle pounds of grace and power—is now recognized as a source of nurturance. It is spending time in the presence of horses that most readily convinces people of their potential to inspire and heal us. Scientific studies have increasingly supported this therapeutic function of human interaction with horses, and there is, consequently, a developing discipline of equine-assisted therapy.[3]

The horse's distinction as a prey animal makes it a vivid mirror of its surroundings. Its heightened awareness, curiosity, and willingness have been elemental to survival. The domesticated horse complies most often with humans because of its communal instinct,[4] making it a cooperative partner for human educational purposes. Its large size makes the horse an effective partner for teaching people about the significance of body language because it is easy to see when one is being effective or ineffective. Although the immensity of the horse makes its body language easy to read (when one knows what to look for), people less often consciously read one another's body language. This is, perhaps especially, the case in the classroom.

Oftentimes in the learning process, fear of the unknown or seemingly unknowable can paralyze students. Fear can manifest as boredom, disengagement, or even aggression: the young woman half awake with her head on the desk; the blank-faced boy staring out the window; the girl who snickers, challenging the teacher's every move. Because a horse's or person's fear of new experiences can manifest in ways that are not overt, close listening—or reading—is essential for creating a productive learning experience. The practice of horsemanship can foster such skills. When humans attempt to communicate with horses they must, out of necessity, relinquish their dependence on spoken language. In so doing they have the opportunity to rediscover the power of bodily communication. A deepened awareness of body language can create connective openings for students who manifest their fear in ways that chafe against traditionally accepted behaviors in schools. Instead of chastising or dismissing students' physical behavior as somehow oppositional to the classroom process, reading students' body language can offer educators across contexts additional avenues for initiating teachable moments.

READING BODY LANGUAGE AS PART OF A "LISTENING STANCE"

Here the term "reading" is used in an expansive sense. As we read books and newspapers, essays and articles, drawings and paintings, films and screens, landscapes and signs, we also read bodies and the spatial significance around and between them (Brandt, 1990, 2001; Cheville, 2001; Gee, 2007, 2008; Hull & Katz, 2006; Hull & Rose, 1990; Jewitt, 2003, 2011; Leander, 2004; Schultz, 2003; Shohamy & Gorter, 2009; Street, 1984). Reading occurs within and beyond the classroom, it is part of all human environments and it happens both consciously and subconsciously. This expansive understanding of reading resonates with the "listening stance" put forth by Katherine Schultz (2003). She uses the term "listening" in two ways:

> [B]oth literally (teachers pay attention to students' voices and how they are distributed across time and space) and metaphorically (teachers attend to children's verbal and nonverbal interactions; they read their facial gestures and the ways children move through space alone and together). Listening to the rhythm and balance of a classroom takes into account the temporal and spatial dimensions of the formation of community. (p. 44)

Arguing that a listening stance is essential to rethinking a pedagogy receptive to students, Schultz's book, *Listening: A Framework for Teaching Across Differences*, discusses listening over long periods—semesters and years. Building on Schultz's ideas, the case studies in this chapter will focus on reading in both equine and academic contexts. This expanded notion of reading encourages teachers to recognize and analyze opportunities for educational and personal growth in new and useful ways. Those who consciously read body language can use their observations to become more aware of how they themselves embody communication. I suggest that teachers who practice this kind of awareness can enrich their students' experiences of learning and deepen their own experiences of teaching.

The following section explores how working with horses can provide opportunities to recognize, and take advantage of the power of the body to make meaning. The practice of reading as I describe it here creates collaborative learning, where knowledge is co-constructed between students and teachers. It is this communicative exchange that the dedicated horsewoman aims for with her equine partners; wherein the horse and rider share in the curious play of moving together, performing and training collaboratively.

THE FARM: WORKING WITH FERAL HORSES

In 2007, I was working at a non-profit horse rescue facility in the State of Washington—sixty acres of grass and intractable blackberry, with a stream that flowed heavily in the winter and was cold and quiet in the summer. There was a feeling of fluidity about the farm: finding a different language to speak with the horses, sharing the sunny afternoons with youngsters, I was in constant motion, walking or jogging an acre just to catch a horse, deeply breathing in the breeze filled with the smell of hay. I had a keen awareness of life at the farm, of open sky and the feel of a horse's soft coat on the palm of my hand. There was a simple joy in my work that was hard to describe but easy to live.

Though I grew up riding, familiar with the domesticated horse, this was an altogether different experience. The rescued horses were bought from farms in Canada that collect pregnant mares' urine to create hormone replacement drugs. The aging mares and foals are a mere by-product of the farm's breeding program.[5] Each year the farm purchased a dozen yearlings to rescue them from slaughter. These feral horses, who had had little to no human contact, would not allow even the simplest human touch, which is taken for granted with most domesticated horses.

Though some in the equine world would object, many agree that horsemanship is not about domination but rather about creating opportunities for the horse and rider to learn and develop collaboratively. Thinking about horsemanship as a partnership that involves choice and agency, or as a collaborative learning experience, opens the possibility for the mutual engagement of horse and rider. (Similarly, learning is often more engaging when both teacher and student feel reciprocally invested and responsible for the choices they make in the classroom.) At the rescue facility, agency and choice were essential in "gentling" the yearlings gradually and developing amiable relationships that would benefit both the horses and their future owners. This gentling was an arduous task requiring a perspicacious and patient person.

GENTLING YEARLINGS: A LISTENING APPROACH TO HALTER BREAKING

It was a cold spring in the Northwest; mud abounded and the huddling group of manes and tails inspired sympathy. Because the feral yearlings were not yet halter broke they were kept separately in a small pasture.[6] Our goal was to have each yearling halter broke so we could move them into a larger meadow and introduce them to the herd by summer. The smaller pasture enabled yearlings to become accustomed to humans, of whom they were wary, due to limited and often negative interactions. The first few times I entered the pasture I focused simply on being there, reading their movements in close proximity, but not immediately pressing further. Just as new horses are kept on the perimeter of a herd before being accepted, I wanted to offer my presence rather than exert authority; thus, I kept to the edge of the pasture until my coming and going became familiar. In a pasture, the energy can shift from calm to anxious in an instant, so I watched for the "curiosity, pleasure, boredom, tension, fear, anger and aggression [which] are all expressed, though silently, with body language" (Rodenas, 1991, p. 22). Inside the pasture, I needed to read individual horses as well as the dynamics of the entire herd.

Oftentimes, I would sit on the fence, throw hay, and watch the yearlings play. It was important to create a situation where they did not feel pressure. In Figure 1, I practice replacing pressure with patience as I work with an Arabian mare named Beaurita. At the beginning of the session, when I began to free longe[7] her, Beaurita's energy was high and unfocused. Here I dropped my energy: notice the direction of my head and eyes, and my hands at ease with the whip. Bringing my body to rest—not facing, but rather angled open to Beaurita—she no longer focused on escaping the pressure of my requests. Instead, she came to a stop and focused her attention on me. Similarly, with the yearlings, I spent time walking around the pasture practicing patience, sometimes sidling closer without directly approaching them. When the herd ceased gathering to watch me, when they began to groom or nibble at hay, I knew my presence had become non-threatening. It was in one of these relaxed sessions that one of the yearlings moved toward me.

The first contact I had was with a leggy bay filly who reached out to touch me with her nose. She flared her nostrils, swept her soft nose across my wrist, and gently tickled me. It was a slow process, with several sessions of just letting her approach me, but we became comfortable with each other. As she accepted my touch I began to move slowly back and forth along each of her sides, standing at her shoulder— where I would position myself when I would eventually lead her—and running the palms of my hands over her body.

Figure 1. Dropping pressure, Erica practices patience with Beaurita.

I always started and ended sessions by tugging gently on her mane, scratching a bit at her withers, stroking the ridge where the mane ends between her shoulder bones—actions that mimicked the grooming habits of horses that are bonded within a herd.[8] Some grooming habits I could readily employ, such as imitating the nipping at the withers of another horse by tugging the mane with my hand, which is more akin to scratching an itch than providing any grooming for the mane. Other habits were less easily imitated. In hot weather, when the air is teeming with flies, two horses will often stand head-to-tail, swishing flies from each other's faces. After the young filly accepted my imitation of bonded horse language, it was difficult to swat her nose away when she began to mouth my shirt because she wanted to groom me, but I had to make clear early on that while we could work together, expressing affection, there were necessary safety parameters for our interactions.

While I was teaching her appropriate human-horse interaction during halter breaking, she was also teaching me how to be a better horsewoman. She showed me the importance of patience. When I decided too quickly that it was time to halter break her and attempted to put the halter on over her ears, the instant she felt something foreign on her face, her neck muscles contracted and she quickly pulled away. I should have taken more time, let her see, smell, and touch the halter before attempting to put it on her. But, I was in a rush. Because I lacked attentiveness to the yearling, preoccupied with my own goal of putting on the halter, she moved away from me.

I took a step back. I put the halter over my shoulder, walked around the corral a bit, pretending to examine the mud, the feeder, and the latch on the gate. She came nearer. When she accepted my hands on her again, and we meandered around a bit, I let the halter slide slowly down into my hand and just held it there, waiting. It wasn't long before she was nosing the halter. After just a couple sessions, stroking her neck with the halter in my hand, rubbing her face with it, she let me slide it up over her ears, and fasten the buckle. My Girl, as we soon named her, quickly became the most easygoing and willing of the herd.

READING TO REASSESS: CREATING COMFORTABLE ENVIRONMENTS FOR CURIOSITY AND CHOICE

In gentling My Girl, the importance of choice became apparent to me. In the session where I prioritized my personal desires as her trainer (rather than my concern for her), our session was not productive. However, when I moved away from the time-pressures associated with halter breaking and refocused on helping her to become familiar and comfortable with humans, she willingly participated. Allowed time to adjust to a foreign object and the independence to determine her movement, My Girl took the initiative to nose the halter in my hands. As her fear diminished, we steadily progressed.

This experience taught me that a trainer, or a teacher, must remain attuned to whom he or she is working with.[9] Teaching is oftentimes about reading our students. We might have a lesson plan with required goals for our classes, but the importance of being able to read and react spontaneously to students' needs is an essential element of education. Back in the pasture, My Girl likewise exhibited this need for spontaneous adjustments. Her fear, which momentarily detracted from our progress, was easily recognizable: the halter was new and scary, and she balked when I attempted to put it on her without slowly introducing it. My Girl's wariness of the unknown was instinctual, connected to the survival of her species. The importance of recognizing the instinctual source of a horse's body language is not something universally valued in horse training. Similarly, spending the time and energy required to understand students personally is not universally valued in academic contexts. Yet, such understanding can positively affect each of these learning environments.

Before drawing out the parallels of this kind of reading in an academic context, following are two more equine examples, the first demonstrating misreadings of the motivation for certain body language, the second delving into the subtleties of communication via stance and tone.

READING FEAR: WHEN "MISBEHAVING" MAKES SENSE

One day at the farm, a woman who was interested in buying a horse came to try out one of the older trained horses, Red. It was a windy day. Leaves swirled in chilly gusts; the clouds moved across the sky, creating a chiaroscuro of sun and shade across the dirt arena. Though Red was usually calm, that particular day he had all the taut coiled energy of metal springs, making the woman a nervous rider. He loved to jump, and after warming him up, she pointed him over a couple of small cross rails. His energy mounted. Flying over several more jumps without a problem, Red suddenly spooked coming around a turn, jumping sideways and twisting underneath the rider. Momentarily thrown off balance, she pulled on the reins, jerking Red's mouth. She stayed in the saddle and, regaining her seat, shortened her reins. Turning him sharply, she used the short crop to swat his haunches, resulting in a resounding **thwack**. It seemed to me that the noise probably unsettled Red more than the short sting of the crop.

The rider wheeled him around and cantered in the same path, a circle toward the jump; more nervous than the first time, Red skittered out again at the turn. A sidestepping horse, moving quickly, can be enough to dismount a rider, and the woman clung tightly to the reins once more, whacking him again behind the saddle. Visibly nervous, the rider was trying to correct Red using her crop. Red's neck glistened darker where sweat gathered. He held his head high, ears swiveling quickly; his tail arched up, flagging out behind him. His nervousness only increased, but after a couple more attempts to aim Red at the jump around the turn, the rider finally succeeded in haphazardly putting him over the rails and completed her ride. As she cooled him down, walking—Red still moving sideways at moments— the rider seemed as agitated as Red.

At the turn where Red spooked, there was a flower box where bright red and yellow artificial flowers fluttered in the occasional breeze. Up until that point, he had been going along somewhat excitedly but willingly and smoothly. He loved to jump and offered no resistance to the course the rider was putting him through. But this blind turn combined with the fluttering flowers surprised him; subsequently, he did what most horses (and humans) would do when frightened: he balked. Rather than alleviating his fear, the rider essentially enhanced the presence of fear by hitting Red with the crop. When the pair went around again, Red was not only nervous about the flowers, but he feared getting hit as well.

By taking into account why a horse spooks, a rider will be able to address the situation in a way that is productive and logical for the horse. Though the horse's movement in this example was undesired by the rider, if she had understood that the horse was not willfully misbehaving but rather behaving as a horse, a kinder and more effective response might have been possible. Oftentimes, the strategy for overcoming fear is simple: if a horse can touch whatever is frightening her, her fear is usually alleviated. Encouraging a spooked horse, gently and firmly, to approach and touch whatever it is that is frightening her allows some freedom of movement. It is often the restriction of space and movement that escalates a horse's fear. Through tactile interaction—not illogical punishment—the horse will release its fear, and the rider can continue with the lesson at hand. Reading body language holistically—in a manner that considers both context and motivation—and in responding to the root of the problem, riders can more productively train and interact with their equine partners, an approach that humans would also benefit from using in all areas of their lives.

It was such observations, coupled with reading the yearlings and the larger herd at the farm, that initially taught me about the significance of bodily communication, both with horses and with humans. Through my experience gentling yearlings and familiarizing teaching apprentices with equine contexts, I found that promoting a keen awareness of the body enriched the young women's—and my own—educational experiences. Educational experiences with horses that involve attention to touch, space, orientation, posture, gaze and gesture[10] offer young people opportunities (multiple, over time) to develop personal awareness. This was the case with Diana, a young woman who came to the farm to join the Apprentice Program.

THE APPRENTICE PROGRAM: DIANA'S FIRST DAY

After months of gentling yearlings, building fences, and getting the herd through the roughest months of Northwest rain, summer bloomed green and warm with new opportunities. I'd spent the winter and spring working with the horses, learning each of their seventy-two names, and spinning ideas with the two women who ran the farm. We created an Apprentice Program for anyone who wanted to learn about horses but couldn't afford lessons. Apprentices were given tasks that ranged from feeding to exercising horses, depending on their ability. The inexperienced apprentices spent most of the day cleaning, fixing things around the farm, and walking the fence line to check for jutting nails and any damage done by the herd. It was after long days of chores that apprentices earned lessons with the horses. Diana was one of these inexperienced apprentices, with a family who couldn't afford to support her expensive desire to ride and work with horses.

Diana was fourteen. She had shiny blue, rubber-banded braces and short dark hair, always slicked tightly into a perfect ponytail. She was thin, with large, dark eyes and a rounded nose. Diana was quiet, sweet, and avoided eye contact as much as possible. On her first day at the farm her mother and I made polite introductions, then I put a hard bristled brush in Diana's hand and asked her to follow me out to the main pasture, where I showed her how the water troughs should be cleaned. She nodded at all of my instructions—bouncing her chin at my questions or shaking her head.

"Why do you want to be an apprentice, Diana?"

Nod yes. Pause…

"Do you like being out of the city?"

Nod yes.

"Do you like horses?"

"I love horses."

Diana looked at me, up and then down. She said it again, "I love horses," without as much emphasis but clearly, as if I hadn't heard her the first time.

"I love them too," I smiled. "Can you tell me what it is that you like… I mean, can you tell me why you love horses?"

Diana stopped her scrubbing. She looked at me again, and then away. As if on cue, My Girl ambled over to inspect the water trough. A dark bay with a blaze of white from the tip of her right ear across her nose and one startling blue eye, My Girl loved to be scratched between her ears, right on top of her head, and now she nosed Diana's hand that held the brush. Diana, who had seemed to be holding her breath, began to breathe deeply. She smiled, touching My Girl's long face gently, with the ends of her fingers, as if My Girl might break.

"They are so beautiful. Horses. They're so beautiful, tall and strong and friendly. They're beautiful."

I nodded my head. Smiled.

"Clean that trough like I showed you, and don't forget to turn off the hose. My Girl is just fine there, but swing that rope in a circle to keep the other horses at a distance if they come exploring. When you're finished, come find me."

Diana nodded once more to me, finished tracing My Girl's blaze of white with her fingers, and bent down to scrub the trough.

My observations of Diana's body language began that first day on the farm when walking her through basic tasks. This informal assessment was an important part of adjusting my own body language and determining the effectiveness of certain activities and interactions.

LONGE LESSON: CONSCIOUSLY READING AND ENACTING BODY LANGUAGE

Apprentices often spent a couple weeks working before they received lessons with the horses. This provided time for the girls to reveal more of their personality, thus enabling the equine educators to observe and to approach lessons with the appropriate horse and situation. It was imperative to pair the novice apprentices with the right horse, in the safest situation possible, because of the inherent risk involved in working with horses.

In the following weeks of basic chores and safety lessons around the horses, Diana's quiet diligence continued. When put to tasks with other apprentices, she hardly spoke as the other girls chatted away. Walking with her eyes cast downward as if quietly attempting to go unnoticed, her body language displayed submission to every being around her. I decided against working on leading a horse, where close bodily proximity requires a practiced awareness and response to horse behavior. Instead, I chose to demonstrate longeing.[10] That way, there would be more distance between Diana and the horse, allowing her to read the horse's entire body while also thinking about her own.

I paired Diana with Red. A chestnut thoroughbred, lean and tall at seventeen hands high, he had one perfect white sock. I had been working with Red for about six months. He was a bit goofy (he would flap his lower lip noisily, bouncing his head when he saw me coming with carrots), and though he required encouragement to work, he was a fairly willing partner. It was important that I also knew what could change that sweet demeanor: riding over jumps and working too closely with other horses could send Red into panic that only experienced riders could handle safely (as described in the example above). Red was the right horse for Diana in this case because he was calm, not pushy, and also easygoing enough that it took a confident person to convince him he should have to work. Observing Diana interacting with the other young women and horses, I also predicted that interacting with Red would provide ample opportunity for us to address the importance of body language in communication.

I clipped a longe line to Red's halter and led him into the center of the arena, telling Diana to stay close behind me, though I didn't need to—Diana was my shadow during her lessons, fusing smoothly to my side. I explained that although we often use longeing to exercise horses that cannot be ridden or to warm up a horse before we ride, longeing is most useful when we think about it holistically. It is a good tool to prevent injury, a productive way to learn the gaits of a horse and observe any ill-fitting tack (such as halter, bridle or saddle) or atypical movements before climbing astride. Some people only use longeing to let their horses 'get their kicks out' before riding, but others utilize it to communicate, or 'sync up' with their horses. It was this latter experience I wanted for Diana.

I held the longe line in my right hand, a long whip in my left. As I asked Red to move out from the center of the arena into a circle, a light tap with the end of the whip on his haunches communicated hey, I'm here, get moving. Though a thoroughbred, a breed known for speed and energy, Red was often calmly inclined to slower paces. His muscles twitched under his coat where the whip touched him; he took a quicker step, moving out along the circle. As he walked, I spoke to Diana, showing her where I kept my body in relation to his. To keep him moving forward as he was, I kept my body in line with the center of his. To ask him to slow down, I positioned my body further toward his shoulder; to ask him to increase his speed, I moved my body further back, at his hip to drive him forward.

Asking Red to transition from a walk to a trot, I made a short clucking sound, and with a rising tone said, "trot." Then back to a walk, I dropped my voice, "aaand waaalk," saying the words slower, mirroring in my tone the desire for him to slow down as well. I asked Red to trot again, then asked him to transition into a canter; I gave two quick kissing noises and said "canter" with my voice rising. I explained to Diana that longeing was not simply helping Red to warm up his muscles, but it was a way for us to connect.

"Even though Red is a good-natured boy," I explained, "he's still a horse and riding a thousand-pound animal is dangerous. It's safer for me to ride Red after I can tell that he is listening to my voice and reacting to my body language on the ground, so part of making sure he's listening to me is also listening to him. I have to adjust the tone of my voice and the energy of my own body depending on how Red is feeling."

After an initial tap with the end of the whip, I only occasionally lifted it to point out my body position in relation to Red. Diana stood on my right, slightly behind; her arms entwined across her small chest, nodding at my words—her enormous brown eyes peering up, toggled back and forth between my body and Red's, moving out along the circle.

"So, how do you think he's feeling right now? Excited, relaxed? Anxious?"

"Umm…"

"Where are his ears?"

Recalling our previous lessons on horse body language, she answered, "He's listening to you. His inside ear is inside."

"Yes, his inside ear is pointed toward us, and his outside ear is flicking forward and back, right?"

I briefly reiterated how a horse's ears are their antennae, and you can tell where a horse's attention is by observing the direction of their ears. Although a horse will move to face the direction of a threat or engage with a person or another horse, their ears are the more subtle signals of their constant awareness. This is helpful in anticipating their movements and in evaluating their mood.

"What else should I look for to see how he's feeling?"

Diana was quiet. I waited.

"He's pretty relaxed I think, his head isn't high and he's kinda slow."

"Good," I agreed.

Our first lessons had covered the nature of the horse, its inclinations and moods. Diana was slowly and comfortably drawing on her knowledge of the horse's body language to read Red.[11] She rightly gathered that Red was "pretty relaxed" because his head was lowered, with one ear swiveled toward us, leaving just his outside ear to keep tabs on his surroundings.

After I'd demonstrated the three basic gaits, I asked Red to come back to a walk: I positioned my body so that I was ahead of his shoulder, and he came to halt along the circle. I gently pulled on the line toward my body and faced him, slightly turned. Whereas squarely facing him would have been confrontational or halting, my open body language was inviting instead. Red turned and began to amble toward the center of the circle. Diana stepped further behind me. When I wanted him to stop I faced him directly, stepping forward and bringing my right hand up to gently rub his forehead. I turned to Diana.

"Any questions?"

She shook her head. It took several minutes to help arrange the whip and longe line in her small hands, the pale skin glowing damp along her hairline. Diana took a step back, held the line in the direction she wanted Red to turn, the whip pointed at his opposite shoulder. Red just stood there.

"Tap his shoulder with the whip."

Diana looked at me, and I nodded. She lifted the whip higher, awkwardly, like it weighed twenty pounds instead of less than one; she poked him in the shoulder. He stepped back; she blushed, but Red got the idea and headed out to the larger circle. He began walking, lazily; Red knew I'd handed the line over to Diana.

"Alright, go ahead, get him moving."

Diana wobbled the whip toward his hip, "Trot?"

Red continued walking. Diana looked at me. I raised my brows and nodded, encouraging her to try again.

"Trot." It didn't sound like a question this time but still more of a suggestion than a command.

Again, she tentatively said, "Trot."

Red came to a halt and turned toward us.

Diana looked at me, reddening, stumbling over her words, "Wh... why won't he trot when I say it?"

What she was beginning to perceive was that it's not what you say, it's how you say it.

"Let's do it together," I said. "You keep the longe line and I'll handle the whip," I took the whip and stepped up even with Diana, "let's wake this boy up."

I kicked up a little dirt with the toe of my boot and gave a few clucks, "Come on, Red, get movin'!" He gave a little jump, trotted a few steps out to the circle again, and then came back to a walk. I smiled. Red wasn't going to listen to Diana if she was only offering suggestions. Diana was overwhelmed, and as horses are extremely sensitive to their surroundings, Red could feel how unsure she was; he wasn't misbehaving so much as reflecting Diana's physically embodied emotional state back to her.

Figure 2. Erica uses body language to ask Sherpa to walk.

I pointed the whip at his hip, telling Diana that we needed to position ourselves farther back on his body to push him forward. In Figure 2, a young quarter horse gelding, Sherpa, has responded to the combination of a verbal cue and the alignment of my body with his haunches, moving out at a trot. His outside ear remains forward, while his inside ear is tilted toward me, demonstrating a focus on my communication. This detailed attention to the spatial relationship between horses and humans draws on knowledge of how horses communicate within a herd. Body language between horses can be as violent as a horse's hoof striking out but most often as subtle as the angle of a horse's haunches. Standing at a distance from Red, Diana and I were working on this effective, but much subtler, means of communication. While she held the longe line, I stayed ahead of her and began to put Red to work again, changing the words and intonation.

"And pop!" I snapped the whip at his heels; Red began trotting.

"Aaand corn," lowering and slowing my voice, Red came back to a walk. Diana stifled a giggle.

"Hmhmhmhm," I kept an upbeat hum, and Red continued walking steadily.

"Popcorn, popcorn." There were more, barely audible giggles coming from Diana. I smiled, continuing to watch Diana carefully. Red's energetic movement told me I only needed to lift the whip slightly as I asked him to transition again; he took a couple steps and leapt into a canter. I positioned myself in line with his hip, driving him forward, watching the dust rising from his hooves as he encircled Diana and me with a steady rhythm. I took a step forward, lining myself up with his shoulder.

"Hmhm, hmhm," Red dropped down to a walk, his body swinging loosely. I took one more step forward and told Diana to tug gently on the line. He stopped and turned into the circle; I turned toward Diana who was half-smiling, a little guiltily.

"It's not what you say Diana, it's how you say it," I reflected. "You can use any words you want. The thing you need to learn is that your voice, your tone, your body will speak louder and mean more than words." She looked at Red and back at me. Her face was serious; she nodded vigorously.

"If you're not sure, he won't be sure either."

We began again. I continued to handle the whip but stepped back behind Diana. Without the distraction of the whip, she was able to focus on her voice. She spoke more clearly, her intonations exaggerated but much improved, as evidenced by Red's responsiveness. I used the whip, pointing or snapping it lightly, and, side by side, we worked together with Red. As Diana felt more comfortable with her verbal commands, she began to embody them as well, reducing the need for additional encouragement. After a few more sessions of helping Diana manage the longe line, whip, and body positioning, she began longeing Red on her own.

EYE TO EYE: OBSERVING DIANA'S GROWTH

At first her body movements were small and unsure. Her shoulders seemed to fold in on themselves like the feathered wings of a tiny bird. When Diana first attempted to move Red with her body positioning, knowing she needed to be more assertive, her attempt often manifested itself in an awkwardly aggressive lurch. It was at first a mimicked authority but with each successive communication, Diana became more and more confident, her body movements becoming smoother and more natural.

As she spent the summer with the community of horses and people at the farm, she continued to emerge. Shifts were visible in her stance, in the way she walked, and in the way she interacted with horses and people. The necessities of communication with Red had, it seemed, slowly lifted Diana's shoulders. Her collarbones began to open up, and her chin released away from her chest. The longeing exercise with Red required that Diana practice multiple kinds of stances and gestures, among them, aggression, invitation, passivity, and neutrality. Whereas Diana used to arrive with a faint nod, seamlessly sliding into her chores, as the summer progressed, she began to make eye contact and say "Hi." In the first weeks of her work as an apprentice, she was reluctant to try new tasks or work alone and with others, but after she began comfortably working with Red she showed a vibrant, though still quiet, eagerness to engage—attempting new tasks by herself or amiably asking others to help her out. Concurrent with this more open stance, Diana spent more time with the other girls at the farm, sitting and chatting together during down time.

Through horsemanship, it seemed, Diana was learning to embody a confident stance that was informed by a deepening awareness of communication patterns. Reading these changes in Diana and her interactions, I gathered that she was simply more comfortable—in her body, and in her interactions. This ease of being developed concurrently as engagement with horse activities and her peers increased. By the end of the summer, the heat fading with the swirling of autumn leaves, when I called Diana's name she looked me right in the eyes.

These changes in her body language, suggesting growth in Diana's positive self-image and confidence, would take on greater meaning for me as a teacher a couple of years later.

RESONANCES IN READING ACROSS CONTEXTS

The embodied learning experiences at the farm sharpened my awareness of how to read others' body language and how to use my own, effectively instilling in me the notion that through reading bodies we can better understand horses (as well as humans) to create collaborative learning experiences for both students and teachers. Identifying this reading as socially and educationally significant, the academic examples below offer views of how educators can consciously embody meaning while teaching and suggest how students can, as a result of embodied teaching practices, gain knowledge to strengthen their growing sense of self in the world.

THE SIGNIFICANCE OF SPACE IN THE CLASSROOM

In my first year as a Teaching Associate in the Sonoma State University English Department, my pedagogical approach in the composition classroom mirrored elements of my reading-centered approach to working with horses. Perhaps most deeply rooted in my approach to teaching English is an attention to my own body language and spatial orientation in the classroom. A typical day included,

- Maintaining circular seating while moving several times during a class between larger and smaller groups of desks.
- Crouching next to students at their desks. Moving to sit close beside a student who displayed "attitude" or seemed disengaged.
- Sitting on the floor, looking up to students or sitting next to them facing the board together during difficult moments in discussions.

My choices about seating and movement were aimed at creating a collaborative environment; however, I also brought my body language into play to teach specific lessons.

EMBODYING LANGUAGE IN LEARNING

Akin to Catherine Kroll's multimodal grammar lessons (see her chapter in this volume), where she employs exercises using colors, shapes and symbols, I likewise involved heuristics and embodiment in teaching the concept of signposts in writing. A "whole-body" learner myself, I am also a "whole-body teacher." As a lifelong athlete, like Kroll, I have a predilection for multimodal learning. While we did not utilize color in our lessons, we did use symbols, drawing, and our bodies. To teach my students to recognize and employ signposts in their writing, I utilized my own learning experience of embodying language to communicate what signposts do for readers. We worked on recognizing how these words helped us to decipher the meanings of difficult sentences in reading a variety of texts. I gave my class a handout of common signpost words—thus; similarly; and; therefore; heretofore; while;

however; despite; in contrast; unfortunately; but; although; unless; rather; yet; previously. We then discussed how these words signaled to us as readers if the content (or argument) of the sentence was moving in the same direction or if the author was going to shift direction. We also noticed how these words cued us, suggesting how a text is likely to move at the rhetorical level (Bean, Chappell, & Gillam, 2011; California State University Expository Reading and Writing Curriculum, 2008).

The first day we did this exercise, I likened the signposts to physical movement and did an impromptu skit: I embodied two sentences we had written on the board. When I was embodying the direction of the first sentence (walking along in front of the class) and I came to the signpost, "thus," I took a small jump forward, gesturing ahead with my palms open,

"Ta-dah! Right? Thus tells me I should keep moving forward in the same direction." Again, I began walking across the classroom, asking, "what should I do if in the middle of the sentence there was a "but!?"

At "but" I stopped and pivoted my whole body around to face the opposite direction. Once we had diagramed the basic directional structure of the sentence, we would figure out what the first part of the sentence said, then utilize the directions of the arrows (the signposts) to help discern the meaning of the second portion of the sentence. Pulling out sentences that were difficult to understand, we wrote them on the chalkboard and drew rectangles around the signpost words. If the word indicated the same direction, we would draw a line from the start of the sentence, looping around the rectangle and continuing forward with an arrow pointing to the end. If the word indicated that the sentence was changing direction, we would loop the line around the rectangle and draw an arrow facing the opposite way. In motion—written and embodied—we found our sense of play in the classroom.

Embodying signposts is one strategy that makes teaching enjoyable; through this modeling I aimed to engage my students in "whole body" ways. Kroll notes that, "students' own creative learning strategies" are stimulated by observing "their instructor's engagement and play with the material" (see her chapter in this volume). For me, a sense of play in teaching and learning comes directly out of the effectiveness and simple fun of engaging my body in the practice of horsemanship.

ORGANIZING DYNAMICS IN LEARNING

Reflecting on interactions with students revealed to me that there were strategies I had learned in my work with horses that carried over into my teaching approach. My equine work required that I stay attuned to who I was working with; reading body language helped me to settle on an appropriate approach to the day's lesson. Paralleling my method to gentling My Girl, in which I often waited for her to take the lead, in my classroom I aimed to engage students in initiating their learning through a similar patience. If I refused to take up the reins, students could direct discussions or express their concerns about texts or difficulties in homework; waiting amidst quiet was essential.

This is, of course, easier said than done when considering the pressures of course requirements or the standardized tests of K-12 schooling. Still, in the course I taught, I found spaces of freedom within and between the requirements in which I could incorporate my students' influence. Reading my students required that I sometimes wait for the voices that would emerge when I resisted filling the silences with my own speech. In an effort to bolster their engagement, I created certain spatial structures to encourage participation.

Though I had told my students that we would always sit in circles, not in rows, at our second class, on autopilot they sat in slipshod rows. I asked them to move into a circle again. Shuffling, they reluctantly acquiesced, shoving bags aside and moving their desks into a haphazard oval. Thinking back to high school, I realized that all the classrooms I had ever been in had this conventionally structured seating: all students facing the front of the room. This recollection helped me see my students' resistance to sit in a circle as learned behavior rather than as misbehavior.

By sitting in a configuration without a "front" everyone has an equal hand in the class (if only spatially at first). Schultz supports this reorganization of the "dominant paradigm" with her argument for listening which, "alters the role of the teacher and the nature of the pedagogical interaction. Listening shifts the locus of activity away from the teacher, without taking away the responsibility to teach" (p. 14). Drawing on concepts from feminist pedagogy and my experience as a facilitator for a class in the Comparative History of Ideas Department at the University of Washington, I wanted to upset the traditional idea that I was there to give them knowledge, and they were there to receive it (cf. Freire, 1970, 1993; Luke & Gore, 1992; Gore, 1993).

Along with the seating structure, I attempted to lead my students into interactive learning through other various spatial moves, such as sitting in different seats at each class meeting to disrupt the physical manifestation of hierarchy, thus removing a direction in the room from where authority or knowledge is expected. And they moved frequently, often taking the seats of other students as they went to the board to write or do group work. I physically enmeshed myself within the class in order to create a classroom where my students felt invested and active in their learning experience. Some of this was accomplished in discussions by listening, asking leading questions rather than offering statements of knowledge, and speaking from spatial positions within the circle of my students. When discussion slowed, and students found text difficult, I would crouch down to examine the text with them;

I would ask a question or repeat one of their questions. Just as I had harnessed curiosity to draw My Girl toward me in the pasture, I demonstrated my own curiosity or confusion with a text in the classroom to snag my students' interest and nurture their own inquisitiveness. I waited, sometimes seated in silence, looking to my students for direction. Squatting down next to them, I asked students to wonder and grapple out loud. Although an educational hierarchy still exists, focusing on body language keys me into understanding how to more skillfully read and subsequently incorporate more of my students' voices and desires into learning.

INTO THE COMPOSITION CLASSROOM & CONSIDERING TEXTS

In a lower-division writing course I taught at Sonoma State University as part of a new stretch program—two semesters of linked classes English 100A/100B—many of my students were part of the EOP (Educational Opportunity Program); they were the first in their families to attend college and/or came from low-income households. On our midsized campus (approximately 8,000 students), which is 68% Caucasian, the majority of my class self-identified as non-white. The EOP offers support to these students through a variety of programs and counselors, with whom I kept in close contact throughout the semester.

It was my students' backgrounds—what one EOP advisor called "disadvantaged"—that I considered when choosing readings for my course. Mike Rose's book, *Lives on the Boundary*, kept coming to mind. Rose's narrative, which grapples with his personal learning and that of others' on the margins of education, demonstrated that the selection of texts can be of central importance to students' experiences. Rose discusses a teacher who had taught the classics, books that were not a part of his home life. Referring back to this teacher throughout the book, Rose clearly felt empowered by access to what was outside of his upbringing. In an attempt to create such an experience for my own students, I sought a balance of materials in my classroom: providing them with canonical texts that were inspiring and difficult (though possibly foreign) as well as texts that reflected their individual cultural experiences (though not considered by some to be academic). Sometimes it felt more like precariously teetering than balancing as class schedules derailed into discussions exploring the texts and issues of my students' daily lives.

Early in the semester, I decided to share an excerpt from Immanuel Kant's work with my class. I chose it as an example of good writing and a classic philosophical text that had inspired me as an undergraduate. Though some suggested that Kant would be "too difficult" for this group, I wanted to show my students my confidence in what they were capable of rather than deny them access to a text because of assumptions based on their backgrounds or test scores. While I sought to expose them to texts that may not have reflected their own cultural identities, I continued to read their interests, whether they coincided with our materials or not. Although Rose felt empowered by access to texts outside his background, other students might have felt intimidated. This consideration arose early in the semester, during my class's first discussion when one of my students expressed feeling something other than inspiration as a result of reading Kant.

"BORING" TEXTS: FOLLOWING ANGELICA'S LEAD

Angelica had attitude. She was smart. Her rebellious behavior was subtle but undeniably vacillated between what felt like apathy and antagonism. Her long dark hair either shaded half her face, or was twisted up between her fingers. Though short in stature, she seemed taller than five feet, three inches, even when she was seated. If her body language was any clue to her self-presentation as a high schooler, Angelica must have been audacious—and it seemed she wanted me to know it. She had two habitual stances:

- Slouched back, her tail bone tucked under at the edge of the seat, legs shooting out to the sides, knees akimbo, arms crossed, chin down and tucked to one side or the other, eyes gazing aslant, sometimes her index finger pulling at a braid; or
- Upright, sitting against the back of the seat, legs crossed at the knee pointing askew, one arm across her chest with the other resting at the elbow, and a jutted chin resting at the edge of her palm.

Both of these postures suggested that she was, perhaps, not a completely willing participant. Her reading of me was immediate: she could sense that I would not stand for a direct challenge to my authority, but that I was aiming for amicable relations, and I would not call them out on subtle transgressions. It was early in the semester when I assigned Kant's "What Is Enlightenment?" Our discussion began:

"So, how did you guys feel about the reading?"

Silence. Feet shuffled under chairs, eyes falling to the book. Quiet. Angelica was the first to respond.

"It was boring."

Angelica looked me right in the eyes as she spoke, then her gaze shifted somewhere behind my head. I turned toward her, paused a moment, then nodded.

"Yeah? Which parts were the most boring?"

Eyes came up from desks. Angelica looked at me for what felt like a full minute. Another student, Tyler, lifted his hand. Still ingrained with the rules of high school, he was unused to speaking up in our class when he had something to say, and instead he waited for me to call on him. I nodded encouragement.

"In the middle. The whole middle part is a bit… well, it's the part I had a hard time reading."

I asked the class to turn to the part Tyler indicated, two lengthy paragraphs midway through.

"Alright, so let's read this aloud together, and try to figure out why this part is so boring."

We read a few sentences aloud and discussed what they meant. Students took turns rephrasing the content aloud in their own words, a practice we utilized often. In order to fully explain what these paragraphs were doing, we needed to solidify our understanding of what enlightenment was, and so we returned to the beginning of the essay. Again, students took turns putting Kant's sentences into phrases that readily made more sense to them. Together, we established a common understanding of the term *enlightenment.*

"So what is Kant saying in this first longer paragraph?"

We revisited the section that bored us again, identifying the examples in this paragraph regarding the different positions that enabled a person to speak her individual mind; they discussed how enlightenment could depend on the person's role and responsibilities in society. I asked the class which of Kant's examples helped them to better understand his definition of enlightenment and which ones seemed superfluous. Kant determines that while a pastor is bound to preach according to the church, a scholar is just in his duties when he expresses his own thoughts. But Kant argues, "that the people (in spiritual things) should themselves be incompetent is an absurdity which amounts to the eternalization of absurdities" (p. 266). From this we understood that enlightenment is too important to have individual freedom of thought hindered by one's private duties or profession. We decided that these examples were mostly useful, especially when Kant clarifies that the intellectual binding of the pastor to the church should not preclude his higher duty to nurture enlightenment in himself and, in certain cases, the public at large. Many of the students expressed the wish that Kant had been more concise in his explanation. Nevertheless, they began to appreciate the clarification of these lengthier paragraphs.

"So looking at the whole essay, what do you notice about the first few paragraphs we read last class, and the two here that were the most boring part?"

Silence.

I clarified that I just wanted to know what they noticed from a visual perspective, "what about the length? That's the first thing I noticed."

Two students quickly agreed.

"Yea, the middle is super long."

"He just kinda goes on and on here."

I nodded. "So, going back to the examples Kant uses: when we looked at them individually, they all seemed like good examples, yeah? Do you think that this part is more difficult to stick with because it's so long?"

A collective, "Umm," some nodding heads, a moment or two, and then, a few "yeah, yeahs." We discussed the purpose of the paragraphs and the different ways that Kant could have structured them. In small groups we underlined the most interesting sentences and paragraphs, identifying what makes strong writing.

By listening to Angelica's comment and embracing her attitude, we were able to embark on a rhetorical exploration. When Angelica said, "It's boring," although it sounded as though she was saying that the text wasn't interesting; as other reading researchers have observed, it is more likely that she was indicating the text was difficult (Schoenbach, Greenleaf, Cziko, & Hurwitz, 1999), and I inferred that she was a bit scared of failing and looking foolish in front of her classmates. As her teacher I had to listen closely. As Schultz might say, it was my responsibility to read beyond her words for the intention behind her seemingly rebellious comment. Simultaneously validating Angelica's perspective and drawing her into discussion, I asked her to be accountable for her thoughts by questioning her further. There was also a sense of surprise: Angelica was caught off guard when I responded to her comment with genuine interest. By taking into consideration what might be informing Angelica's response, I was able to listen more thoroughly and surmise that her attitude toward the reading (and the class more generally) possibly stemmed from fear. With this knowledge, I could choose to respond in a positive way that would engender opportunity for her to participate rather than punish and alienate her from the classroom. To engage Angelica with the text, I wanted to validate her feelings rather than shoot them down as wrong or engage her in a power struggle over her attitude.

READING WITH AND AGAINST THE GRAIN, OF STUDENTS, HORSES, AND TEXT

Perhaps all teachers, at one point or another, find themselves in an educational scuffle: where nothing seems effective in motivating their students. This certainly happens in the equine world, where no amount of strength overcomes the power of the horse, where no amount of force inspires genuine improvement. What might have happened in the example of Red and the nervous rider if the woman had recognized Red's fear and reacted with curiosity rather than assuming his behavior was rebellious and punishing him? Just as we sometimes have to follow a horse's lead, we sometimes have to follow a student's lead. This strategy of following can be employed astride a runaway horse. I've experienced the unsettling helplessness of trying to stop a frightened horse, whose instincts are propelling it fast and far away from what it fears. A childhood trainer taught me that following and then re-directing a horse's energy is more effective than straining to stifle it. Sometimes the surest method is to encourage the horse forward, crouching your body into the jockey's flexed spring stance, matching the horse's movement with your own; then smoothly, in sync, slowing your own rhythm. In each instance (Red's behavior, a runaway horse's flight, and Angelica's comment) there are two sorts of reading occurring.

Teachers, trainers, and those who practice horsemanship must often "read with the grain" of their students (Bean, Chappell, & Gillam, 2011) and equine partners, assuming that they know where they're headed, and agreeing to go along for the ride. More broadly, reading with the grain might involve not only taking an author's position but also stepping into a student's shoes, or feeling for those four hooves, and assuming that there is good reason, knowledge, and emotion influencing body-based expressions and reactions. Red's reaction to the rustling flowers was logical, and there was also logic in Angelica's stances within the classroom. Reading Angelica involved reading against the grain of the text I had assigned, disagreeing with Kant and questioning his stance. Though Angelica described the text as uninteresting, when we followed her lead our classroom discussion deepened, becoming anything but boring, which subsequently allowed us to reframe a very difficult text.

READING TO CONNECT

As the semester progressed past Kant, it was Angelica's tutor who gave me insight into her interests. Angelica was a fine basic writer. She wrote simple, grammatically accurate sentences, and she was developing a unique voice—her essays were full of strategically employed slang. As part of the requirements for my class, Angelica had a weekly appointment with a writing tutor. I often asked her tutor, Molly, how she was doing and if the assignments were clear. Molly confirmed that Angelica completed the work but that her behavior was often sassy or apathetic during their tutoring sessions. During their sessions, Angelica vacillated between the two stances previously described and commented on the "boring"-ness of the texts and assignments. Following one such response Molly detoured from the assignment at hand and asked Angelica what she liked to read and write. Angelica liked poetry. After Molly shared this conversation with me, I had a conference with Angelica. We discussed her recent paper, including her strengths (voice and analysis) and her weaknesses (repetition and informal speech). Shifting registers even as we spoke, Angelica smiled, and rolled her eyes, "My high school teacher was always sayin' that I was usin' too much slang in my papers." I asked her what she liked writing outside of school. She said she liked poetry because you could write however you wanted to, and it was fun. Poets can take or leave the rules of grammar, play with rhyme and reason as they wish. Poets are free to make meaning as they dare, but writing papers in college has so many rules. Rules you have to follow for success. When Angelica rolled her eyes, she was communicating a feeling that I discovered (in writing conferences) was shared by many of her classmates.

I scrapped my syllabus and structured the next four weeks around poetry: reading poetry, writing poetry, and composing an analytical essay. I handed them Tony Hoagland's poems, "Dickhead" and "Beauty." They did close readings in class, exploring how he made meaning in these poems that dealt with constructions of masculinity and femininity. I gave them short poetry writing assignments and shared my own work with them. It was in the few minutes we spent at the beginning of class reading our work that Angelica began to emerge from her habitual stances.

The assignment was simple and open: to write a free verse poem about a meal that conjured a memory. I had already shared with them a poem about being homesick during my first year in college and how the smell and taste of butter melting on toast reminded me of my mother. So, at the start of the following class, when I asked if anyone would like to share, Angelica relinquished her slouch, sat up, elbow on the desk propping up her poem, one hand raised, "I'll read." And she did. With sass and vibrant voice, she read her poem. When she finished the last line, "MmMhm, Gramah's sweet pies!," the class immediately began clapping, smiling, and shaking their heads in wonder and appreciation. A student, prominent among his peers, a cool customer with hip square glasses, spread a long smile and offered approbation: a quick northward jerk of the chin, "That was gooood."

During our work with poetry, there were additional shifts in Angelica's body language. While her stances retained elements of the two previously described, during later classes, she shifted her body to face the center of the room and the board. And she did something else I hadn't noticed her doing before; she stretched her arms above her head almost every class. And most of the time, when Angelica twisted her wrists up overhead, my attention would fall on her, asking, "yes?" and she would smile and shake her head, "nothing." Though she still sometimes slouched back in her seat, she more regularly sat up during class discussions and would make eye contact with me. When she did look me in the eyes, she didn't keep the straight face she had always presented before, rather she often smiled. A shy smile.

Her tutor and I discussed this vacillation: a kind of chin thrusting, side-ways stance, and this shy, smiling warmth, which was sometimes accompanied by a giggle. Whereas she used to shift between tough and then careless attitudes, the carelessness seemed replaced by this somewhat insecure, almost flirtatious giggle. Giggling? How does one read the bubbling shyness I've described? It accompanied Angelica's engagement in class discussion, in tutoring, in one-on-one conferences.

By engaging with the work, she was taking a chance. This giggle seemed a signal of nervousness—the kind of nervousness that accompanies the risk inherent in learning. Katz discusses such risk in learning when she asks in her chapter on dance (in this volume), "What would it take for young people to feel that they have permission to experiment and play [in schools]?" The reading approach described in this chapter is one answer to this question. Approaching texts and engaging in discussions collaboratively—jointly curious in the endeavor to question and comprehend—create opportunities for such experimentation and play. Katz suggests that, "For youth to learn and grow and change, they need spaces that are emotionally and psychologically safe, where they can work at the edges of their evolving abilities" (see her chapter in this volume). Such a space requires that students can risk making mistakes, and such a space requires that sassy comments like Angelica's stimulate a curious and questioning response rather than a stifling punishment.

Though Angelica still demonstrated audacity (in banter with her classmates, in reactions to assignments), her apathy diminished. Her contributions to discussion and comments on the readings were predominantly expressions of irritation or arched eyebrows of disbelief, but they seemed genuine. Whereas I read her comment about being bored with Kant as an attempt to disengage herself from further discussion (or from responsibility for having to make anything of the text), I interpreted her willingness to share her moments of frustration as a sign that she was genuinely engaged. I am still unsure of how to read Angelica's stretching. Was she more relaxed in the class? Did she simply need to stretch? Whatever else the stretching signaled, it seemed to indicate an increased sense of comfort, and it was accompanied by a positive shift in Angelica's attitude. Taking up more physical space in the classroom went hand in hand with taking up more intellectual space—with her poetry, questions and comments during discussions. I came to know that I could always count on her to offer candid thoughts and reactions to reading assignments, and she came to understand that she could count on me to listen.

HOLISTIC TEACHING: READING IN RIDING, READING AND WRITING

The seeds of this chapter have long been germinating in my journeys through pastures and classrooms. These case studies and personal experiences are intended to demonstrate and encourage the expansive possibilities for reading, broadly conceived in teaching. By expanding our sense of reading and taking a listening stance, not only in teaching but in all of our interactions, we are making room for perspectives and experiences beyond our own. It is this desire—to communicate and connect—that resonates with many of those who are drawn to work in the equine world. And it is, not surprisingly, this same hankering that draws many of us to teaching.

Strange bedfellows yet kindred spirits, horse trainers and teachers share a desire to help others reach their potential. What I learned from my time spent working with feral horses and young women at the farm has not only influenced my pedagogical approach, but my orientation toward life. Because the act of teaching is political by nature (and therefore personal), my approach within and outside of the classroom originates from a heightened awareness of body language: a practice that beckons for understanding and compassion between humans and animals. Through sharing these case studies and personal journeys, of reading in riding, and reading and writing, I hope to encourage fellow educators to join me in expanding communicative repertoires and broadening notions of reading to include the body and, in so doing, positively shape the lives of our students.

Notes

1. Although some may balk at the likening of students to horses, I do so in order to explore the role of body language in learning experiences.
2. See Paula Rodenas' *The Random House Book of Horses and Horsemanship* for a brief and accessible introduction to the horse and contemporary equine disciplines. For a more detailed discussion of the long history of horse and human interactions, see *A History of Horsemanship* by Charles Chenevix-Trench.
3. Programs in which the horse is a central aspect of teaching or therapy are still being developed. These include the various fields of Equine-facilitated Psychotherapy, Equine-assisted Learning and Equine-assisted Therapy. Non-profit Equi-Ed (http://www. equi-ed. org/) located in Sonoma County, California, is an organization that utilizes the therapeutic capacity of horse-human interactions to positively affect the lives of people with disabilities.
4. The individual horse should be approached holistically with the understanding that "horses are intensely social, and the herd, the band of mares with its stallion and outcast adolescent males, is the basis of their society. In the herd is their comfort, their protection, and their pleasure… it is often said that the cruelest thing you can do to a horse is to keep it alone…. Training is the language of physical response, and this communication is what supports the horse in its activities away from the herd" (Menino, 1996, pp. 101–102). Speaking thoughtfully through the body is elemental when introducing the horse to new experiences.
5. Equine Advocates, a non-profit horse rescue and educational facility, makes use of the PMU (Pregnant Mare's Urine) industry as part of its mission to promulgate information to the public about horse abuse and rescue. http://www. equineadvocates. org/
6. Horses are halter broke when they accept a halter on their heads and are willing to be led.
7. Longe lining is a technique in which the horse has a long line attached to its halter, bridle, or cavesson, which is held by a person on the ground. This person gives commands to direct and exercise the horse, who primarily moves in a circle around the person. Free longeing offers this practice without any line and is most often carried out in a small round arena.
8. "They touch each other constantly, grooming each other with their lips and teeth, brushing away flies with their tails. There are social rankings—the boss mare, the second mare, the young lieutenant stallion—and a horse's status is part of its identity and personality. But a herd is not a pack, and a horse is not driven by status as a dog, which cannot see another creature without

determining through some means which of them has or shall have more status. Friendship is important to a horse" (Menino, 1996, p. 101).

9. As Schultz (2003) writes, teachers, especially young teachers, can become caught up in how they are doing as teachers rather than focusing their energy on listening to their students' needs. This is an example of when my desire to reach a goal overrode my listening stance with the yearling.

10. Much like the expanded repertoire of stances women gain in the self-defense courses Keli Yerian describes (see her chapter in this volume), working with horses provides people with an opportunity to play with and practice using body language that may be unfamiliar to them.

11. As a prey animal, the horse has a powerful "fight or flight" instinct. A fearful horse will keep its head high, hollowing its back and watching for predators. A relaxed horse will lower its head, engaging different muscles. This body position is associated with relaxation. A calm state is almost always the most productive for both horse and human interactions (both on the ground and in the saddle).

Works Cited

Bean, J., Chappell, V., & Gillam, A. (2011). *Reading rhetorically.* Boston, MA: Longman.

Behler, E. (1986). *Immanuel Kant: Philosophical writings.* New York: Continuum. (Original work published 1784).

Birdwhistell, R. (1952). *Introduction to kinesics: An annotation system for analysis of body motion and gesture.* Louisville, KY: University of Louisville Press.

Brandt, D. (1990). *Literacy as involvement: The acts of writers, readers, and texts.* Carbondale: Southern Illinois University Press.

Brandt, D. (2001). *Literacy in American lives.* Cambridge, UK; New York: Cambridge University Press.

California State University Expository Reading and Writing Curriculum Task Force (2008). *Expository reading and writing curriculum* (ERWC). Sacramento: California State University and California Department of Education.

Chenevix-Trench, C. (1970). *A history of horsemanship.* Norwich, UK: Jarrold and Sons.

Cheville, J. (2001). *Minding the body: What student athletes know about learning.* Portsmouth, NH: Boynton/Cook-Heinemann.

Freire, P. (1970/1993). *Pedagogy of the oppressed.* New York: Continuum.

Gee, J. (2007). *What video games have to teach us about learning and literacy.* New York: Palgrave Macmillan.

Gee, J. (2008). *Social linguistics and literacies: Ideology in discourses.* London; New York: Routledge.

Goldin-Meadow, S. (2003). *Hearing gesture: How our hands help us think.* Cambridge, MA: Belknap Press of Harvard University Press.

Gore, J. (1993). *The struggle for pedagogies: Critical and feminist discourses as regimes of truth.* New York: Routledge.

Hall, E.T. (1966). *The hidden dimension.* Garden City, NY: Doubleday.

Hull, G., & Katz, M.L. (2006). *Crafting an agentive self: Case studies of digital storytelling. Research in the Teaching of English, 41*(1), 43–81.

Hull, G. & Rose, M. (1990). "This wooden shack place": The logic of an unconventional reading. *CCC, (41)*3: 287–298.

Jewitt, C. (Ed.). (2003). *Multimodal literacy.* New York: Peter Lang.

Jewitt, C. (Ed.). (2011). *The Routledge handbook of multimodal analysis.* New York: Routledge.

Katz, M.L. (Spring 2008). Growth in motion: Supporting young women's embodied identity and cognitive development through dance after school. *Afterschool Matters, 7,* 12–22.

Kendon, A. (2004). *Gesture: Visible action as utterance.* Cambridge, UK; New York: Cambridge University Press.

Leander, K. (2004). *Spatializing literacy research and practice.* New York: Peter Lang.

Luke, C. & Gore, J. (1992). *Feminisms and critical pedagogy.* New York: Routledge.

McNeill, D. (2005). *Gesture and thought.* Chicago: University of Chicago Press.

Menino, H. (1996). *Forward motion: Horses, humans, and the competitive enterprise.* New York: North Point Press.

Morgan, M. H. (1894). *Xenophon: The art of horsemanship.* London: J. A. Allen.

Rodenas, P. (1991). *The Random House book of horses and horsemanship.* New York: Random House.

Rose, M. (2005). *Lives on the boundary.* New York: Penguin.

Schoenbach, R., Greenleaf, C., Cziko, C., & Hurwitz, L. (1999). *Reading for understanding: A guide to improving reading in middle and high school classrooms.* San Francisco: Jossey-Bass.

Schultz, K. (2003). *Listening: A framework for teaching across differences.* New York: Teachers College Press.

Shohamy, E., & Gorter, D. (2009). *Linguistic landscape: Expanding the scenery.* New York: Routledge.

Street, B. (1984). *Literacy in theory and practice.* Cambridge, UK; New York: Cambridge University Press.

CHAPTER SIX

36 Jewish Gestures

NINA HAFT

GESTURE AS A FORM OF IDENTITY: JEWISH IN THE MIRROR

Not long ago, I choreographed a dance about a Jewish family from the 1950s, set in the Jewish community (and mob culture) of Las Vegas. As it turned out, only one of the dancers cast in this piece had grown up in a Jewish family herself, and I was thus faced with the unlikely task of teaching the dancers how to move and act like members of my own Jewish family. To complicate matters, I cast all the male roles with female dancers, so some of the dancers were also learning how to move convincingly as males. Together we scrutinized the movement, language, and signatures of gender and culture, to bring this project to life.

I was not entirely new to drag performance at the time—I had once created a physical portrait of a boxer in another dance—but I was curious about how to articulate a form of drag that was convincingly Jewish. This was perhaps when I first started to ask: is there such a thing as a Jewish gesture? Do we embody desire and loss in identifiably Jewish ways? The hands, the postures, the facial expressions—what does our movement say about us?

I frequently recognize Jewish gestures, and in fact have become somewhat obsessed with collecting them. If I am comfortable with someone, I will spontaneously ask her "what's your favorite Jewish gesture?," but mostly I just see people perform them and then I surreptitiously practice their gestures until I can reproduce them in detail. This may sound essentialist to you; it does to me. The fact that it is my own cultural group gives me some comfort, but the truth is that I really don't want to believe that the way I move reveals the way I have lived. But the body speaks even when the mouth is silent. My movement signature may be entirely unique to me, but it also embodies information about gender, age, and ethnicity, among other things. Tracing the origins of my movement signature has been central to shaping my identity narratives. It has also been instrumental in my work as an artist, director, teacher, and cultural activist.

I have spent countless hours observing and imitating movement, not only as a performer and educator but also as an observer of human idiosyncrasy. Full disclosure: I have taken guilty pleasure in performing detailed imitations of other people's signature movements. As an adolescent at summer camp, I was able to perform the gait and posture of many of my friends on demand. I hoped my 'act' would be taken as proof of my detailed (albeit immature) attention to what made each one of us unique. It seemed popular among my friends, but perhaps they watched in order to make sure they did not themselves become the subjects of my performances.

My curiosity about body language has endured and feeds my work as a choreographer and performer. Today, I experiment in rehearsals with what theatre director Ann Bogart (2001) calls "putting a fire under" stereotypes, in an effort to transform them into the underlying stories that drive human behavior (p. 93). I am less interested in whether the stereotypes are verifiable and more invested in understanding how they reveal our contradictory fears and desires.

How does gesture mark identity? Gestures can be read as a set of non-verbal codes broadcasting who we are in the world. For example, whether or not a female crosses or uncrosses her legs can be interpreted as unguarded innocence (in a 3-year-old playing with dolls); coy flirtation (in a teen eating ice cream at a carnival); striking a butch pose (by a 20-something in overalls with hammer in hand); or uncouth forgetfulness (in an old lady watching TV in her nightgown). Our beliefs about sex and age intersect in these moments with our perceptions of power in society. We internalize these beliefs about possible, proper and powerful body language in any given situation, and we choose our gestures accordingly—albeit, sometimes subconsciously.

Are these gestures anything more than reified stereotypes? This has been my underlying question throughout the research, creation, and performance of my solo dance performance piece, "36 Jewish Gestures." I wanted to find out how much of my movement could be reduced to code and just how far I could push the meaning behind such movements. Performance is an exquisite crucible for this kind of investigation because the contexts in which we make this shift in observable ways: the venue we play in, and the audience that meets us set the context for the work anew each time. The same work can read as flat caricature or nuanced rendering, depending on these elements.

Bogart (2001) writes about the power of stereotypes in her work, challenging their association in the theatre world with lack of originality and inherited cultural memory:

> When approaching stereotype as an ally, you do not embrace a stereotype in order to hold it rigid; rather, you burn through it, un-defining it and allowing human experience to perform its alchemy. You meet one another in an arena of potential transcendence of customary definitions. You awaken opposition and disagreement. (pp. 104–105)

What does heating up stereotypes look like in my rehearsals? When working on solo material, I have experimented with distilling people I know into single-gesture portraits (old habits die hard). I have also studied gestural sequences harvested from iconic movies and my own family gatherings. I repeat and exaggerate these gestures, often finding myself unable to remember them unless I simultaneously voice the words out loud that give these gestures emotional resonance. Even in performance, I have found it impossible to perform "36 Jewish Gestures" without muttering under my breath, which has turned out to be the perfect grace note to most of the characters in the piece.

Rehearsing Jewish gestures has become an artistic strategy that triggers sensations and memories of feeling jocular, erudite, and occasionally too loud. Honestly, I practice each gesture until doing so makes me feel very Jewish. Feeling very Jewish feels like many different things to me, but it is always a relief to get there. When I move and speak and think in this way, I release a tremendous amount of energy that I have discovered is tied up in presenting myself as a postmodern, abstract and 'culturally neutral' mover. Today I understand that it is not possible to be culturally neutral as a mover or to remove the time and place from the training or the person. However, my early training in ballet and modern dance presented itself as such. As a young dancer, I strove to erase my idiosyncrasies, and to compensate for my physical and technical differences by cultivating a classical standard. In contrast, when I allow my even earlier influences from Yiddish Theatre and Borscht-Belt comedy to surface in my work, I find a form of expression that is broad, informal, and celebrates idiosyncrasy.

In company rehearsals, I have asked my dancers to break down exactly how to carry their head, shoulders, wrists, and pelvises to convey character, motivation, and intention. The goal: to read onstage as specific Jewish characters. This experiment becomes something we all look forward to. We are literally cultivating new ways of moving while challenging assumptions about our own power and identity. Women become men, Gentiles become Jews, and we all delight in being literal for a change, tossing the postmodern, antirepresentational aesthetic to the wind. In this space, we find new artistic freedom.

MATCHING MEANING AND MOVEMENT

Gesture is not only a performance element; it is an embodied practice that links our felt experience to our oral speech. We all speak with a multitude of facial and bodily gestures—witness the miscommunications that take place when we 'talk' by telephone or email and the non-verbal cues drop away. A good deal of what we say is conveyed by our gestures, which literally add dimensionality to our voices.

For example, when someone declines your offer of dinner or a ride, you might 'instinctively' recognize the gestures they make in tandem with the word "no" as evidence of a veiled rejection or, conversely, of a genuine disappointment about a missed opportunity. Yet movement analysts would argue that what we call instinct is often our interpretation of someone's verbal idiosyncrasies and kinesthetic gestures. The subtexts created when our words and movement are not completely in agreement can lead to emotions running high. We hear "oh, I am so sorry to miss it!" voiced with postural and facial gestures that hint of retreat or attraction, and we are intrigued, offended, or confused. The timing of these meanings in relation to one another is what sometimes renders our 'miscommunication' funny or tragic. The relationship between gesture and speech is theatrically fertile; playwrights, directors, and actors are trained to bring subtexts to life, tracing threads of the story through actors' unspoken drives and inner conflicts. In western cultures, traditional tragedies and comedies rely heavily on subtexts or the mismatching of words and intention.

The relationship of speech to gesture is also of great interest to scholars who examine the 'mismatching' of gesture and speech for insight into language, thought, and learning. Goldin-Meadow & Wagner's work (2005) points to such mismatches as indicators of cognitive transformation and change. Because these mismatches are rarely interrupted or challenged in any way by speakers or listeners, they may be powerful indicators of a speaker's "below-the-radar" shifting understandings, feelings, and states of mind (Goldin-Meadow & Wagner, 2005). From an anthropological perspective, these same gesture-speech mismatches may be evidence of the rapid migration of gestures across generations and continents, where language and movement are instrumental to those assimilating into a new country, socio-economic class, or kinship arrangement (Sklar, 2008). We may barely notice that we are allowing our posture, gestures, rhythmic phrasing, uses of space, and movement to change. It is often when someone from 'back home' takes notice that we realize our stance in the world has transformed. We now inhabit this new social space from the inside out. As we enter new social spaces, we literally embody old and new places.

As Sklar (2008) concludes about Efron's study of New York City immigrants, transplanted people often relinquish their 'native' gestures in a single generation and come to "play host to the gestures that live and circulate within the American site…" (Noland & Ness, 2008). In this way, gesture is an enactment of belonging somewhere.

Gestures can telegraph likeness—"you look just like your mother when you do that" or "I can tell you're angry." Gestures can also broadcast difference. Have you ever witnessed a friend change in the presence of a peer group to which you do not belong? It is not just the palpable alteration of speech patterns we detect but also the shifts in movement repertoire that we parse into aspects of the body, effort (energy), shape and space. In the early 20th century, it was Hungarian-born Rudolph von Laban's Movement Analysis system that first organized movement pattern recognition in terms of these four main categories: body, effort, shape, and space. The category of body concerns the parts of the body articulated and held, the underlying patterns of connection between limbs, and the sequencing of these articulations. Effort describes the use of different dynamics within the parameters of time, space, weight, and flow in movement. Shape looks at the kinds of shapes in the movement, along with the ways these shapes change and relate to self and the world. Finally, space circumscribes the uses of directional pulls, planes, three-dimensional patterns, and the volume of space around the body itself (von Laban, 1975).

Laban was particularly interested in making connections between the expressive capabilities of human movement for connecting our inner and outer worlds. Understood this way, a gesture might function as an emissary between our felt experience and communication with others. Gesture is thus an utterly potent form of shaping as well as expressing identity.

GESTURE AS WORLD VIEW: 36 JEWISH GESTURES

Faced with the challenge of teaching Jewish gestures, I was happy to find that I am not alone in discerning a signature style of movement that constitutes Jewish gesture as it is practiced by the ethnic group to which I belong—Ashkenazi Jews from Eastern Europe. In a groundbreaking study conducted in 1941, anthropologist David Efron analyzed Eastern European Jewish and Southern Italian immigrants in New York City (Efron, 1941/1972). Efron literally sat on a popular street corner and observed the movements and speech patterns of pedestrians. From this work he was able to 'profile' the spatial and rhythmic characteristics of physical gesture as they coordinated with oral speech.

Efron found that gestures rapidly changed as each cultural group started to assimilate. In this way, he showed that gesture was not biologically, psychologically, or racially based but rather a cultural artifact of the worldview of the speaker/gesturer. Significantly, Efron's early work on gesture refuted key concepts of racial purity and cultural essentialism advanced at that same historical moment by Hitler's Nazi Socialist party and lent credence to Rudolf von Laban's ideas about movement, identity, and relationships (von Laban, 1975). Efron substantiated the expressive power of movement and its ability to link a person's inner and outer worlds (identity and relationships) through physical expression.

Discovering Efron's work emboldened me to start collecting Jewish gestures and inspired me to present them as my 'findings' in a solo autobiographical performance. I took equal inspiration in this endeavor from a seminal contemporary dance theater solo by choreographer Joe Goode, titled "29 Effeminate Gestures," which premiered in San Francisco in 1987. I developed "36 Jewish Gestures" as my homage to Goode, who happens to be a former teacher of mine. Goode's piece, and his innovative approach to integrating text, movement, and social commentary, provided me with a uniquely suitable framework for my project. The structure of my solo deliberately mimics that of Goode's by opening with a short song ("Bei Mir Bist Du Sheyn"), a chair, some contemporary dance, a sardonic treatise on my professed topic, and an explicit subversion of boundaries between masculine/feminine and performance/experience.[1]

I soon realized, however, that I needed to look beyond my own experiences to create this piece, so I began asking people I knew—who self-identified as Jewish—what their favorite Jewish gesture was. This was a great exercise. I not only learned some new gestures but also got to learn from non-dancers, who took great pleasure in seeing me work hard to master their own spontaneous movements. As a dancer, I have had many years of experience observing and replicating movement, but this form of artistic research was a unique experience. In these exchanges, I revealed myself to be a clever observer and merciless chronicler of others' movements, yet I ran the risk of being seen as someone who mocks other people, exaggerates their foibles, or worse—perpetuates racial stereotypes. Certainly, none of these is a good behavior to sport as a movement educator or as a friend. Fortunately, my keen interest in the details of each gesture (i.e., not only the movements but also the stories behind them) convinced most people that I was an ally, genuinely interested in their movement.

Part One of "36 Jewish Gestures," begins when I address the audience in my Borscht-Belt 'drag queen' persona, modeled on aspects of Sophie Tucker (burlesque, vaudeville, and film/radio star of the early 20th century), Bea Arthur (of TV's *Maude*) and my late aunt Yetta. I invite the audience to laugh and cringe at my favorite Jewish gestures which build in a medley of stylized, dance-like movements punctuated by bawdy, hammy gestures. By breaking the fourth wall that traditionally separates the viewer from the performer, I clue my audience into the fact that their experiences of gesture matter here.

Part Two is my 'lecture,' which draws on Efron's study in its comparison of Eastern European and Italian gestures, complete with a mockingly erudite voice-over and vaudevillian physical theater. I perform Efron's findings by voicing them in the tone of a professor and dispassionate researcher while simultaneously punctuating my comments with a barrage of stereotypical yet laughably identifiable gestures or what I call "gestural thought bubbles." The following passage from my script summarizes highlights of Efron's results:

> Efron's landmark study tells us that Jewish gestures embody a speaker's inner thoughts and feelings. Humor, sarcasm, argument and innuendo are just some of the nuances that gestures add to our speech. Traditional Southern Italian gestures, for example, often symbolize actual words, such as 'walk backwards,' 'stupid,' 'I insist,' 'rage,' 'don't ask me,' etc.
>
> Gestures observed in Polish, Litvak, Russian and other Ashkenazi Jewish groups tend to revolve around the axis of the wrist or elbow, punctuated by small movements of the neck and head. These Jewish gestures occupy the near reach space in front of the body, somewhere between hip and shoulder height, growing smaller and more direct during heated discussion. Neapolitan and Sicilian gestures, however, occupy more space to the side and back of the body, hinge at the shoulder joint, and grow larger as tempers flare. As both groups [Jews and Italians] assimilated, they continued to gesticulate, only in ways that were less culturally specific."[2]

In delivering this pompous stretch of scholarly discourse, I hoped to heighten awareness of each audience member's habits of gesture, movement, gender, and culture. What I discovered by performing it is that my father's movement signature is more deeply embedded in my body than my mother's, and thus my "feeling like I am Jewish" often entails moving like a man. As the script for my solo continues, I share my own musings on migration, assimilation, my relationship to my father, and the Middle East conflict.

The work concludes in Part Three, where I perform a constellation of Jewish masculine gestures, postures, and characters in my male drag king persona. The tenderness and barely contained rage in this last section is accompanied by a prayer, which is traditionally chanted on the Jewish Day of Atonement, Yom Kippur. "Hineni" is traditionally chanted in synagogue, led by a male cantor—a singer and prayer leader—on Yom Kippur. It is here that I wrestle, quite literally, with what it means to me to be a good Jew.

JEWISH GESTURE ON THE SILVER SCREEN

In addition to observing gestures in conversation, my creative research methods also emulated Efron's by my study of iconic images from the stage and screen. I harvested and memorized gestures by Molly Picon in archival Yiddish films such as *East and*

West and *Yidl Mitn Fidl*, Fanny Brice in vaudeville and early movies, Barbra Streisand in *Funny Girl* and *Yentl*, Sarah Jessica Parker in *Sex and the City*, Groucho Marx, Gertrude Berg, Lenny Bruce, Joan Rivers, and Milton Berle in archival television footage, and many others. I was especially interested in Jewish performers whose genius was in subverting American ideas about masculinity and femininity within the rubric of Jewish culture.

Bruce and Berle challenged stereotypes of cerebral and disembodied Jewish masculinity by being raunchy, sensual, confessional performers, who got rich making Americans laugh and squirm about their own secret desires. Picon and Streisand famously played iconic Jewish male roles in drag (*Yidl Mitn Fidl*[3] and Yentl[4]), while being sexy and flirtatious though tough about business. Parker's Carrie Bradshaw heats up the stereotype of the Jewish American Princess by chronicling her unabashed materialistic pursuit of love in a format reminiscent of the women's pages of *The Jewish Daily Forward*.[5] Rivers does it all, virtually becoming a drag queen version of a Jewish housewife who openly remodels her body into that of a *shiksa* (Yiddish for "non-Jewish girl," i.e., dyeing her hair blond and surgically altering her Semitic facial features, etc.) while being as bawdy, bullying, and belligerent as Lenny Bruce.[6]

Jewish masculinity and femininity were uniquely vulnerable to change when translated onto American soil. No doubt all immigrants encounter challenges to gender and family roles when relocating into new communities and economies. For Jewish families, the traditional division of public (male) and private (female) spheres was further complicated by the Old World injunction for men to study and pray (sacred sphere) and for women to keep both the home front and the storefront running smoothly. In the New World, Jewish men were portrayed as effeminate and bookish or as thwarted and villainous. The old Jewish male stereotype of "brains without brawn" spawned distinctly disembodied antiheroes in literature and cinema,[7] while Jewish women were often presented as fleshy creatures who lured men astray (like Lilith did Adam before Eve came along), or who complained loudly about their materialistic desires. These stereotypes are what made actors like Lenny Bruce and Fanny Brice so subversive.

When Lenny Bruce offended people he gestured up and forward sharply with his chin, just like a *yeshiva bokher* (Jewish male religious student) arguing the Talmud. He leaned on the microphone stand with a fey bent wrist, but in his other hand he wielded the phallic microphone itself, heckling his audience preemptively. He spread his legs and took large strides, in contrast to the *luftmenschen* (Yiddish for "impractical dreamer") who walked to synagogue while lost in great thoughts. Bruce embodied a distinctly American swagger that evoked sex, aggression, and power.

Vaudevillian Fanny Brice traded broadly in stereotypes of Jewish femininity, pioneering a style of performance that helped us laugh at the *griner* (Yiddish for "recent immigrant") and gender-dysphoric person in all of us. Brice's exaggerated lack of physical grace and sensuality disarmed her audiences. Her knock-kneed, bony-legged and sexually naive characters such as Baby Snooks (a vaudevillian-style toddler) established her as the un-womanly star of stage, radio and film. Never the irresistible dame or dangerous siren beauty, Brice used her talent and business acumen to stay squarely in the spotlight. Her performances could be described as post-*shtetl* form of drag, as she pushed at the boundaries of Hollywood, burlesque, and clowning using the accent of a recent Jewish immigrant. One only has to look at her unflattering costume, squared off posture and gawky waddle in "It's Gorgeous to Be Graceful" to understand how subtle Brice's mastery was of the gestures of gender and culture.[8]

Sex, gender, and language were thus often the favored tools of Jewish physical comedians. In 20th-century America, these tools were the catalysts of social change, engendering new gestures of identity and community. What these Jewish artists performed was a surreptitious critique of the American immigrant experience. Their identities migrated across gender and class boundaries precisely by standing out—as Jewish, awkward, defiant. Their gestures also migrated via television and film and were ultimately embraced by mainstream American culture.

PERFORMING IDENTITY: GESTURE AND PLACE

A nosy Jewish mother drawn from my aunt Yetta, a drag queen resembling Harvey Fierstein in the film *La Cage aux Folles,* a taciturn Italian mobster inspired by my brother's friend Albert, Cher Horowitz from *Clueless,* Joe Pesci in *My Cousin Vinny,* vaudevillians Sophie Tucker and Ethel Merman, and Isaac and Ishmael of the Old Testament. These are some of the many characters I perform in "36 Jewish Gestures." I literally embody these characters onstage, some for just a brief moment/gesture, others for the length of an entire vignette. I concatenate these personae as a way of underscoring how each gesture we use in daily life in some way sums up an entire world of meaning.

Of course, not all Jewish gestures look alike. In conversation with others who study gesture and culture, I have come to realize that some of my gestures in this piece may be regional as well as cultural. For example, a Lebanese Christian friend of mine who is married to an Italian diplomat attended a performance of the work. Afterwards she commented on how surprised she was to see how Jews, Israelis, Lebanese, and Italians share an especially similar gestural language using their hands and heads. My performance apparently included gestures that she and her children would recognize as their own. Coming from the mother of a family that moves around the world, with the diplomatic assignment (in part) to export Italian culture, I found her comments intriguing. Might her gestures 'migrate' across boundaries in a way that speeds up the process by which we normally acquire new gestural expressions? If mothers are the first people with whom we experience identity, connection, and language, then mothers might also become the bodies through which gestures are first transported. Are the gestures, tastes and taboos of each new post grafted onto my friend's Franco-Arabic roots differently than they are onto her children, who have never lived in any one place for long? Will her son and daughter identify with gestures learned, in crucial places and at crucial times, more so than with gestures from the Mediterranean?

I have also looked to artists inspired by Levantine culture.[9] For one colleague whose parents migrated to the U.S. from Iran, her family's Jewish gestures seemed to her to be more Persian than Germanic (i.e., Sephardic, as distinguished from Ashkenazi Jewish culture). In her own work as a filmmaker, she described the challenge of representing Jewish life on screen in ways that a wider Jewish community might recognize. For example, what looked like a quintessentially Jewish series of gestures to her in a film we both saw did not look the same to me. For my colleague, this portion of the film was crucial to her buying into the director's message about Iranian Jewish ideas about marriage, whereas I thought the film really said more about mother/daughter conflicts. This was because I was captivated by the dissimilarity of gestures between the mother and daughter. In hindsight, I believe I was observing the rapid assimilation phenomenon by first-generation immigrants that Efron (1941/1972) noted in his work. Not knowing much about Persian Jewish family life, I could not recognize that both women were making and understanding each other's Jewish gestures.

For some of my Palestinian colleagues, the individual gestures, rhythms, and dynamics of their folkloric dance (*dabkeh*) were regarded as quintessentially Palestinian. Not only the steps and the rhythms but the dynamics reflect a synthesis of bodily experiences of place (in what Laban [1975] would term "efforts" or Sklar [2008] might call "vitalities"). These movements are passed on to each generation, often as a way to preserve the memory of traditional Palestinian life before the *Nakba*.[10] The Palestinian artists I have worked with are committed to performing their dance form (and their gestural language) for the express purpose of 'inhabiting their homeland' and reminding others of their right of return. They literally see the act of dancing as a way of preserving and inhabiting the land inside their bodies—a striking inversion of the usual positioning of bodies within social landscapes. Many peoples who have experienced genocide regard remembering as a sacred act of dedication to those who perished, along with their ways of life. That memory of a place might be 're-membered' or re-embodied *through dancing* is a provocative idea. The possibilities for site-specific performance as migrated through the dancers' bodies has great potential—if a demolished house or orchard can be 'seen' through the eyes of a grandparent's memory and description, then perhaps we can inhabit places past, present and future through our gestures and dances.

Traditional Palestinian dances tend to have fewer sources from outside of Palestine influencing their vocabulary and presentation than traditional Israeli folk dances. The newly formed State of Israel deliberately drew from its largest immigrant populations (Yemenite and Eastern European) when formulating its new physical culture. When interviewed, most of my Israeli colleagues in contemporary dance did not identify anything as particularly Jewish or folkloric about their movements, though some cited their Eastern European or North African heritage as key reference points in their physical imaginations (Haft, 2007b).

"My father was from Morocco, but that does not really make any difference in my work…although I did have a belly dancer at my Bar Mitzvah," quips choreographer Sahar Azimi. While hyphenated identities (such as 'African-American') are not generally embraced in Israel, I thought it significant that Azimi was one of only a small number of dance artists I met there who expressed interest in Palestinian dance. Another Israeli choreographer I interviewed, Renana Raz, cited her Polish parents' life with other immigrants on a *kibbutz* as key to her "fascination with folk dances and how they tell a different story than contemporary dance." Her work stood out in the contemporary dance scene for its embrace of political dance theatre and its overt exploration of culturally based dance forms with the expressions of gender these forms allow. Barak Marshall, a choreographer working today in both Tel Aviv and Los Angeles, is uniquely aware of the hybrid nature of Israeli identities. His mother, Margalit Oved is from Yemen and is revered in Israel as a dancer and singer.[11] Marshall notes that Jewish Israeli audiences and presenters sometimes show discomfort when his mother sings traditionally Arabian music in his pieces (as she often does). He attributes this to an ambivalence that many Israelis have about music native to a culture that is common to many Middle Eastern Jews yet has been stigmatized as belonging to enemies of the state (Haft, 2007b). Marshall's performances are unique in Israel for their deliberate mashing-up of references to his mother's (Adenite) and his father's (Eastern European and American) heritage in his works.[12]

AUDIENCES RESPOND

Many viewers of "36 Jewish Gestures" commented on my gendering of the gestures, marveling that they could really see me transform physically as I adopted the movements and mien of my father in Part Three of the piece. The labile essence of

Sample gestures from Nina Haft's performance piece, '36 Jewish Gestures.'

my gender, regional origin, age, and intention as revealed in these gestures is exactly the point of my piece. Though we are "being ourselves" when we gesture, we are also per/forming—i.e., arriving at shape or identity through the ritual of public expression. What we share inevitably evolves from the material, habits, and personalities of the many people and places embedded—and embodied—in our movements.[13]

I have performed "36 Jewish Gestures" for a wide range of audiences: dance, and theatergoers, LGBT and non-queer folk, academic conferences with undergraduate students, graduate students, and faculty of various arts and humanities disciplines, Jewish and non-Jewish scholars and culture mavens, Italians, Filipinos, Latinos, Arabs, Israelis, Americans, and others. Most of the time people either laugh in recognition or grow uncomfortable with the characters that I portray in this piece. My suspicion is that audiences who identify as coming from an immigrant family find the piece resonant. Those who take pleasure in standing out—or in understanding an exclusive set of non-verbal signs—seem to enjoy it the most. Others seem to be uncomfortable with the defiantly non-assimilated forms of expression that I use in this work. My performing may heighten their awareness of culturally inflected movements they themselves enact. It is also possible that by performing, I am opening up an insiders' gestural language for outsiders to interpret or, in some cases, judge, and perhaps this evokes discomfort for viewers who would rather not have subconscious gestural habits brought to light.

Although I have not collected anonymous audience responses, I have noticed that older Jewish viewers of my father's post-Holocaust generation do not seem to find "36 Jewish Gestures" at all funny. I have thought a great deal about this, as this audience represents the group of Jews I feel most kinship with and most indebted to in making this piece. I imagine their discomfort may in part be due to the political questions I raise in the work about gender, power, and the conflict in the Middle East. I suspect as well that their discomfort has to do with explicitly performing my Jewishness; standing out as identifiably Jewish was a choice that was complicated for them by the events of World War II, and by the silence, complicity, and horror they once witnessed. We don't speak much directly about it, but I recognize their quintessential Jewish gestures after the lights come up, and when I see their *farbissena punim*, I imagine that these sourpuss expressions of disapproval I see on their faces are directed at me. Some of my more cheerful older Jewish viewers are quick to approach me so they may point out the Jewish gestures I have omitted in my research. They are the ones who are excited to converse with me about gesture and identity.

One of the more provocative debates I have encountered in my work in New Jewish Performance is about what makes a dance Jewish. For me, my dances are Jewish because of my choreographic 'lens'; the way I see and investigate and layer and textualize my work derives as clearly and strongly from my identity as a Jewish woman as it does from my identity as a dancer. A Jewish dance may also be one that engages form and/or content relevant to Jewish history and experience, such as liturgy, religious or historical narratives, images of Jewish art and life, etc. More obviously, a Jewish dance may be one that uses culturally Jewish artifacts, such as klezmer music, Hebrew or Yiddish text, characters speaking in identifiably Jewish accents, etc. Finally, perhaps a Jewish dance might simply be any dance made by a Jewish artist. Yet for some of my viewers, my dances are not Jewish unless they are performed by Jewish bodies.

What constitutes a Jewish body? In Judaism, according to most religious authorities, a child is not considered Jewish unless one is born of a Jewish mother. I would argue however, that a Jewish body is a culturally mediated one.[14] The dancers I have worked with may not 'look Jewish' to mainstream Americans, but that is partly my point. Must racial, ethnic, and religious affiliations qualify us as Jewish enough, and who sets these standards? The migration of Jews over centuries has resulted in a veritable rainbow of Jewish cultures. We do not all look alike. People of all skin colors, hair and body types look Jewish, not only to their mothers but to anyone who lives next door to and intermarries with us. Jews of North African, Asian, African, and even Middle Eastern origins frequently encounter disbelief and sometimes exclusion by their (more) European counterparts.

From those who see "36 Jewish Gestures" and do not identify as Jewish or Italian, I have heard that it makes them reflect on gestural repertoires that run in their own families. This type of kinesthetic literacy is precisely the kind of endeavor I hope to inspire with my performances. We all learned how to move (and how *not* to move) from people who are important to us, and we carry these formative people (and the places they came from) within our muscles, our movements, our gestures. Deidre Sklar (2008) writes about this as embodied cultural knowledge, the "cultural organizations of kinetic vitality [that] occur as a 'ghost' in all gesture" (p. 101). This knowledge may migrate between visual and kinesthetic modalities, and between people and places.[15] According to Sally Ann Ness (Noland & Ness, 2008) this knowledge also "allow[s] us to conceive in sharper images how place-like bodies can be, and…how gestures may come to possess the agency to migrate into new bodies"[16] (p. 278).

GESTURE AS TEACHING AND LEARNING TOOL: MODELING MOVEMENT

Teaching is a vital and energizing aspect of my artistic practice. Whether I am communicating how I move to my students, or 'reading' their choreographic compositions to understand them better, teaching informs my relationship to movement. The dialectic between codifying my own movement and being a vehicle for the movement of others is one that has trained me to notice habit and choice. I use this sensitivity to honor the gestural and cultural foundations of my students' dance styles and to push them to excel at their own chosen ways of moving.

For my students, the contemporary dance technique and choreographic frames I offer are new. This has helped me to apprehend my own art in a new light. I no longer see my technique and theory classes as a foundation curriculum. Instead, I teach my advanced contemporary dance technique class as I would a martial arts class, where students of all levels and backgrounds may engage the material on different levels. For some, I offer a new way of moving or a new approach to the act of choreography. Others are learning about applied anatomy and how to move from that knowledge in their own dance languages. Still others see what I offer as 'technique' in contrast to their own spontaneous—and equally virtuosic—practice of free styling and improvising.

I share my work as a performer with my students and invite their feedback. These exchanges are my way of modeling art as a form of investigation. I talk with my students about how their challenges are similar and different to mine, and I talk openly about how I have dealt with limitation and biases in our shared field. What I hope to convey is that there is truth and magic in repeating things: by examining what happens in a familiar gesture or movement, they too can find the roots of their kinesthetic impulses.

As a teacher, I provide one possible sounding board and the experience of learning a system of movement along with a critical examination of its biases. We can all laugh at the arbitrariness of a pirouette or a clichéd floor move, but we can also embrace the rigor and joy of mastering a new, technically difficult physical challenge.

In this way, I hold space open for students to synthesize their influences and honor their dance ancestors while finding their own signature movement within their discipline of choice. As a teacher, this is how I believe empowerment arises.

Over the years, my students have spanned ages 5–75 and consisted of people with and without disabilities, a multitude of ethnicities, genders, and religions. In teaching dance and choreography, I have observed that movement is a key to constructing, claiming, and sharing one's identity. When I talk with my students about how being Jewish, being feminine in non-traditional ways, or being from New York City informs my movement and my art, their ears perk up. They talk about their own adventures in identity formation, their experiences with invisibility, stereotyping and intergenerational communication. They talk about their encounters with rules about age, gender and culture in their movement. These experiences become part of their creative work and continually shape the way they see themselves as learners and as leaders.

For my college students, dance and movement are central to understanding the world around them and who they are within it. Many of my students are immigrants or first- and second-generation children of immigrants. In addition to their focus on education and economic self-sufficiency, these students often turn to the movement and music of their cultures of origin. They build bridges between old worlds and new ones, paying respect to previous generations while instantiating contemporary identities. They respectfully learn the steps their forebears once took, while eagerly embracing the American dance *lingua franca* of hip hop and free styling that will make them feel confident, sexy, visible, at ease with themselves and others.

One of my students immigrated to California from the Philippines at the age of seven; Grace is bilingual in English and Tagalog and took her first formal dance class in college. As she pursued her talents in hip hop, and started combining contemporary dance and slam poetry, Grace created a powerful piece for her senior project about Filipino soldiers who fought for the U.S. in WWII being denied their veterans' benefits. Her work was a cutting-edge tapestry of art forms about place and identity, forged in a hip-hop aesthetic that was entirely American. Her choreographic style is a unique amalgam of Asian, Pacific Islander, European, African and American idioms, a movement language that strategically addressed both her elders and her peers. Grace views performance as a space where she can articulate her voice as a woman, an immigrant, a mother, and a daughter. In a conversation we had recently about her company's new piece on mental illness and motherhood, she explained, "We're just trying to create some chaos in order to achieve some peace. MEnD Dance company exists to fix, repair damages, to heal and recover, to mend: we hope to do this not only for our audiences and ourselves, but also for all those whose stories have been lost" (personal communication).

My own creative work has been directly impacted by my students' identity and movement practices. My bias towards set choreography over improvised material or towards abstract movement over dancing to words has started to shift; I now strive to help my dancers reconnect with the spontaneity and musicality that's supported by dance forms grounded in 'feeling the music.' When I invite an advanced student to teach a variety of ethnic dance that they know well to their peers in my classroom, I take the class too. They see me as a student, as someone who wants to learn how to move like them. Not only does this subvert the usual power dynamic between professor and student, it also gives me an opportunity to model focused training behavior and an educational ethic I learned long ago from my kung fu teacher: to earn one's Black Belt is to commit to being a public student.

As a secular Jew trained in a postmodernist dance tradition, I have confronted my own bias against 'dancing to the words' and found new inspiration in my students' intricate dance conversations with Jesus Christ. As I teach—and learn from—my students about dance as physical culture, I have started to incorporate cultural dances from places I have traveled into new experimental movement narratives about the places I carry inside me. This has led me to create two works about my travels in the Middle East: "SKIN: One Becomes Two," and "T:HERE."[17] Each of these works integrates contemporary dance with *dabkeh* and illuminates my understanding of how Israel, Palestine, and America live inside my own movement and sense of self. This dance research and performance would not have evolved were it not for the conversations I have had with my students about what it means to bridge the cultures and generations they negotiate daily.

When my students see "36 Jewish Gestures," they see me talking about my family, my culture and the neighborhood I grew up in. They see me mining my roots to define who I am in a series of moments, a.k.a. life. They see me come out as gay, as conflicted about Zionism, as tender and violent and bawdy and sarcastic—characteristics I sometimes mask in my efforts to be an accessible educator. In so doing, my students begin to see me as negotiating the same shifting territory of finding and performing identity that young adults everywhere confront. Many have never met or known someone well who was Jewish before studying with me. By the time they graduate, they are all experts in the details of how I move, how I speak, and how I see the world. They may not know much about being Jewish, but they, too, can recognize my Jewish gestures.

CONCLUSION: GESTURE, TEACHING, AND POWER

My study of movement has helped me to craft my own intersecting narratives of identity. After more than a decade of making work about the body as a site for identity and culture, my artistic research has evolved to include how we embody place. My work brings New York City, Chernobyl, and Chattanooga into the studio. My students bring Africa, Asia, the Middle East, Central, South and North America, Europe, and many other places into our work. When we learn movement together, we are given a window into how these places dwell inside each one of us. Hip hop, ballet, folk dance, ballroom, and contemporary dance idioms alchemically combine the places we carry inside us with the spaces we inhabit.

As I gather and share movement-based tools with my students, my teaching practices draw on these experiences. Together we use these tools for negotiating the complex social worlds we inhabit, and gesture continues to be a wonderful resource in this endeavor—it is something deeply personal that at the same time connects us to community, family, tribe. Our gestures are ferries from another time and place to the here and now; they help us understand where we come from and where we are going. Such knowledge is power. With my students, I aim to cultivate practices of seeing, expressing, questioning, and understanding the many worlds of movement. Such practices will send them back to their most private forms of gesture and forward into the world as articulate and embodied visionaries. Their voices are evolving, as movement artists and as citizens. They aim to move us, and we will each decide whether to listen. I can't wait to see what happens.

Notes

1. To view an early version of this work, visit http://conneyproject.wisc.edu/videos-2009/
2. Nina Haft, Script from "36 Jewish Gestures: For Joe with Love" (2007).
3. http://www.youtube.com/watch?v=XthFTDMi020
4. http://www.youtube.com/watch?v=QwCPA05e_F8
5. *"A Bintl Brief"* was the women's advice column in *The Forward,* a daily Yiddish-language newspaper (still in circulation), founded in 1897 in New York City. The column covered topics ranging from the importance of unionizing for garment workers to intimate advice about how to negotiate life as new Jewish immigrants to America.
6. Joan Rivers in 1967: http://www.youtube.com/watch?v=EpPCFoXXhF0&feature=related; and again in 2007: http://www.youtube.com/watch?v=iGVJnL3uuLE&feature=related
7. Cf., protagonists Neil Klugman in Philip Roth's novel *Goodbye, Columbus* (1959) and Fielding Mellish in Woody Allen's film *Bananas* (1971).
8. Brice in "It's Gorgeous to Be Graceful" (1930): http://www.youtube.com/watch?v=whJUDe32yEU&feature=related.
9. By Levantine, I refer to countries bordering on the Eastern Mediterranean Sea from Turkey to Egypt. I have studied and performed in Yafo, Tel Aviv, Jerusalem, Ramallah, Amman, and Dheisheh Refugee Camp near Bethlehem. I observed dance events and also interviewed choreographers about their work. My conversations with choreographers Sahar Azimi, Renana Raz, Barak Marshall, Khaled Elayyan, Ziad Abbas, and Wael Albuhaissy have informed my ideas about regionalism in gesture, movement, and dance.
10. *Nakba* is an Arabic word meaning "catastrophe"; it commonly refers to the formation of the State of Israel in 1948 and the subsequent dislocation and exile experienced by Palestinian families.

11. Marshall's mother, Margalit Oved, is from the Gulf of Aden (located on the tip of the Arabian peninsula), where women's devotional songs were considered the most beautiful of all liturgical music. Oved was an early principal dancer in Inbal Dance Theater, a professional dance company founded in Israel in 1949 that famously syncretized Yemenite folk dance, indigenous shepherd dances, and contemporary Israeli folk songs.
12. http://web.me.com/barakmarshall/MONGER/Barak_Marshall.html
13. The work of Katharine Young (2002) on somatic psychology and modes of embodiment within families informs my thinking about the migration of gesture from one generation to the next.
14. There is a growing corpus of intriguing scholarship on the Jewish body; see, for example, works by Sander Gilman (1991), Melvin Konner (2009) and Meira Weiss (2002).
15. In "Remembering Kinesthesia," Sklar (2008) writes about the embodiment of gesture as felt experience, distinct kinetic vitalities which migrate across our senses and interact with social circumstances to create cultural patterns.
16. In her concluding chapter in *Migrations of Gesture*, Ness (Noland & Ness, 2008) deftly investigates how migratory movement predetermines all other embodied experiences, including that of gesture, because these movements are basic to life itself, and to the abstraction of self in relation to other.
17. www.ninahaftandcompany.com/works.htm

Works Cited

Bogart, A. (2001). *A director prepares: Seven essays on art and theatre*. London: Routledge.
Efron, D. (1941/1972). *Gesture, race and culture: A tentative study of some of the spatio-temporal and "linguistic" aspects of the gestural behavior of Eastern Jews and Southern Italians in New York City, living under similar as well as different environmental conditions*. The Hague, Netherlands: Mouton.
Gilman, S. (1991). *The Jew's body*. New York: Routledge.
Goldin-Meadow, S., & Wagner, S. M. (2005). How our hands help us learn. *TRENDS in Cognitive Sciences, 9*, 234–241.
Haft, N. (2007a). 36 Jewish gestures: For Joe with love. Script from live performance piece.
Haft, N. (2007b). Dance and cultural identity in Israel and Palestine. Unpublished manuscript.
Haft, N. (2010). *Works*. Retrieved from http://ninahaftandcompany.com/works.htm.
Konner, M. (2009). *The Jewish body*. New York: Nextbook/Schocken.
Marshall, B. (n.d.). *Adenite music*. Retrieved from http://web.mac.com/barakmarshall/symphonyoftincans/Adenite_Music.html
Noland, C., & Ness, S. A. (Eds.) (2008). *Migrations of gesture*. Minneapolis: University of Minnesota Press.
Sklar, D. (2008). Remembering kinesthesia: An inquiry into embodied cultural knowledge. In C. Noland & S. A. Ness. (Eds.). *Migrations of gesture* (pp. 85–111). Minneapolis: University of Minnesota Press.
Von Laban, R. (1975). *Principles of dance and movement notation*. Princeton, NJ: Princeton Book Company.
Weiss, M. (2002). *The chosen body*. Stanford, CA: Stanford University Press.
Young, K. (2002). The memory of the flesh: The family body in somatic psychology. *Body & Society, 8* (3), 25–47.

Thinking With Your Skin

Paradoxical Ideas in Physical Theater

ELIOT FINTUSHEL

In the tradition of physical theater—commedia dell'arte, mask theater, mime, and the theater of clowns, buskers, and saltimbanques—you have to think with your

body. The conceptual mind is just too slow, too shallow a device to be able to handle the barrage of shifting information—proprioceptive, social, and environmental—to which a performer must respond. All in an instant, she makes her audience nod, gasp, sigh, weep, or fall down laughing. How is this possible? It may sound mystical or New Agey, but the main ingredient is a kind of selflessness: *hollow flexibility* (a phrase borrowed from my old teacher, Philip

Kapleau (personal communication). The successful performer has learned to surrender to gravity, to inertia, to the floor, and to other performers' bodies. The student of physical theatre takes herself to the edge of abandon, almost out of control (that "almost," of course, is crucial, and distinguishes performers from mystics) in order to achieve the responsiveness at the root of good stage work.

Some of the basic ideas in physical theater sound like riddles, but they are written in our bones. Here, for example, is a precept for improvisers in trouble: You find yourself onstage feeling like a deer in the headlights, your fellow actors and the audience staring, waiting. The flop sweat is gathering. You're in a bind without a clue as to what to do or say next. Now what? The rule is: "Physicalize at random." Here, "physicalize" is a term that means to express something intangible—an idea, a feeling, a mood, a thought, or a sentiment—through posture or gesture. If sadness makes my chest cave in, then I have physicalized the sadness. If, thinking of release, I open my chest, spread my arms and let them undulate like wings or like beating flags, then I have physicalized optimism. If, imagining a miser, my eyes narrow and my whole body curls in like a dead, dry oak leaf—there, in the body, is miserliness.

"But that's just crazy," you want to say. "What meaning can come out of physicalizing *at random*? Won't it be a mishmash of tics and flailings?"

No.

As a matter of fact, we humans are all but incapable of saying or doing anything arbitrary as Freud and Rorschach knew! Everything in us works together—until we obstruct it with scruples or civilization. Try this experiment: ask a friend or a student to relax her arms, letting them swing at her sides in the ordinary way people do when walking and to stroll around the room. Now ask her to walk on the outer edges of her feet, then, after a while, on the inner edges. If you watch her hands as she does so, you will observe that they rotate in and out along with the feet. It's just this body of ours doing what it does best: working as a whole, each part echoing, reflecting, or taking up the theme that another part has announced.

In fact, we say "Physicalize at random," to trick ourselves into dumping the mental and physical inhibitions into that wonderful functional unity that everybody's born with. In fact, the resulting gesture is always the right one, and the leap out of the constraints of convention and into that rightness can be exhilarating both for performer and for audience.

When I was a student member of an upstate semi-Equity touring company, working alongside seasoned actors hired out of the Big Apple, I took part in an improvised scene about factory workers. I was the big boss, telling one of the workers what to do—but he wouldn't do it. The character's resistance to my character was so strident that it started to bleed over into the realm of the personal: actor versus actor, toe-to-toe, and shouting. I was about to wilt under flop sweat and trepidation when the god of commedia, horned and grinning, kicked me in the butt: "Physicalize at random."

And I cried—that is, my character did. It was a cloudburst, a thunderstorm. Now the ball was in my brother actor's court. But what could have been tastier than this reversal of status, the boss become vulnerable, the worker omnipotent. My stage partner was a pro—he (to be precise, his character) *comforted* me; the audience howled.

What makes it so difficult to respond with such spontaneity? Young children at play are as wild and varied in their movements as a waterfall. They use not only their own bodies but one another's bodies, freely and without restraint. They no sooner think of a thing then they *are* it. Here a child has become a lion, a pterodactyl, a thunderstorm, or a princess, and there a toddler turns into a mountain that another child climbs. Then a landslide knocks the other down, and both are swimming without water. The thing is, such apparent randomness isn't safe or useful. We can't go around like that; actual lions, actual thunderstorms, and so on, have obliged us to impose restraints. So the question becomes, how can we relax those restraints when we want to, when it really *is* useful and safe to do so—onstage, for example, or in the magic circle of a classroom activity? We want to invoke the natural freedom of childhood but with mature circumspection as well as mature intellect and motor skills.

Yes, there is craft involved here. A parlor comic is generally dead meat onstage. The playground Superman, simply translated to the stage, is a chaotic blur. To transform play to art, we have to play *consciously*, with informed intention, cognizant of fellow stage artists and of the audience, among many other things. These are the higher-order activities that performers study in acting schools. But it is possible to learn all those sophisticated skills and still be dead wood onstage—in fact, it's the rule!—if you haven't recovered what small children know in their bones...try some of the following physical theater exercises and see what happens.

Here's an experiment—and a great classroom exercise—"Emotion in Body Parts." Pick any body part and any emotion, and ask a student to physicalize it. For example: angry hand or happy shoulder. Many combinations, like the ones just given, are easy for just about anybody at any age. But as you go down the list, demanding expressions of this or that emotion in this or that body part, you will encounter a definite divide. There are combinations for which grownups simply draw a blank, whereas children, especially small children, K-2, all perform with gusto—and convincingly! A jealous elbow, no problem! An angry butt, here it is! A stomach in love, just look!

In the life of the imagination, there are no mistakes. I don't know exactly how the rush and roil of the child's mind bifurcates into right and wrong—every thought a plaything, every mood a paint box color, but I know how to find the way back. And I know how to chalk a magic circle around our dangerous native genius in order to invite it, without harming us, to serve us. When we can do that, then we can risk everything. Although I encourage my adult students to 'look stupid,' with young children such advice isn't necessary. The curriculum for my college course requires of every student that she experience in front of the class, at least once, embarrassment to the point of blushing and feeling hot. Until middle school, at least, there is no need to trick people into taking risks. Anybody will be up for anything. (After that, people are generally more guarded, perhaps especially in schools.)

There is a game well known to improvisers that's called, "Prop Rounds." (Though a professor of mine liked to call it "Tubular Metamorphoses"—take your pick!) Instructors show the class any common object—for example, a broom, a basket, a hula hoop, or a traffic cone. The rule is that it can't be the thing we always think it is, but it can be *anything* else—what is it? Children take turns demonstrating what the object is, not saying, mind you, but demonstrating—showing—using it for the thing they see it to be. One child makes the broom into a microphone and sings the "Star Spangled Banner." Another sees it as a horse and rides it around the room. Another plays it like a slide trombone. The hula hoop becomes, in turn, a gigantic earring, a halo, a toilet seat, a porthole, and the sun. The basket may be a belly, a baby, a hat. Every embodied idea is both possible and good.

In fact, it's common to see children who are slow to learn academic subjects excel at an exercise like this. Their teachers see hidden qualities emerge. In a way, it's accidental, isn't it, that grammar and arithmetic have come to be considered more essential elements of the grade school curriculum than creative drama? It's not hard to imagine a world where those priorities are reversed—only think of traditional societies in which people spend more time sculpting, painting, chanting, or dancing than doing business. Then those who fall 'behind' in our current order might actually be the ones out in front.

It is necessary to be serious about silly things.

Let's take a step further. Suppose the props we transform are one another or ourselves. The mime Tony Montanaro used to say: "Wrap yourself around the image." He meant become the thing you're thinking of. In the game "Sculpture Garden," children pair off and take turns being the sculptor or the clay. No words are exchanged because, after all, clay can't see or hear; the sculptor has to just mold with his hands. Tilt the chin, press back a shoulder, lift an arm, push at the back to make the chest stick out. At a signal, the work is finished, and the statue has to be as still as stone while the rest of us, the sculptors, walk among the statues and have a look. Sometimes we give them names: The Mountain Climber, The Ballerina, The Stomachache, The Stegosaurus. In this game the children who play the clay and those who play the sculptors learn complementary lessons, both of which are important. The sculptors have to embody a vision, a thought, or even a joke in another human body—mind to matter. The clay has to yield to a partner's touch, sensitively and judiciously, while maintaining balance, and be ready to become *anything*. This is one form of the skill I've called hollow flexibility. This protean skill is available to everybody, exhilarating to all who exercise it, and is amazing to those who watch. We thought we were just one thing, but it turns out that we're everything!

Even more surprising are the transformations that appear—and easily—in the game I call "Polaroid," because there is no sculptor, no director, and no consultation. The players create a definite picture together, often with wonderful nuances and symmetries, spontaneously, and in an instant. First, the teacher introduces his camera, which, unlike other cameras, can take pictures not only of things in front of it but also of things on the side or behind and at any distance—for example, on the moon or in the next universe over. It can also take pictures of things that happened yesterday or last week or last year or a million years ago, and things that will happen tomorrow or next year or a million years from now. It can even take pictures of things that will never happen, things in books or in the imagination.

The secret is in the film, of course: it's made of people. Four or five or more players stand shoulder to shoulder against the wall (in the "film compartment"). The teacher, or someone else, by invitation, says what she wants a picture of. For example, she might request to see the end of the world, the age of dinosaurs, a child's future wedding day, the Bolshoi Ballet, flying cars, or General Washington at Valley Forge. Next she counts slowly to three. With each number, the "film" takes a step forward and nearer to one another, all the while morphing into the shape of the picture until, at three, they freeze into a tableau.

No planning or discussion is permitted by the people who are the film. Their bodies work it out together along the way. They "think" it through physically as a group. The teacher can also push the sound bar (mimed), which makes the picture audible and silences it the instant the bar is pulled back. Interestingly, once the operation of the sound bar is explained, children, whether they have become yowling wolves or a screaming tornado, unfailingly silence themselves the instant it's pulled back. Here's an example of discipline that arises naturally out of fascination and delight. How can a group of players spontaneously create such an interesting tableau? How does each know what the others intend, so that they end up, in the photograph, as coherent parts of a whole in about five seconds? No doubt, a lot is going on under the surface—peripheral signals are passed among them by sight, sound, and touch, and a universe of shared experiences shapes their reactions to phrases. If the group's mutual sensitivity and responsiveness can be dulled by fear, self-consciousness, or anxiety about being judged—as is often the case in high school, for example—it can also be sharpened by craft as in the following exercise.

"Stop and Start Together" begins with the class walking about silently at random. When the teacher says, "Stop," everyone must stop and then go when the teacher says, "Go." Once this pattern is established, the teacher drops out. The instruction is given that when anyone, on their own impulse, stops, everyone stops, and when anyone starts walking again, everyone has to walk. In a variation of this game, the class as a whole or in smaller groups may try to walk across the room all in a phalanx, stopping and starting by the same rule as before, and reaching the other side together. When this exercise is understood, the effect is remarkable; an onlooker would swear that everyone secretly was wearing earphones and listening to a common command or else executing pre-set choreography.

There may be interesting difficulties along the way. One or two children may dominate, always initiating the change, obliging the teacher to adjust the rules in order to make the game more democratic. Notice what has gotten in the way: anxiety about putting oneself forward has dulled the group's sensitivity. Something personal and psychological has impeded the purely physical awareness of movement and rest and the simple, natural give and take that arises out of that sensitivity. Watch a flock of birds turn on the wing or migrate great distances together by sensing, each and all, the pockets their wings make in the air.

The familiar "Mirroring Game" cultivates the ability to harmonize one's own will with another's in the arena of physical movement. The class pairs off, and the members of each pair face each other at a distance of only a foot or two. There are three stages to this game. First, partner A is instructed to lead and B to follow, switching after a while. The leader has the sophisticated challenge—although she is allowed to do anything at all—of doing something in such a way that her partner is able to follow along. Slowness and continuity of movement, we discover, are a big help.

The mirror's challenge is the same as that of the clay in the statue exercise— be "hollow" and "flexible" to let oneself flow with the partner's initiative. In the second stage, the partners are instructed to give and take the lead as they like. The best is to be able to do that with continuity, so that the lead passes fluidly back and forth without any break or pause. In the last stage, the partners are coached: "Both lead and both follow," or "Nobody lead or follow; mirror each other." By this time, their bodies will understand what that means. Every movement is part of the flow. Active and passive, initiation and response, no longer mean anything as opposing terms: It's just one dance. This may sound like metaphysics, sentimental mysticism, hocus-pocus, but, in fact, it's a commonplace of everyday life. It goes on everywhere people do things together. The only extraordinary thing is that here we are doing it consciously, with no end other than moving as one.

If into this mix we add the voice, things become a little more raucous—and a lot more fun. The production of voice is a kind of human movement, after all, and shares the qualities of movement. For example, Rudolf Laban's classification of styles of movement applies just as much to our voices. Laban was a choreographer as well as a pioneer of industrial time and motion studies. Using Labanotation, a system he devised in the 1920s for precisely recording dance, Laban was able to describe any human movement with reference to a few simple elements, roughly: weight, shape, and speed. Each of these elements can have two values; thus, every movement is heavy or light, straight or curving, fast or slow. These three two-valued qualities combine to produce, like corners on a cube, eight types of movement, from "punching" (heavy, straight, and fast), through "pushing" (heavy, straight, and slow) and so on, down through "floating" (light, curving, and slow). One can easily witness the "punching" style of movement among businessmen late to work, "pushing" in the slow burn of customers en route to the complaints window, and "floating" among lunch-break window shoppers. Every part of the body partakes of the Laban dynamic of the whole. Remember the walking experiment in which, unconsciously, hands tilted to match the tilt of the feet—the voice is no different. The puncher's voice punches; the pusher's pushes; and the floater's floats.

In fact, in mask performance, where the goal is to physicalize the shape and rhythm of a particular mask, an internalized cadence or quality of voice can guide the physical characterization. For example, the miser's whine, the trickster's chuckle, the lover's lyrical sigh—they all have voice even though no one ever hears it. The performer harmonizes movement to imagined sound: sound ensouls the movement.

In mask performance, the goal is to physicalize the shape and rhythm of a particular mask.

My mask teacher, Leonard Pitt, studied mask theater in Bali and performed for a while with a Balinese company. He once told us that the director sometimes stood in the wings, just listening, and critiqued the masked performers by the sounds their bodies made onstage.

In the game of "Name Shapes," students embody their voices as they voice their body's movement. Standing in a circle, each person, in turn, says her name in an extended, exaggerated way and moves in a style that goes with it. Without tutoring or preparation, qualities of sound find their perfect correlates in movement: loud goes to large, tremolo to trembling, legato to fluid. Notice how often words that primarily apply to sound or music are borrowed to describe movement in space, and vice versa. This is just as true for the vocabularies of emotional and physical qualities, as we'll soon discover in the treatment of "neutral mask." The effort is to have body track voice in as much detail as possible. After each individual Name Shape "performance," the whole group together repeats that person's name and movement in exactly the way that the person just did it.

These days we actually understand some of the science behind empathy (Iacoboni, 2008). When we see a gesture enacted, "mirror neurons" in our pre-motor cortex fire in the same pattern that would accompany our own performance of that gesture. Whether or not, in our shifting and evolving scientific understanding, this schema ultimately holds true, our ability to identify with others and to let their voices and movement influence our own—as if they *were* our own—is undeniable. We experience this in both the "Mirroring Game" and in "Name Shapes." (Also see Kroll's chapter, this volume.)

"Voice Puppet" enlarges on the discoveries of those games. In it we are animated by a voice or a sound that isn't our own. It's possible for adults who play this game to experience sensations of release, fluidity, or clarity as a result of momentarily handing over control to another person and diving into delicious free-fall. This is yet another instance of hollow flexibility. "Voice Puppet" is played in pairs—puppeteer and puppet. The puppeteer stands behind the puppet. The puppet bends over, torso, arms, and head hanging down loosely from the pelvis. If the person playing puppet sees the floor, it means that there's too much tension in the neck; she should be looking at her knees or shins with arms just hanging down. This is the puppet's position of repose. Whenever there's no sound, even for a short moment, the puppet falls back into this position.

The puppeteer manipulates the puppet by means of her voice and any other sounds she may make, for example, by whistling or stamping or slapping her own stomach or a puffed cheek. The puppeteer may coo, roar, grunt, hum, yodel, or cluck her tongue, and it's the puppet's job to embody the sound, to become a sort of human oscilloscope. The puppet's torso may undulate and rise, it may shake like jello or flap like a flag. The arms may shoot up or beat like wings. And every time the puppeteer lapses into silence, the puppet falls into repose. The movements should be responses to the sounds, not to any idea the sounds may represent. The exchange is physical, not conceptual. If a sound is dog-like, the best response, within the spirit of this game, is to become not a dog but *the sound of a dog*.

This vibrant responsiveness at a level more basic than ordinary thinking is the foundation of a good deal of the actor's and improviser's craft. Thinking is just too clunky, and the result is terrifically unaesthetic. When a performer thinks, the audience knows what she is trying to express, but they don't feel it: the performance is wooden, artificial. There are many theatre games that cultivate the ability to respond below thought; the most interesting are for adult students.

Consider the game that Viola Spolin (1963), in her seminal book, *Improvisation for the Theater*, called "Contrapuntal Argument." An actor sits between two others and carries on two completely unrelated conversations, left and right, at once. It is often just as surprising to the middle actor as it is to the audience that she was able to accomplish this; one certainly can't think one's way through it. It's also a chore for the two on either side to maintain a conversation uninfluenced by the other— but that's quite a different skill.

In another exercise, which I like to call "Stealing Faces," we set up an imaginary situation between two people—a job interview, for example. The actor playing the interviewer is tasked with running through a gamut of emotions, while the job of the other is to mirror those feelings. To do this, she has to work upstream against the tendency to be *conceptually* responsive.

Suppose, for example, that the interviewer shouts, "You arrogant twerp, why should I hire you, anyway?" Then, "Because I'd do a good job, sir," or "I'm sorry if I've offended you," would not be responses in the spirit of this game even though they might be *sensible*. The sort of response this game requires would be an emotional retort like, "I don't give a hoot if you hire me or not, you fat oaf!" The actors have to cut under the superficial process of thinking to the visceral push and pull of the situation onstage.

In conventional literary theatre, the sort of theatre in which actors memorize and deliver lines that someone else has written, it is, of course, essential for the actor to memorize his lines very thoroughly. But, again, if all he does is deliver the memorized lines—even if he has worked on them with thespian craft to enrich them with his own feeling and associations and has analyzed everything for objective and motivation and so on—the audience will still see little more than a golem, the creature of which the Talmud says, "It walked like a man, and it spoke like a man, but it was not a man."

In fact, to achieve miraculous life onstage, after learning the lines by heart, you must forget them. The actor finds herself onstage confronted by people and situations that evoke a definite response, she confronts them with hollow flexibility. She feels impelled to speak and the words that come out of her mouth, not mimicked but authentically arising from the situation, happen to be exactly the words in her script! This is the deep trick at the heart of naturalistic acting and its central paradox: spontaneous authenticity that arises from exhaustive preparation—studying and memorizing, then forgetting.

In physical theater, the theater of gesture and movement, we say: "Think with your skin."

It's like surfing, riding the waves of attention from fellow performers and from the audience, and responding with an acuteness of which thought is seldom capable. Like the old joke about the first principle of comedy—what is it............? Timing. You have to be able to feel the moment ripen, and for that you have to be empty yet receptive. (Once more: hollow flexibility.)

Here is a further refinement of the "Voice Puppet" game in which the whole class can be puppets at once: "Atmosphere Puppet." Everyone assumes the posture of the voice puppet in repose and simply listens. There is no puppeteer. Instead, the puppets respond to ambient sounds, floorboards creaking, heat ducts rumbling, a passing truck, a birdsong, someone clearing her throat halfway down the hall. The sounds are the puppets' strings: the world is the puppeteer. Even very small children have no trouble learning this game, and graduate students find it fascinating.

Tony Montanaro, in his magic barn in the woods of South Paris, Maine, where maskers, mimes, clowns, buskers, and saltimbanques from all over the continent would gather to refine their art, used to conduct the converse exercise to Atmosphere Puppet. He called it, "Plunge." A lone performer would stand before the rest of us and respond in movement, gesture, and speech to every inner impulse. We watched motifs sprout, stir, ramify, explode, transform. Sometimes stories emerged, and sometimes it was like looking at a sculpture or a painting that morphs through time. It was not about thought, I can tell you. But sometimes Tony would make the performer stop, and she usually acknowledged the justness of his intervention. She knew she had made something up; she had played out some old routine; or she had embroidered around a personal tic. Out of fear or weariness, the performer had cheated: she had left the authentic, spontaneous realm of the body and had tried, conceptually, to invent something: "Horror vacui."

Paradoxically, to achieve wonderful responsiveness onstage, the life of hollow flexibility, you have to see precisely what's thick and stiff in you: the particularities of your own personality as embodied in posture, gesture, and movement dynamics. Alas, this sounds like a ponderous undertaking, but, though difficult, it is intimate and straightforward. Here are two exercises that aim at this awareness. The first, "Neutral Circle," can be performed and enjoyed even by kindergartners, and not without some discernment, though it takes the crucible of adolescence, I think, to really appreciate what it's about. The class forms a circle. Each student steps forward in turn, says her name, and then steps back, with this requirement: that there be no special content or meaning in the performance.

Normally, when you see someone sit or stand or walk or do anything at all, in fact, you see much more than the nominal activity. Jeffrey Bihr, the voice teacher, has given this example: when someone, with drooping shoulders and long face, says, "Pass me the butter," the response is not, "Here it is," but "What's wrong?" And as Ralph Waldo Emerson said, "What you do speaks so loud that I cannot hear what you say." In the present exercise, it turns out to be extremely difficult to just step forward and say one's name. One student looks tired. Another is eager to please. One is terrified of doing it wrong. Another can't stop laughing. One does it like a soldier. Another seems to be angry about something. It doesn't take an expert: you read everything in the shoulders, the chest, the gait, the vigor or flaccidity of movement. It's amazing how much you see in a step and a syllable, when you're given license to look. Reading the body, you feel very much like a mind reader.

Note well: the insights you seem to get into someone's soul when you play this game are an illusion! You don't really know what makes someone lower their head, for example; it could be sadness, or a stiff neck. Hepzibah, a character in Hawthorne's *House of the Seven Gables*, is despised and feared by children because of all the mean looks she gives them, but the truth is that she is near-sighted and has to squint. In this game, we're not learning about souls but about appearances, about correlations of movement and feeling. Whether the feeling is ours, projected, or that of the person we're watching, is not so important. It is a *theater* game.

Especially for adults and for older children, this exercise is as much for the observer as for the person whose turn it is. We are cultivating the ability to discriminate body language. Everyone on the circle gets a chance to experience the vertiginous isolation of the performer, trapped in her own movement repertoire, the chance to see, often for the first time, particular qualities in her own movement made visible by "the look of the Other." Also, everyone gets to see that we're all like that.

In the second game along this theme, we use a so-called "neutral mask." The mask originally designed by the Italian maskmaker Amleto Sartori for the French mime teacher Jacques Lecoq is the model for neutral masks used in many theatre schools. Lecoq's use of the mask was near mystical and aimed at cultivating a fiery intensity in stage performers. The present exercise is focused more on straightforward discovery of how we actually do move.

The neutral mask is as simple as we can make it—fluid, unified—a mask that constrains the wearer to do nothing, or anything, by way of embodying it, a mask without personality. Students, taking turns, put on the mask and, as before, perform a simple set of tasks: sitting still for ten seconds in a chair, then walking to a table, turning over an object that lies there, and, finally, walking back to the chair and sitting again.

It's a minefield. Alone in the mask, when I play this game, I feel isolated and self-conscious. (Good! It wakes me up to my own movement.) The goal is to sit in such a way that someone seeing me, when asked to describe me, can only say, "He's sitting"—not happy, not sad, not anything, but just sitting. Then I have to walk that way, with no special quality, manipulate an object that way, and so on. But what exactly shall I do with my arms, my hands, my knees, my neck? This feeling of being at sea is a wonderful teacher. I become acquainted with my body in an objective way. It's as if I were sitting on the other side of the proscenium, seeing myself from the perspective of the audience.

For the rest of the class, it can be equally revelatory. They are instructed to watch carefully every departure from neutrality—every gesture that means something personal—and to remember it in the form of two words or phrases, one of them the name of the feeling and the other a physical description of the movement that evidenced or evoked it. To see all the flashes of meaning in gestures is easy and absorbing, but marking their origin in the body turns out to be, though doable, difficult. Everyone has something to say, but often, when they try to name the physical part, it comes out sounding like a feeling.

"Yes, OK, you're right: she looked anxious when she walked," I'll say, "but what made her look anxious? What's the physical part?"

The reply: "Her step seemed hesitant."

"That's still an emotional description. What did you *see*?"

"There was something uncertain about it."

"Another emotional term."

"It was jittery."

And here we arrive at the most common case—a descriptor that is at the same time emotional and physical. Our mind can jitter, but so can a platform, so can our bones. "Sunken" can describe a mood or a mattress or a person's chest. The word "buoyant" can describe mind states or water wings.

What does this overlap of emotional and physical descriptors say about us as human beings?

Sometimes, in the simple movements between chair and table, a whole story seems to emerge. A prisoner is waiting to be shot. A princess entertains her suitor. A night watchman hates his job. How much is coming from the performer and how much from the observer? In fact, it is possible to find purely physical terms in which to describe someone's posture and movement:

"His chest was concave."

"One shoulder was farther forward than the other."

"Her torso leaned forward when she was getting up."

"He moved quickly and made a lot of noise with his feet."

It's the other students' job to see how an emotion speaks through the body and to distinguish the one from the other. We're not aiming to establish a list of correlations, a table, or an index—"this" means "that." Rather, we're cultivating a certain inner and outer eye—an aliveness to body language, not only others' but our own. That sensitivity—hollow, flexible—is worth infinitely more than any book of correspondences; it's alive.

Performers have to find in themselves an Archimedian point, a fulcrum below the everyday conceptual mind and below the ideas of who they are or who they're supposed to be, on which they can lever themselves, and the audience, into any imagined situation or character. One name for that fulcrum point is hollow flexibility, and that's a resource, a battery, a fountain of inspiration, not just for stage trotters, but for everybody.

A certain lack of definition is inescapable—and may be of the essence. In the *Tao Te Ching*, Lao Tzu, praising emptiness, said, "A wheel draws its utility from the hub at the center." Every physical gesture is both an intersection and a generator of unlimited meanings, unlimited associations. How terrifying the responsibility and the power of just moving a thumb—in some arenas, from some seats, it may mean life or death! We can't be sure where our gestures came from or where they lead, and yet we act, we feel, we move, we participate in the universal flux. Physical theater comprises a focusing and refinement of that everyday human business and pluck.

Works Cited

Iacoboni, M. (2008). *Mirroring people: The science of empathy and how we connect with others.* New York: Picador, Farrar, Straus & Giroux.

Lao, Tzu. http://www.wussu.com/laotzu/laotzu11.html

Spolin, V. (1963). *Improvisation for the theater: A handbook of teaching and directing techniques.* Evanston, IL: Northwestern University Press.

CHAPTER EIGHT

Visceral Literature

Multimodal Theater Activities for Middle and High School English Language Arts

TORI TRUSS WITH MIRA-LISA KATZ

FOOD IS LOVE: STORY IS NOURISHMENT

Years ago when I was an actor in the Big Apple, I decided to take a course in commercial acting to widen my work possibilities. I distinctly remember the day we covered food commercials. The first commercial was for a brand of ketchup. The text (not great or lasting literature by any stretch of the imagination) was written on a giant tablet, the video camera was ready to roll, and another actor and I were called to the front to act it out. The fifteen-second scene, a conversation between a waitress and customer, was set at the counter of a diner. The dialogue went something like,

"Hey Joe, how've ya been? What'll ya have today?"

"Nice to see you, Marcia. You know, the regular," with the mention of the ketchup brand at some point. The instructor, a formidable commercial actress and wonderful teacher, offered this advice, "All you need to understand is that *food is love*." I knew instantly what to do, how to make something out of nothing. Instead of advertising a brand, we played a mini-love scene, and it worked. Though I did not end up working as a commercial actor, I have never forgotten how revelatory that idea was, that food is love.

Last year, when co-teaching a college course on reading pedagogy for undergraduate English majors who intend to become secondary school English Language

Arts teachers, I was struck with an insight, equally simple and true. To introduce these pre-service teachers to a unit on oral interpretation, I asked them to remember their experiences of reading aloud or being read to as children. Approaching the discussion as an acting exercise in "sense memory," they closed their eyes and were guided through the memory of the event with sensory questions: "What is the first thing you hear? Who are you with? What do you see? Smell? Touch?" Tapping the specificity of our imaginations in this way heightens the memory and revives the bodily experience of it in a present-tense manner. After a minute or two of writing/reflecting we talked about their memories.

Their responses were startlingly heartfelt. One young woman described the comfort and safety of having her father all to herself for bedtime reading, "I remember being read to by my dad, it was so great...his voice, being with him. . . ." Another recalled cozy moments with siblings, "We'd all get under the covers with a flashlight when we were supposed to be asleep and I'd read to my sisters." A third remembered her parents, "When my mom washed the dishes, my dad read the newspaper to her. In fact, when I think about it, that's my image of them being together." And the memories continued, "I'll never forget the book my 4th grade teacher read to us every day after lunch." The discussion among the students was vibrant, full of laughter, short reminiscences. They excitedly interrupted one another, heads nodding in recognition of book titles. Their comments revealed an intimate and fundamental relationship with literature that was surprisingly tender for college students, and was as much about the important people in their lives as about the story being read. It struck me, then, that the sharing of literature can be as intimate as the sharing of food. It is an act of love and nourishment. The idea that literature is love now guides my course development in both Theater and English Language Arts. When we look at literature as an opportunity for social and emotional engagement and development, we expand the "nourishing" potential of literacy, perhaps especially so when that engagement occurs through collaborative multimodal theater activities.

For most of us, most of the time, our way of taking in literature is through solitary reading. The reader is pulled into another world alone. While a satisfying experience for some, it can be brutally difficult for others. For both novice and experienced readers, voicing the text aloud changes the interaction by making the literary experience social rather than solitary. More importantly, it can add an interpretative dimension to the text. Voice creates tone, character, suspense, emotion, and meaning. Too often in the classroom, however, this exercise is a tedious chore for everyone involved. As one student recalled of her elementary days, "I hated when we sat in a circle with our books and took turns reading aloud. It was slow and boring and I wanted to skip ahead." How, then, can we provide the kind of structure and training where "reading aloud" is experienced as dynamic and engaging for both reader and listener?

I suggest that using dramatic forms of reading to lift the words off the page and into the body can open up possibilities for a host of learning opportunities that can enhance literacy. Such practices demystify and invigorate the text in ways that are developmentally relevant and interesting to students, perhaps especially for older learners. In fact, the performance of literature (including improvisation, creative dramatics, oral interpretation, and readers' theater) can lead to energized and often transformative communication as well as deeper comprehension of the text. This chapter aims to embolden teachers and teacher educators to incorporate more embodied performance and theater techniques into their language and pedagogy classrooms. Offering readers multimodal access to literature and other kinds of texts while fostering personally meaningful connections to the texts via embodied, multimodal approaches can increase engagement and motivation, and deepen literacy.

The Power of Live Performance

Performance is potent: it has transformative power for both performer and audience. Ideally, the actor/reader is given tremendous focus by the audience, a kind of attentiveness that in turn encourages her fullest commitment. The performer frequently transcends her own personality within the larger and cohesive structure of a text. Embodying the text involves the full person—not just the intellect but also the emotional, sensory, kinesthetic, and sometimes even the spiritual being of the student. She articulates thoughts and feelings at many levels and through this process can develop a deeper relationship to works of literature and a greater understanding of herself.

With non-professional actors this kind of experience can be very significant. A beginning acting class I teach at the college level always includes several non-theater majors. They enroll for a variety of reasons—as a break from the rigors of their own discipline or sometimes because they performed in shows in high school and miss the camaraderie and applause. I remember one extremely quiet accounting major whose reason for taking the class was to develop his confidence as a public speaker. For his final scene, he worked on the role of Peter in Edward Albee's *Zoo Story*, about an unassuming, mid-level publishing executive and a down-and-out artist who have a chance encounter on a park bench. The students performed the climactic finale when troubled artist, Jerry, irrevocably challenges Peter's complacency by forcing the mid-level executive to participate in Jerry's suicide. The darkly existential scene evokes the difficulty humans have in communicating their innermost selves and highlights how painful it can be when life lacks meaning. The performers—both non-actors—did incredible work. The audience wasn't simply shocked by the surprise ending, they were moved by the playwright's ideas, touched by the characters' suffering, and amazed by the level of commitment and believability in their classmates' work.

After the final performance the accounting student hung around the classroom unable to leave. In part, Martin (a pseudonym as are all proper names in this chapter) wanted to enjoy the congratulations his classmates proffered, but mostly he didn't seem to know what to do with himself. Like an athlete who's just won an important race, he needed a moment to "cool down." Having been momentarily transformed by the experience of performing, of connecting to another character, another world, of communicating so completely with a group of people, he was both incredibly gratified and also a little disconcerted. It was evident that Martin wanted to talk it over with me, yet he was completely speechless. I tried to help him clarify the experience by sharing what I'd observed in his performance. We discussed how, in committing to the story, the actions of the character and his fellow actor, Martin no longer had to think about his lines or the audience: it was as though it was really happening; it was effortless. Martin's work was beautiful because he and his acting partner let go and allowed the play to "play" them (what Fintushel calls "hollow flexibility," this volume). An actor's involvement is physically focused and demanding. The more physically committed a performer is, the more expressive his performance is likely to be.

What Martin experienced occurs with some frequency in the final showings of acting classes: performance forges connections between the material, the performer, and the spectator. In such moments, student actors can exceed their training and skill level by going deeply into the text. This deep human understanding is a kind of literacy or knowing that involves the whole being—the mind, the body, the heart, emotions and spirit. The whole being is affected by what some might have considered merely words on a page.

As a teacher, actor, and audience member, I've come to recognize these moments as precious and fleeting. One hears it in the reverential quality of those listening—a quiet that is full of energy, a hyper attentiveness; the group and performer become one. In a classroom setting, it could be a brief fifteen seconds or a full two minutes before the quiet shifts to more conventional classroom listening. In that short time, the group galvanizes, develops a communal awareness that what is going on is important, and everyone is inclined to be completely present. From my perspective as a teacher, what's really happening is that there is a collective acknowledgment of meaning that resonates beyond the immediate moment, reaching from the theater classroom or stage into the lives of participants and back again through the practice of embodying text.

In language arts classes, people often say that there are 'universal human predicaments' and that literature seeks to conjure those for the reader. I understand this to mean that the reader doesn't simply identify with the protagonist; rather, the reader can sense her own life in relation to the story—a real-life struggle, a moment of joy, sorrow, or awe is echoed. This brings meaning to the reader, going beyond the fiction to tap into a broader human experience. In a theatrical setting, the experience can be all the more exhilarating and gratifying because it's shared by a group of people.

INTEGRATING AWARENESS THROUGH LISTENING AND PLAY

Our brains, bodies, and lives are so complex that we regularly listen and respond to all kinds of stimuli simultaneously. As a result, we rarely give our full attention to any one thing, especially in a classroom. An actor, on the other hand, has to listen fully onstage; otherwise the scene will seem lifeless or fake. The old adage 'acting is reacting' is true insofar as actors need to be very responsive. Onstage, the more open and receptive the actors are, the more responsive and "alive" the drama will be. Listening, then, involves all parts of the person—the senses, the physical body, the emotions, and the imagination—and all focus on the dramatic moment. It's a kind of backwards perspective of the educational theory of multiple intelligences (Gardner, 1983). As educators, we seek to identify and teach to the unique "learning styles" of our students. Many students self-identify their learning strengths, saying things like, "I'm an auditory learner," or "I have to move around in order to concentrate on the lesson," or "If I see it written on the white board, then I can remember it." Essentially, they are labeling themselves as auditory, kinesthetic, or visual learners. Actors strive to open up and utilize *all* the learning pathways for expression through body, mind and emotion. When an actor listens fully and is present to the moment, the direct result is increased commitment and responsiveness; it yields a creative and fully engaged state of being.

Though impulsive reactions are ideal for the stage, impulsive behavior is not always beneficial in a classroom full of young people. In fact, it may seem like a recipe for chaos. The trick is in a skillful harnessing of that energy for creative work. Look at language itself—a chaotic assortment of sounds clattering and oozing together, configuring and re-configuring to form words, which in turn, form phrases, then sentences, and eventually stories and discourses. From the seeming disorder of vowels and consonants emerge incredible, sane, wondrous, smart ideas that fuel civilization. By going back to the primal clatter and ooze of "sounding," we can build a fuller understanding of language's complexity. As linguist Roy Blount (2008) says, language has juice: "[A]ll language, at some level, is body language....Alphabet juice. The quirky but venerable squiggles, which through centuries of knockabout breeding and intimate contact with the human body have absorbed the uncanny power to carry the ring of truth." Sound also has energy, and meaning emerges from playing with the energy of spoken language. Sound play is both subtle and grandiose, not just in the mind, but on the tongue, in the lungs, in gesture that extends beyond pointing a finger or flicking a hand to being felt through the chest and pelvis and down into the feet. It plays along the hairs on the skin's surface, crackles in nerve-endings, and courses blood-like through our veins. It gurgles in digestive bile and stretches through muscles, tendons, and ligaments.

To dynamically explore sound is a delicious, profound kind of comprehension that actually transcends words. When we take a writer's language and play it out *physically* and *vocally* in a performance setting, the words begin to ring with a different kind of truth. We tread on personal territory; the performer puts herself in a vulnerable position to do the work, and, in so doing, reveals something of herself as well as something of the literature. A nuanced performance by a skilled actor can actually improve a text by adding complexity and depth through the body. Text and performer inform each other. Two examples follow.

PERSONAL TRANSFORMATION IN THE STUDENT

As a parent volunteer in my daughter's 6th grade class, I contributed to a curriculum unit on the Ancient Greeks. Our project was to take the Persephone myth and put it on its feet, so to speak. *D'Aulaires' Book of Greek Myths* (D'Aulaire & D'Aulaire, 1992) was our sourcebook. Some students barely cracked it open; others inhaled it. One student had read it over twenty times since her first encounter with the text in the 4th grade; she could quote whole passages verbatim from memory. She became our dramaturgical expert for the show and could keep track of the soap opera lives and complications of the gods, heroes, and assorted animals. Our performance was site-specific—not on a stage or in the classroom but in a non-theater space that would lend itself to the story. The playground structure, made up of of swings, ladders, rings, and spinning parts, became the Underworld of Hades. The "stage" continued up a grassy hillside with oaks, fir trees, and paths leading into the open space of a watershed—our "Mt. Olympus," as it were. The kids were quite happy to be outside in May. Though it was considered "way too elementary school" to hang out on the play structure at recess, they were thrilled for the excuse to play on it for the performance.

Before attempting a production, I began with several creative dramatics games—imitative, imaginative, interactive, and simple—to feel out the students, get them comfortable in front of each other as performers, free up creativity and expressiveness, and introduce acting concepts and terminology.

We played a game called "In the Manner of the Word," which involves three to five participants who secretly select one emotion to play (happy, sad, angry, and so forth). The audience then suggests an action for the players to do "in the manner of the emotion word." Afterward, the remaining classroom members who make up the audience guess the emotion. For example, a small group of student actors prepare to perform. Out of audience earshot, they might choose the phrase, "heart-broken." When they are ready, audience members suggest several possible "actions" to perform, and I select one for the onstage group of actors to embody. "Play basketball 'in the manner of the word' (as if you were heart-broken)."

It can be an absurd challenge but also a creative one. "Brush your teeth 'in the manner of the word.'" Or "Sneak out of the house at midnight 'in the manner of the word.'" Players perform two to three different actions in the manner of the word before the audience is allowed to guess the word. (This has the additional benefit of teaching audience etiquette—students learn not to shout out the word or wiggle or wave their hands wildly in the air; rather, they become quietly and deeply involved with the onstage action, keeping their focus on performers' movements and gestures.) Though the players are onstage together, each works silently as if she were alone. Each is aware of but does not include the others in her actions or emotions. I may ask them to incorporate sounds or talk their thoughts aloud. I "freeze" the others to focus on one player mid-action and continue throughout the group until everyone has "gone solo." This provides a low-pressure opportunity to perform alone for a few seconds without actually being alone onstage. Sometimes, I let them play together and a scene spontaneously develops. Note this very important detail: the thoughts are alive in their bodies *before* they are allowed to use words. Students jump into performing the simple action with a particular emotion, and then, almost effortlessly, they begin to create a back story to justify the action and the manner in which it's being performed. Why is this heartbroken person sneaking out of the house at midnight? She's running away from her parents because they won't let her go with her boyfriend, who is moving across the country. The imagination answers the 'why,' and they conjure as they go. Because the actors are at first constrained from talking, the body does the speaking (think of the highly animated acting styles of early silent movies). As Fintushel says (this volume), "The conceptual mind is just too slow, too shallow a device to be able to handle the barrage of shifting information—proprioceptive, social, and environmental—to which a performer must respond." I used this game as an icebreaker in my daughter's class for our Greek drama work. It is also a quick diagnostic that can assess the performing comfort level of individual students.

One 6th grader, Maria, was terrified of acting in front of her peers. The teacher described to me how uncomfortable she was doing oral presentations. Middle school is a time of ferocious self-consciousness, and these particular students had to navigate some tricky, powerful cliques. This girl would rather have suffered a Spartan punishment—have her liver eaten, for example—than go onstage in front of her peers. Nevertheless, when she finally agreed to go up for "In the Manner of the Word," she visibly suffered and worried through it, barely able to focus on the imaginary task. But she did it! As I ended the day's session, I talked to the class about how hard it is to perform and how brave one has to be to get up, how we give courage to one another by supporting the person onstage, and so forth.

Over the years, I have learned how important it is to go slowly and simply, to create an atmosphere of trust. I assure them repeatedly that there is no failing. The acting student must feel free to behave on impulse rather than be motivated by fear of reprisal or correction from peers or teachers. The idiosyncratic first response is usually the most genuine, creative, and unique. Growing up conditions individuals to curtail or temper first responses out of respect for others and as a way of demonstrating 'good manners.' This process manifests in politeness, sharing, obedience, compliance; through our 'appropriate' behavior, we adopt 'civilized' behavior—embodying social interactions that may be both good and bad for us, sometimes both. Unfortunately, it is anathema for the actor to clamp down on the first impulse; it separates her from the character, the drama, the conflict, but worst of all it distances her from her own imagination.

The overall format of the Persephone myth project was to perform the story, section by section, in small groups. Each group brainstormed, improvised, and built the script for their small portion of the story, and we patched the pieces together and performed it for one another. Approximately fifty students from two classes were involved. As it happened, painfully shy Maria was assigned to the section where Hades cracks the earth open, grabs Persephone, and drags her down to the underworld. In our staging, Hades ran up the hill to the path where Persephone had wandered away from the spring dancing, grabbed her, fought a swineherd with a sword, and dragged her back down the hill to the play structure. The D'Aulaires' version included an illustration of that particular moment with a couple of pigs falling into the hole alongside Persephone. Maria, who had mostly avoided any eye contact with me from the first day, suddenly ran up bright-eyed, begging to play the part of the pig so she could roll down the hill. She then wholeheartedly volunteered to play the violin for the earlier section where Persephone dances with her friends.

Here was a child who was terrified to be seen as being "foolish" by her peers, actively finding a fun, safe way to publicly present herself. How did this transformation occur? Maria shifted her focus from self-consciousness—"What do I do?

Everyone is looking at me?"—to a specific, simple, and playable objective ("I want to roll down the hill, I know how to do that and it's fun"). She accessed the text through simple, doable actions, in this case, connecting to the illustration of the pigs, which opened up possibilities for her. In some sense, then, the written text and pictures afforded her a way to express herself as well as to have a personal breakthrough. By performing this story, Maria learned something about risk-taking, perhaps not immediately relatable to the text but immediately important to her growth, sense of accomplishment and self-confidence.

She will no doubt be required to do oral presentations throughout her schooling, and possibly the pain of them all will be lessened because she got to play a pig rolling down a grassy hill in the story of Persephone. In cases like Maria's, performing literature through embodying the text can teach one how to move beyond (or through) fear by offering opportunities to take on an enticing range of possible selves.

TRANSFORMING LITERATURE

In an example demonstrating the inverse, where the performer illuminates the literature, I offer a scene from the college course for pre-service English teachers mentioned at the beginning of this chapter. The assignment was a classic oral interpretation: a solo performer brings a two- to four-minute text selection of her choice to the music stand, introduces herself and the young adult novel she is drawing the excerpt from, briefly explains why she chose the passage (why it is meaningful to her), and then performs it aloud. A key feature of the assignment is that the selection *must* have personal relevance, and the performer *must* give a reason for it in her introduction before the performance. This accomplishes three goals: first, the student understands the material on a personal level, which increases affective commitment to the performance; second, the performer reveals something authentic about herself to herself as well as to the audience; and third, the class' experience of the performance is anchored directly in the framing provided by the performer's introduction to her excerpt of choice.

According to their skill level and willingness to take risks, students perform in variously layered ways. Some simply read with expression; others readily add gesture and movement, memorize sections, and delineate characters and the narrator vocally and/or physically. Some boldly leave the comfort of the music stand to use the full stage, creating an imaginary locale in space in which they mime the actions of the story. It all depends on the student; there is no failing.

For the pre-service teachers in this college-level English methods course, the challenge was not the literature itself, but the vulnerability of publicly performing a selection (and some trepidation about having to guide their future students to do the same). A quiet, young Latina, Maricela, who professed to know nothing about performing and rarely spoke in class, chose a passage from the prose poem novel, *Out of the Dust* by Karen Hesse. Like many of her fellow students, Maricela felt nervous and vulnerable. And like them, she was putting herself on the line. There is nothing like solo performing to do this. In her introduction, she stated that she would perform the section of the story where the narrator is burned and disfigured by a kerosene fire, a catastrophic incident that propels the novel. Maricela explained that she had chosen the text because she, too, had been badly burned by boiling water in an accident as a child. Of course, this put us all on alert; fellow classmates and friends were immediately fully attentive. We watched as through a full-voiced reading and gestures she surrendered herself fully to the story, letting her own truth mingle with the fiction. Her performance took on a visceral authenticity that was riveting to the rest of us. The text was utterly alive; the language was vibrant with suspense, pain, fear, anguish. It was her story *and* the character's story. She had no formal knowledge about the techniques of oral interpretation—how to pantomime or employ the vocal tricks of projection and phrasing or how to manage the logistics of getting her paper from the music stand to the ground; but none of that mattered. She transcended the mechanics of the craft to take us to the heart of this significant event—hers and the character's.

The experience Maricela portrayed had the feel of catharsis—for her and for us. In the dramatic tradition of ancient tragedies, catharsis has to do with invoking fear and terror in the audience. It involves a purification that sweeps beyond the imagined event, to a core identification of universal human struggle. In this circumstance, the classroom audience experienced the characters,' the performers,' and their own fear and pain. We were simply, in the parlance of my students, "blown away." We not only had a deep regard for Maricela's commitment but also gained a new understanding of the story's power. As a performer, Maricela had brought something of her experience to vivid life through the safety of someone else's text. The story allowed her to explore her own experience more deeply. But there's an important distinction: by physically enacting the story in front of an audience, she moved beyond her private understanding of the character to a public sharing of meaning. In essence, she had transformed the text into a visceral encounter not only for herself but also for everyone else in the room.

FOSTERING THEATER IN SECONDARY AND POST-SECONDARY CLASSROOMS

These teaching stories seek to illustrate the premise that sharing literature is a loving, nourishing, and courageous act. A performer is given tremendous attention by the audience, which in turn encourages the students' fullest commitment—an ideal learning situation for both teachers and students. In actuality, however, students frequently avoid this kind of attention because they often feel that too much is at stake. Moreover, many teachers don't feel they know enough about making theater to build the trust, cooperation, and skills students need to feel comfortable performing for one another. We can't simply say, "speak loudly with emotion" and expect to get a committed performance. Nor can we turn students loose to figure it out themselves because this kind of work takes teaching. And for that matter, many teachers are reluctant to use performance in the classroom without some kind of training in theater-making processes. Why? Because the consequences for the teacher, too, are high stakes (and can range from getting a headache to sheer panic): there's too much noise; nobody can settle down; people's feelings could get hurt; someone might feel humiliated; one person can actually physically hurt another; a fight can break out, there could be a breakdown of order, "Oh my God, it's *Lord of the Flies* in my classroom!" Why would an educator take carefully, painstakingly constructed boundaries (classroom rules) and fling a few of them aside for the sake of some romping around? While bedlam is possible, given slow, careful work on fundamentals and attention to the unique strengths and challenges of the group, multimodal theater activities in the classroom lend a visceral dimension and depth to learning that can't be matched.

Pre-service English teachers enact a scene from *Out of the Dust*, by Karen Hesse.

Yet students need structure, and the dramatic process, like anything, needs to be scaffolded. I use simple improvisation games, sometimes called creative dramatics to lay the groundwork (also see Blank & Roberts, 1997; Johnstone, 1979; Lindheim, 2011; Novelly, 1985; Stockley & Belt, 1993). Through these accessible exercises, students learn how to move around freely and purposefully, listen with their bodies, pretend, play, and actively imagine together. They learn about breath and about how sound is made in the body. They play with vocalization, then articulation, words, and slowly build to text. We use call and response, do tongue twisters, and recite a wide variety of texts ranging from rap lyrics to Shakespearean sonnets. We move and gesture while we speak, integrating bodily expression with language.

All this requires a measure of risk taking for both students and teachers. Not only for the sake of performance but also for understanding the literature itself, I model and teach acting techniques—how to respond with the first impulse, how to actively and responsively listen, how to build a character with voice and body, how to transform oneself, how to imagine being someone else, how to play a character's objective or need. As with all human beings, characters want something—a kiss, some money, to be king, to leave that podunk town, to get revenge. The actor must figure out the fundamental objective of the character in order to bring the role to life. For an actor to create a believable character, she must become someone else. The transformative process, developed by the renowned Russian director Constantin Stanislavski is sometimes called, "the magic if" (Stanislavski, 1937/1983). The cornerstone of modern acting springs from asking a very simple question, "If I were a character in this situation with these specific circumstances, then what would I do?" It is essentially an invitation to cultivate empathy in and through the body. By imaginatively and safely going beyond the familiar in physical as well as intellectual terms, we expand our understanding of the world, enrich our sense of self, and learn as well not to fear the 'Other'—whomever or whatever the Other may represent.

MAKING LITERATURE ACCESSIBLE TO THE SPECIFIC NEEDS OF THE GROUP

We know that when texts are personally relevant to students, they are likely to be more deeply engaged in reading them. But what happens when the issues can actually overwhelm a classroom? Years ago, a friend of mine, who had lived in a small, predominantly wealthy town and had been educated in a very affluent, predominantly white university, had gotten employment in a poor inner-city public school. She quickly discovered that every single improvisation activity the students enacted evoked depictions of guns. So she made a rule: you can't choose to solve a conflict with a gun. I thought that was a wise decision but an onerous one. After all, is it fair to deny students their real world, their real point of interest and attentiveness? Did my friend spoil their fun, or did it open up new venues for their imaginations? I don't know. Now, twenty teaching years later, I would urge my friend to find the literature that could crack open the conundrum, perhaps something by one of young adult literature's award-winning authors (Walter Dean Myers, Christopher Paul Curtis, Chris Crutcher, Sherman Alexie, Gary Soto, Jacqueline Woodson, Angela Johnson). I would encourage her not to run away from the apparent point of blockage but to face it creatively, to venture into it, unravel it, embody it, and in so doing, release its visceral stranglehold.

I have faced a similar challenge, which taught me how important it is to tap into the unique strengths and experiences of each group. I got a position teaching acting to a handful of 'at-risk' middle school boys at a predominantly African American, low SES K-8 school in the middle of an extremely wealthy, predominantly Caucasian neighborhood.[1] I was completely unprepared to deal with the energy of these young men. Their hormones were raging full tilt; they wanted to fight each other all the time and to make me out to be the fool (which I was, because I didn't know what I was doing). There was so much showing off and taunting that it was nearly impossible to get them to work together, much less to do theater. My lesson plans and improvisation games were useless. The fact was, these young people had no point of reference for the kind of theater I was versed in; thus, the particular theater skills I was trying to teach seemed completely irrelevant to them—and in hindsight, they were. They considered the games infantile and thought that acting was for 'sissies.' Furthermore, their educational experience differed vastly from mine; whereas I'd loved school, they hated it. I needed help. So not knowing whether it would work but hoping it would, I looked to the storyteller I loved when I was young: Homer.

The Odyssey centers on warriors who are smart, lazy, and arrogant, get into and out of trouble, and become heroes by their wits as well as by their ability to fight. They take care of each other and find faith and humility in a larger cause. At the time, I wondered if these stories could possibly capture the interest of these young men or resonate with their perceptions of themselves in the world. We dumped the curriculum I'd planned and took up the story of Cyclops,[2] getting rid of most of the desks and turning the whole classroom into both story space and production shop.[3] The young men constructed a giant one-eyed puppet out of papier-mâché, poles, and cloth and strung a clothesline between two walls, draping it with a blue tarp and cutting out a cardboard boat to sail across the tarp. One corner of the room was Cyclops' cave with painted rocks creeping from the floor all the way up to the ceiling. But best of all, a colleague, an actress trained in stage combat, came in to work with us. They wanted to fight and after developing and writing a script, I wanted them to be able to put it into action, but it had to be done safely.

The boys were scared to put themselves up for ridicule as actors, so they devised the staging so as to enable anonymity—through voices behind tarps and puppet manipulators. When they did appear on stage it was in combat and circus-style gymnastic performances. As the wounded Cyclops, they even got to throw a cardboard box boulder at Odysseus, which landed precipitously close to the observing principal. Eventually the design and the spectacle making became the chief means for exploring the text. Theater was the conduit for expressing the real interest and concerns of the students and the hook for the literature.

SAFETY AND RISK-TAKING IN THE CLASSROOM

Students are more willing to take creative risks, which are essentially personal risks, when they feel safe and valued. Whatever the teaching situation, I work to create a congenial social space in the classroom where people have intellectual as well as physical room to move. In addition to pushing aside desks, we craft an atmosphere of structured yet playful experimentation, showing students that there is no failing in this kind of imaginative play. As Fintushel claims (see his chapter in this volume), in the world of the imagination, "there are no mistakes." Such dramatic pedagogical exercises can inspire creativity and enable students to collaborate in unexpected ways that may break through habitual behavior and relationships and deepen students' sense of belonging in as well as outside of the classroom.

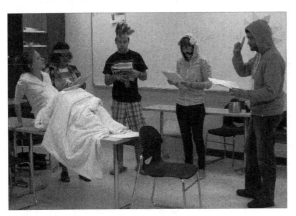

Pre-service English teachers enact a scene from *Out of the Dust*, by Karen Hesse.

Above all, I encourage students to connect viscerally—to engage texts personally, emotionally and physically. Although inspiration and creativity can have a chaotic feel that may at times seem antithetical to traditional notions of classroom order, in courses where multimodal pedagogy involves students in lifting the words off the page and into the body, students' individual and collective movements and social exchanges help them 'master the script' on multiple levels. The kinds of preliminary warm-ups and improvisation exercises described above can lead to important discoveries that often reach beyond the literature curriculum itself, enabling young people to gain not only a greater sense of expertise in relation to texts but also a growing sense of agency and self-efficacy.

As an educator, I continue to reflect on what, exactly, I am preparing my students for. I recently decided to leave my job at the university to become a drama instructor at a private K-8 grade school in Marin County, across the Golden Gate Bridge, just north of San Francisco. The 7th/8th grade faculty met to discuss what they consider to be the most important challenges students face today. The question quickly led to ruminations on what our students need from us in order to help them prepare for productive and fulfilling adult lives. One math teacher expressed concern about students' ability to grapple creatively and freely with complex ideas or problems: "I can't stop thinking about when I recently gave the students an open-ended question. There were no parameters, no rubric, just a question. They didn't know what to do, and were so worried about being wrong in their approach. I realized how hard it was for them to take risks in their thinking." I often reflect on her insight about the high-stakes testing culture we're currently working in. What holds our students back from their best ideas, from achieving their best learning potential? Often, it is simply the idea of being wrong, which evinces a near-allergic reaction these days.

In *Out of Our Minds: Learning to Be Creative*, Sir Ken Robinson (2001/2011) argues that we need to rethink national education systems to better support creative development and thinking, both locally and globally. In a 2006 TED Talk, Robinson quipped, "Nobody has a clue...what the world will look like in five years' time. And yet we're meant to be educating [children] for it. So the unpredictability is extraordinary....My contention is that creativity is now as important as literacy." Schools, he argues, often dampen creativity by demonizing mistakes. Left to their own devices, he says kids would willingly take chances.

> They're not frightened of being wrong....If you're not prepared to be wrong, you'll never come up with anything original....[B]y the time we get to be adults, most [people] have lost that capacity. They have become frightened of being wrong. And we run our companies like this...we stigmatize mistakes. And we're now running national education systems where mistakes are the worst thing you can make. [T]he result is we're educating people out of their creative capacities. (Robinson, 2006)

Drama, particularly improvisational activities like those described in this chapter and elsewhere in this volume, can provide a kind of structured play that encourages risk-taking and adventuresome thinking. Such teaching tools lend themselves to language and literature classes (although they can be imaginatively integrated across disciplines). When literature is explored through drama techniques, the process and results can be dynamic, powerful, and incredibly nourishing for young people. Dramatic performance provides an embodied and social context for literally *moving ideas*, adding a visceral dimension to literacy and literature learning that involves students holistically and attentively in the revelatory processes of their own becoming.

Notes

1. To explain this sociological phenomenon would take much more than a footnote, but suffice it to say that the landscape was gorgeous and had attracted a diverse population to the region. It had the multi-million dollar homes of professionals and entrepreneurs on the steep hillsides overlooking the San Francisco Bay, a large low-income project in the valley, a community of African Americans who had originally migrated north during World War II to work in the booming

ship-building industry, artsy types who lived on houseboats in the Bay, and military families from the base on the other side of the hill. The rich people would not send their children to the public school. The base closed; the artsy hippy children grew up; and boat homes became gentrified. Eventually most of the remaining public school children were African Americans who were keenly aware of the white flight.

2. Behind the scenes of the Cyclops anecdote, is a terrific educational mentor, Peggy Hirsh, principal of a small public charter school who ferociously protected and created learning opportunities for her students. I watched her break and amend and massage so many rules in order to take care of her students. She was an inspirational, guiding force for my early teaching.

3. Schools generally do not have the space available to devote to a project of this breadth. Many classrooms are full to bursting with equipment, desks, resources, and frankly, the clutter of unused, outdated materials and projects. I can only urge teachers to try to simplify their classrooms and open up the space as much as possible for physical movement, letting students' bodies be the creative resources.

Works Cited

Belt, L., & Stockley, R. (1995). *Acting through improv: Improv through theatresports*. Seattle, WA: Thespis.

Blank, C., & Roberts, J. (1997). *Live on stage: Performing arts for middle school*. Palo Alto, CA: Dale Seymour.

Blount, R. (2008). *Alphabet juice: The energies, gists, and spirits of letters, words, and combinations thereof, their roots, bones, innards, piths, pips, and secret parts, tinctures, tonics, and essences, with examples of their usage foul and savory*. New York: Farrar, Straus & Giroux.

D'Aulaire, I., & D'Aulaire, E. (1992). *D'Aulaires' book of Greek myths*. New York: Delacorte Books for Young Readers.

Gardner, H. (1983). *Frames of mind: The theory of multiple intelligences*. New York: Basic Books.

Johnstone, K. (1979/1987). *Impro: Improvisation and the theatre*. New York: Theatre Arts Book.

Lindheim, J. (2011). *Trusting the moment: Unlocking your creativity and imagination*. Hardwick, MA: Satya House.

Novelly, M. C. (1985). *Theatre games for young performers: Improvisations & exercises for developing acting skills*. Colorado Springs, CO: Meriwether.

Robinson, K. (2001/2011). *Out of our minds: Learning to be creative*. Chichester, UK: Capstone Publishing (Wiley).

Robinson, K. (2006). TED Talk. http://www.ted.com/talks/ken_robinson_says_schools_kill_crea tivity.html?utm_expid=166907–14&utm_referrer=http%3A%2F%2Fwww.ted.com%2Fsearch%3F cat%3Dss_all%26q%3Dsir%2Bken%2Brobinson

Stanislavski, C. (1989). *An actor prepares*. New York: Routledge.

CHAPTER NINE

A Trio

Combining Language, Literacy and Movement in Preschool and Kindergarten Community-based Dance Lessons

JILL HOMAN RANDALL

> To the young child, verbal language and movement are entwined. Preverbal
> movement expression does not cease when a child develops language. The road
> to literacy involves the translation of movement expression and communication
> into words. Language and dance are not separate threads, but are woven together
> and incorporated into a fabric of communication and understanding. (Faber, 2002,
> Standards for Dance in Early Childhood, p. 2)

Dance classes for preschool age children reveal the magical intersection between movement and language. The creative dance class described in this chapter is a well-crafted unit of study involving multiple layers of learning about dance, being in a social setting with peers, and exploring larger early childhood concepts related to language and literacy. Children between the ages of 3 and 6 are going through an important period of life—learning letters, sounds, words, and the idea of written language and story. Through these, they explore and develop relationships to others and to the world. At the same time, children are also exploring and learning the fundamental building blocks of everyday movement—movements that are also fundamental to dance.

Below, I describe a 21-week creative dance class for 3- to 5-year-olds that systematically investigates the intersection of language and dance. I examine naming movement verbally, using written language as a springboard for movement and incorporating children's names as well as nursery rhymes to combine verbal, rhythmic, and kinesthetic learning. These approaches create multimodal scaffolding that is dense with physical learning, vocabulary building, and social interaction. Described here is the look, sound and feel of these richly embodied experiences, which I hope will inspire dance teaching artists and classroom teachers to find their own ways of connecting movement and language meaningfully and coherently to reach students with many different learning styles.

INTRODUCTION

The invitation to contribute to this book inspired me to use my 21-week winter/spring semester in 2009 as a laboratory for systematically exploring the intersection of language and dance. These two classes at Shawl-Anderson Dance Center in Berkeley, California included one weekly 45-minute class for 3- and 4-year-olds, and one weekly 45-minute class for 4- and 5-year-olds. A total of twenty-two children were enrolled in the two classes. With over 14 years of experience as a dance educator in after school settings and public school programs, I have long been interested in how children can learn to physicalize the symbolic, taking literacy in viscerally through movement.

In creative dance classes for young children, multimodal activities are:

- Kinesthetic, physical, in the body
- Tactile and tangible
- Auditory
- Visual
- Verbal
- Imaginary and imaginative
- Structured as well as improvisational
- Rhythmic and rhyming
- Fun and joyful

Although first and foremost I am teaching the expressive art form of dance, I am also teaching an emergent curriculum that involves listening and watching the students carefully so that I can understand and build on their interests, loves, and inspirations. Throughout the semester, I also incorporate the National Dance Education Organization's (NDEO) *Standards for Dance in Early Childhood* (Faber, 2002), considering what are developmentally appropriate dance explorations and vocabulary for young children. Third, I am an adamant believer in incorporating all of those simple, yet crucial, locomotor movements that people use, some of them daily: walking, running, galloping, skipping, hopping, leaping, and jumping. These dance steps used on and off the dance floor lay some of the most fundamental conceptual groundwork for much more complex sequences of movements and dance combinations.

My Personal History and Dance Education Background

While earning a BFA in Modern Dance at the University of Utah, I studied with dance professors Anne Riordan and Mary Ann Lee. Anne Riordan pioneered, among other things, dance classes for adults with cerebral palsy. I also studied with Mary Ann Lee, Director of the Virginia Tanner Creative Dance Program. Mary Ann helped me understand how to integrate dance into a public school program as a part of the regular school day rather than as a separate, stand-alone after-school class. Finally, my participation in the University of Utah's Service-Learning Scholars Program, one of the leaders nationwide in the service-learning movement, really got me questioning and exploring the role of dance in the community. At age 21, I embarked upon a full-time teaching schedule, averaging 20–25 classes a week at a preschool and K–5 public elementary. My own embodied learning over 16 years has included extensive hands-on experience, working side by side with amazing public school teachers, and ongoing professional development as a dance educator that has shaped the way I teach dance, particularly with respect to the intersection of language and movement.

Like many children, I was not initially excited about reading so my current stance on language and literacy is a sweet irony for me. I did what I had to in order to get by in school but was far from enthusiastic about literature or reading until my freshman year of college when I met a wonderful English professor whose passion, enthusiasm, and curiosity inspired me to approach the act of reading in particular, and language in general, in a whole new way.

For the past 16 years I have worked hard to incorporate writing, charts, symbols, words, books, and reflective literacy-based activities into my dance classes. During the 1990s, when I was a young, new dance specialist in public schools, there was a strong push for "arts integration" directly into classroom curriculum—educators wondered how to teach math, English, science, or social studies *through* dance. However, I found, as did numerous teachers, that many attempts felt contrived and failed to be authentic or engaging. But, I also discovered that the intersection of words and movement really made sense to me as well as to my students. Because of my intense teaching schedule (working with 300 students per week) I had many opportunities to experiment with arts integration across subject areas. While the art of dance remains at the center of my work, I have become increasingly convinced over years of teaching that multiple modalities foster students' learning in subject area classrooms. The recent research on arts education and learning bears this out (Burnaford, Brown, Doherty, & McLaughlin, 2007).

To my surprise, I have also developed a deep and abiding love of children's literature, which has now become one of my "specialties"—finding books that might be springboards for dances. Always on the lookout for new texts that lend themselves to movement, I assiduously comb through all of the current books discussed in publications such as *The Horn Book Guide*. In 2011, I created a blog entitled *Dancing Words*, specifically about these children's books, geared towards dance teaching artists, classroom teachers, parents, and librarians of pre-K through 5th grade students.[1]

I know that my way of working is not entirely original; I respectfully credit those dance and arts educators whose practices and ideas I build carefully upon, in particular, Patricia Reedy (2003), Lincoln Center Institute (2006), and Maxine Greene (2001). The information gleaned over the years through mentorship, workshops, observations, and reading continues to guide how I integrate literacy and dance to support learning for children of diverse backgrounds and ages.[2]

A SAMPLE LESSON PLAN

What does it look like to blend literacy and dance? Figure 1 outlines a sample lesson from my class for 3- and 4-year-olds. At each class, I posted my lesson in outline form on large chart paper so that everyone (students, parents, and I) could see. As a teacher, these words help me remember the numerous activities quickly. I also find it important to share a visual with families; the class is about more than bringing one's children in for 45 minutes of "moving around." For families, the outlined lesson plans provide a small window into the world of creative dance—a world unfamiliar to many parents. Posting the lessons offers parents language about dance class format and vocabulary.

This text-rich environment and the various ways of interacting with parents about our dance classes—sharing what I do, sharing lesson plans, and communicating via email—help develop a language between teachers, students, and their families that, in turn, fosters linguistic and movement-based development for the children at the same time that it educates lay people about the language of dance as an art form.

Figure 1: Blending literacy and dance: A sample lesson plan.

I. Introduction/beginnings
  A. Quick reference to last week's class (verbal reflection)
  B. Name and gesture
    1. Everyone gets a turn to say her name and create one simple gesture with the arms
    2. The whole class echoes back, saying each student's name and repeating the gesture
  C. Moving to the sound
    1. I explain, and then we move around the room to different sounds
    2. Drum sounds signal walking to the beat of the drum
    3. Shakers signal turning around
    4. Concertina signals opening and closing the arms (like the concertina opening and closing)
    5. The singing bowl signals spreading magic with a wand in the air, for the duration of the sound
  D. Animal cards
    1. Students move to the far side of the room, by the windows
    2. Students select cards from a deck of animal flash cards (by artist Eric Carle)
    3. Once a card is selected, we make a shape with our bodies like the shape in the picture (positions)

II. Free dance/improvisation traveling in space
  A. Pink tulle fabric (about 24 inches long by 12 inches wide)
    1. Students improvise with the fabric while music plays
    2. I walk around and verbally share back what I see—fabric swirling, turning with fabric, shaking the fabric, etc.

III. Prep for the next activity—hopping
  A. I ask the students to hold onto one of the ballet barres around the room with both hands
  B. We practice hopping on one foot, then switch feet

III. Circle
  A. New hopping rhyme
    1. First attempt at a new rhyme I created about hopping
  B. Running rhyme
    2. Revisiting a rhyme from last semester
  C. Follow me, with music
    1. I lead a silent warm up to music, asking students to follow my movements (reaching, twisting, kicking, etc.)

Figure 1. *continued*

IV. Across the room
  A. "Let's _____ " (walk, run, hop, jump, skip, gallop)
    1. We move together back and forth across the room
    2. I call out new suggestions with each crossing (walking, jumping, etc.)
    3. Students offer suggestions for ways we can move across the room

V. Collaborative choreography to Vivaldi's "Winter" from "The Four Seasons"
  A. Students are asked to improvise to the music drawing on all of the different kinds of movements we have already done in class that day
  B. I quickly write down what I see on a large chart pad taped to the mirrors so that everyone can see
  C. I circle 6 ideas from this list, and this becomes our "dance"
  D. All together, we practice the 6 parts of our dance; I verbally cue the students to switch from one part to the next
  E. We perform for each other (half the class at the time)

VI. Ending—I place large foam dots across the room
  A. Students gather at one corner of the studio
  B. One at a time dancers cross the room
  C. The students walk until they reach a dot. On the dots, they balance on one foot with the other leg extended back (arabesque); repeat at the second dot
  D. I cue students with a drum
  E. Students receive a sticker at the end of class and head out of the room

The lesson plan in Figure 1 shows a basic class format with a clear beginning, middle, and end. The students experience dance as a whole group and individually, in a circle, in their individual spaces throughout the room, and traveling through space. The lesson also includes the five essential concepts described in this chapter (detailed in the next section); a variety of activities keeps students engaged and challenged and provides each student with multimodal experiences of early literacy concepts.

21 Weeks and Five Big Ideas

Below, I highlight five activities described at length in subsequent sections:

1. "Naming" movements verbally, by both learners and teachers in a dance class, helps students identify and articulate what we see and do while expanding our vocabulary and movement options;

2. Cuing and facilitating activities through verbal prompts motivates open-ended dance explorations;

3. Using written language (single words, lists of words, and storybooks) provides a point of departure for movement and supports early connections between print literacy and the immediate social world;

4. Engaging in movement activities that incorporate children's names provides opportunities for recognition, builds an individual student's sense of belonging, and fosters community;

5. Reading and moving to nursery rhymes offers a culturally relevant form of verbal and rhythmic learning for children while teaching widely valued cultural references.

FIRST IDEA: NAMING MOVEMENT

Below I describe the verbal components of my creative dance classes, where students are simultaneously learning by hearing, seeing, as well as experiencing tactilely and kinesthetically in their own bodies.

During at least one activity in each class, I "say back" to the students what I am seeing. I first learned this style of observational feedback from preschool teacher Vicki Carlton at the Mulberry School in Berkeley, California. Instead of saying, "Jill is dancing beautifully with her gold piece of fabric," a teacher can share what she objectively sees, "Jill is moving up and down with her fabric. She just changed her speed from slow to quick." The result of such verbalizing is two-fold: first, observational talk provides an opportunity for the teacher to acknowledge and see each student, who feels individually noticed. Second, this simple verbal interaction continues to develop a rich vocabulary for describing ways to move and dance. Specifically, the 3–5-year-old age range is a prime time for developing vocabulary.[3] In this activity, the teacher is helping to articulate what is going on using the vocabulary common to dance.[4] In each class I include an improvisational, free-moving activity, which provides them with a loosely structured opportunity to build *their own voice*, movement vocabulary, and motor skills.

By naming what I see, and writing it down, I also add to their vocabulary and continue this feedback and learning loop. I acknowledge all students in the class and their many ways of moving. "Isabel is galloping. Leila's legs are crisscrossing. Devon is moving quickly." Taking away "beautiful" and "good" minimizes aesthetic judgment and instead acknowledges in spoken (and written) language what is already being explored in and through the body. The Lincoln Center Institute model of aesthetic education also explores ways of describing what you "see" and "hear" before making any judgment about how you feel and what you think as the viewer or audience member.

Another activity I conducted throughout the semester was a simply structured way of making a dance with the class—"collaborative choreography." Every student has an opportunity to contribute one movement to the dance that the entire class will do.[5] Here's what it looks like.

I sit students down in front of a large piece of chart paper for a few minutes and explain that we will be creating a dance together. Using writing as a memory aid for both students and teacher, I explain that I am writing it down so that we can remember it next week. Each student gets an opportunity to show me one way of moving and then gets to name it. The student might name it something unique (i.e., "Jill's sparkly spin") or a common, basic description like "jumping side to side." The students show their movement and then describe it in words. This offers children another way to develop vocabulary and articulate what and how we are moving while also promoting individual development.

Then, each student contributes one idea—a movement or frozen shape—to a dance. One at a time, students stand up and show their movement. They then "name it," and I document it on the paper where everyone can see it (although the children may not be able to read it just yet). Once the list has been made, we learn the dance and then set it to music. Despite (or perhaps because of) the activity's basic form, it has become one of my most successful activities in the last decade because it gives each student a voice, is child-centered, and creates "a dance." Although dance classes involve skill building and improvisational activities, kids feel like they are dancing and enjoy performing a piece.

One Friday afternoon this semester, I had seven 3- and 4-year-old students. We sat down for five minutes in front of my large blank chart, and I asked for help making our dance. Each student took a turn and showed her idea. Then, we put the motion into words:

- Bunny hops
- Low jumps
- Ping pong run
- Horsey gallop
- Amalie's frozen shape
- Anna's jump
- Fast crawling

Although these movements might seem disparate, what made the dance work was adding music and linking the steps together. For this particular class, we used a section of Vivaldi's "Spring" from *The Four Seasons*. Adding music layers pulse, rhythm, and melody into the dance. As the teacher, I was in charge of linking the steps together. This was accomplished by my verbal prompts from one step to the next, setting the length of time we spent exploring each step. (In real time, each step might only be explored for 20 seconds per step.) The beauty and value of these collaborative choreography activities are that we try movement first, then language—feeling and experience first, then description.

During week four of the semester, I also provided the families with a simple survey to complete while the students were in class. The responses were meant to help me shape the content for the semester (which indeed they did). The survey was also my first attempt to inspire families to articulate their child's experiences of movement and dance. I asked the following questions, with the third question getting to the heart of describing the movement.

1. What are some concepts your child is really into these days (fairies, rainbows, colors, wheels, cooking, reading, costumes, etc.)?
2. What rhymes and books does your child love?
3. Describe two ways your child loves to move.
4. Any other information you would like to share?

Some of the responses to the third question included:

"She loves to run and skip. She's into jumping on the bed and jumping in general. She likes to dance at home."

"slug slithering, leaping creature, frog motions"

"jump, run, roll"

"twirling, expressive arm movement in dance"

"She also takes ballet and enjoys showing me tendu and plié for instance."

Throughout the semester, I revisited the parents' responses to help shape my lessons. As for learners of all ages, when dance for young children relates to their current passions and curiosities they are more likely to participate and explore. Sensitivity to student interests builds lessons that connect with meaning to the young children in the class.

A COMPLETE CIRCLE: IMPROVISING, CAPTURING IN WORDS, "SAYING BACK" TO STUDENTS, AND DANCING AGAIN

This is a basic structure for an improvisation that I have done for years with students in preschool through second grade.

In week four of the semester, we were talking about the seasons, specifically winter. I told the students that I would be playing a "winter song" for them. The students improvised and I quickly captured on chart paper what I saw. I wrote down words and phrases such as: circling legs, snow angels, crawling, and sidestepping. After the students were asked to stop moving, I read back to them my list. Then, very quickly, I selected 6–8 of the descriptions to make our "winter dance." We did each movement together, and then we did it again with music. I moved alongside the students, and my verbal cues helped the students know when to change from one movement to the next.

This activity was effective because it began with students moving based on their own ideas and inclinations. We articulated it, captured it, and then repeated it. In addition, by keeping this list of simple word prompts, we could revisit this activity several times over the coming weeks. Recalling steps and phrases from previous weeks is a wonderful skill to start developing, as dance requires students to remember and repeat movements.

SECOND IDEA: USING VERBAL PROMPTS TO INSPIRE MOVEMENT

In the previous section I described a way to go from movement to language. As described below, the reverse process can also be rewarding.

In the latter half of the semester-long class, I sought new variations of structuring the basic "freeze dance" to inspire a variety of ways of moving and responding to music. "Freeze dance" is an improvisation where students move to music and then stop when the music stops. Once the music is played again, students begin to dance again. In week 20, I used images and music for each idea: a painting dance, an underwater dance, a horse dance, a chicks dance, and a fairy dance. Knowing my students and some of their personal interests (from the parent survey and conversations with the students and parents), I wanted to connect our dance class with some of their favorite subjects, so I used very basic verbal prompts, such as, "When the music begins again, I want to see a painting dance," and avoided more detailed explanations. The invitation to paint, be a fairy, and dance underwater opened up students' imaginations and movement repertoires very quickly. Sometimes the most open-ended verbal prompts can invite students into a rich movement exploration.

Another engaging activity using verbal prompts involved creating a short dance in a circle. After practicing for several weeks we shared it with family members on the last day. I started with a piece of music composed by Moby that was fun, energetic, and had a clear downbeat ("I Love to Move in Here"). Then, I created a movement phrase, and instead of teaching the dance with counts—5 6 7 8....—I distilled the dance into basic words, to create the rhythm of the dance in poem-like form:

Arms, arms, arms, arms
Arms, arms, arms, arms
Legs, legs, legs, legs
Low......lower ......lowest......
Crawl......
Paint....paint....paint. . . .
Spiral;
Sprinkle;
Stand.

As the teacher, I provided these verbal prompts using an animated, expressive voice and clear rhythm when speaking the words. The students became engaged and drawn into the movements. My voice led the way into a joyful, playful activity.

THIRD IDEA: USING WRITTEN LANGUAGE AS A SPRINGBOARD FOR DANCE

During my years in public elementary school programs, working hand in hand with classroom teachers, I gained an understanding of the vocabulary the students were exploring in the classroom. Really looking at their word walls, words of the week, spelling lists, and the like taught me about age-specific vocabulary and helped me to establish connections between the classroom curriculum and dance curriculum. I culled from these numerous lists words that naturally lent themselves to movement, especially verbs and prepositions.

Starting with these words, I then developed movement activities and lessons. The work of dance educators Mary Anne Lee, Ruth Bossieux, and Sheila Kogan in particular have inspired me to create activities that teach relationality (near, far, on, off, close, etc.).[6]

Lists of Words

In March of this particular semester, I worked on "kicking" with the students. Beginning with written language—I wrote a list of words—and then used it to facilitate an improvisational dance. I thought of different ways the students could kick, including:

Small kicks
BIG kicks
Moving kicks (i.e., traveling in space)
Frozen kicks (i.e., students pause)
Floor kicks (i.e., kicks into the air from a seated position on the floor)

As a teacher, beginning with words helped me flesh out my ideas in preparation for the lesson. The list of words also served as a starting point for an improvisation that inspired students to move in novel ways while exploring one simple movement from multiple perspectives.

During that same time in the semester, I also created a word list of some common *opposites* to use as a springboard for warming up. I made the list first and then created movements to accompany the words. The order of words created a rhythm and rhyme for me: high, low, fast, slow, stop, go, yes, no, turn around slowly, to, fro. I taught the class this warm-up by showing the movements and saying the words at the same time, allowing students to simultaneously see, hear, and do.

Over the past decade I have also been working on an as-yet-unpublished manuscript about teaching the alphabet multimodally. As part of my preparation for this work, I once went through the entire dictionary over a period of months to help me create a basic gesture warm-up for each letter. I would read all of the words that started with a particular letter and write down all that lent themselves to movement, especially verbs, body parts, animals, and prepositions. These "Warm-Ups with Words" created a repeatable activity structure that also served as a list of words that reads like an alliterative poem, which could also be used as a starting point for movement. A decade later, I am still refining these lists so that they make sense rhythmically and kinesthetically. During this semester I revisited several of them and incorporated the first letters of students' names. Then, over the course of several weeks, we did a "Warm Up with Words" for the letters A, G, K, M, S, and W. The A warm-up, for example, included:

Ankles
Arms
Arch
Applaud
Accordion
Alligator
Ant
Air

By starting with word lists, dance teachers can begin with a clear sense of *what* we are teaching—direction, level, body parts, and particular actions. This clarity develops the real language of a dance class for the very young.

Figure 2. "Warm-Up with Words." Students explore "S Words" and "W Words" near the lists posted in class, for an activity that includes visual, auditory, and kinesthetic components.

BOOKS

Moving beyond poetic word lists, picture books can serve as springboards for multiple activities in a dance class. Books about the art of dance, for example, offer a complementary component to any lesson. Many picture books, not specifically about dance per se, can also lead to rich improvisations and story dances.

Some of my current favorites, specifically about dance, for children ages 3–5 include:

Dance by Bill T. Jones
Let's Dance by George Ancona
I Am a Dancer by Pat Lowery
Dance with Me by Charles R. Smith

Other picture books include action words or simple stories that literally get students moving. Eric Carle's *From Head to Toe* is an easy first warm-up in a dance class; students will be shaking, kicking, and bending like the animals in the artwork. *Star*

Climbing by Lou Fancher and Steve Johnson includes actions like tiptoeing, leaping, and diving. *The Squiggle* by Carole Lexa Schaefer easily introduces the students to images using one prop—a long ribbon.

During the winter semester, I used the following books as catalysts for movement:

Jumping Day by Barbara Juster Esbensen and Maryann Cocca-Leffler

Star Climbing by Lou Fancher and Steve Johnson

The Giant Carrot by Jan Peck and Barry Root

From Head to Toe by Eric Carle

Jamberry by Bruce Degen

Jamberry is a playful picture book with rhythmic language, about a boy and a bear picking, eating, and enjoying berries of various kinds. *Jamberry* is a book one might not consider to be an obvious choice for a dance class, yet it is particularly valuable. Using baskets in my creative dance classes, I frequently revisit the themes of picking and gathering—themes that appear in dances all over the world. *Jamberry* is one of my son's favorite books because we can both easily repeat the rhythm of

Figure 3. Students sit to hear and see the story,
Jamberry, prior to learning a berry-picking dance.

the words. Over the course of some weeks, I used this story as my starting point, reading it to the class and talking about berries. We made "berry shapes" in our bodies—round shapes on the floor—and using baskets, made a "berry-picking" dance to go with the story.

The dance begins with all of us (students and teacher) picking up our empty baskets and holding them with both hands. We move up and down, high and low, with our baskets four times. Then we turn around once and freeze. We repeat this movement phrase again, and then the students quickly sit down where they are on one side of the room.

I have set up three "stations" with three different baskets. In each basket are some pretend berries—large cut out pieces of paper (about 5 inches around) of raspberries, blueberries, and strawberries. When a student's name is called, she skips to the first basket, and picks one berry to place in her basket. Finally, she skips to the second, and then the third. She then skips back to our starting place. Once every student has had a turn, we repeat the starting phrase: up, down, up, down, turn around, freeze; up, down, up, down, turn around, freeze.

Our berry-picking dance started from a quick read of *Jamberry* and then developed organically into an exploration of shape and learning a beautiful, simple dance in A-B-A form, moving in unison as well as one at a time. In this activity using multiple modalities, students talked about fruits, made shapes like berries, heard and viewed pictures of a rhythmically playful book on berries, and used their imaginations to berry pick within the dance.

Picture books offer great springboards for warm-up activities and also longer explorations. Such books provide students with visual and auditory modes of exploring a concept to work hand in hand with a movement activity.

FOURTH IDEA: USING NAMES TO ACKNOWLEDGE EACH DANCER

So far, I have discussed how action words and descriptions can be used to inspire movement. Below, I describe another literacy resource that specifically acknowledges each individual student in the room and employs another important list of words: students' names. In my classes, each student gets a turn to say his/her name and create a simple movement; the class then echoes it back, saying the name and repeating the movement. This activity acknowledges every child, gives each student an opportunity to lead, and challenges the rest of the class to learn students' names and quickly "see and do" their movements in class.

Other simple activities that incorporate names include a version of Freeze Dance, which I call Someone Says. (This riffs off *Someone Says* by Carole Lexa

Schaefer.) We start moving around the room, and then freeze. I call out a student's name, and this prompts them to think of the *next* way for us to locomote. "Annika says…let's skip…." "Gia says…let's roll on the floor…." I acknowledge every student, each one receives a turn, and students benefit from having opportunities to name dance steps and subsequently embody them, creating new pathways between words and movement.

Figure 4. Name Stations. The class jumps to one student's name posted on the wall as part of the Name Stations activity.

I also sometimes create "stations" around the room. Even in a small dance studio, I place handwritten signs in six different areas. Early in the semester, I made signs with every student's first name on it for an activity I call Name Stations. I would say, "Clara, point to the sign with your name. Let's all go over there." Once we were near a particular student's name, that student would think of one movement we would perform right there by her own name sign, such as reaching, turning, or kicking. Spatializing literacy in this way allows students to identify with their names, receive personal attention and acknowledgment, hear each other's voice in class and provide every student with the opportunity to create and explore.

FIFTH IDEA: RHYTHM AND PLAY WITH NURSERY (AND OTHER) RHYMES

Joanne Rudge Long (2008) in the *Horn Book Magazine* article, "How to Choose a Goose," notes that

> It is a truth universally acknowledged that every English-speaking child is the better for an early friendship with "Mother Goose"—*early* meaning from birth, because nothing boosts language development better than those catchy rhymes and rhythms. Scholars and educators alike praise the virtues and resonances of these traditional rhymes. They are essentials of both popular culture and our literary heritage; they stimulate young imaginations; reading, saying, or singing them draws parents and children together in shared delight. Best of all, those beloved, familiar, playful, nonsensical verses are just plain fun. (p. 49)

As a teacher, I started thinking about nursery rhymes and their potential uses in a dance class when I was hired in 2000 to create an "arts integration curriculum" at Malcolm X Elementary School in Berkeley, California. Several of the kindergarten teachers specifically requested that I incorporate rhymes into my curriculum.

I have grown to love rhymes through experimenting in classes, and I appreciate the natural pairing in a class of the verbal, rhythmic, and kinesthetic. For the first time in my teaching, I am making my own rhymes. This semester, I created rhymes about running and hopping. The students loved animating the rhyme, giggling with pleasure as they accomplished the complex skill of running in place. Without a traditional Mother Goose rhyme about hopping, I decided to create a following hopping rhyme as well.

Running Rhyme (in a sixteen-beat rhythm, each line being four sets of four counts):

run run run run run run run run run run run and STOP
run run run run run run run run run run run and POP
run run run run run run run run run run run and FALL
run run run run run run run run run run run and TALL
Hopping Rhyme:
I touch my two feet,
I stand on one.
I touch my two feet,
I stand on one.
Hop on one foot,
Hop on one....
Hop, hop, hop,
And now we're done.

Throughout the semester I incorporated traditional Mother Goose and other rhymes in order to offer children multiple ways of accessing concepts such as jumping, counting, the season of spring, and more. A list of traditional rhymes used throughout the semester includes:

- Hickory Dickory Dock
- Jack Be Nimble
- Rain on the Green Grass
- One, Two, Three, Four, Five
- Sally Goes Round the Sun
- 12 Buckle My Shoe
- Humpty Dumpty
- Wash the Dishes, Wipe the Dishes

Over the past 10 years working in schools, I have repeatedly heard kindergarten teachers bemoan the fact that fewer and fewer children seem to know these rhymes. Like songs and dances, nursery rhymes are cultural touchstones in many countries. I continue to teach these rhymes multimodally—as the language play with words and the rhythms of these rhymes are embedded in our social worlds, and knowing them supports children's success in school, where background knowledge of such rhymes (whether it ought to be or not) is often assumed.

INVITING PARENTS TO CLASS: THE FINAL SHARING IN WEEK 21

In Week 21, I invited families to attend the last 20 minutes of the final class. Many adults struggle to understand what a dance class for very young children looks like, so opening up our classrooms invites families to see how dances are made and allows them to observe students and teachers in action. On visiting day, we asked the parents to move with us as we did the following:

- Parents with us in the circle—name and one movement
- Polar bear poem ("Bear in There" by Shel Silverstein)
- Parents sit down and we show—"1 through 8" exercise and hopping rhyme
- We show our sunflower dance
- We share our class dance—each student contributed one part to the dance
- To end, we skip, freeze, applause, and finally skip across the room

During these open sessions, the audience got to dance with us—feeling in their own bodies what the students have been exploring; and seeing several short dances—witnessing first hand how verbal prompts can lead to improvisations. They also viewed the class dance we made with every student contributing a movement and naming it, which helped them understand vocabulary development, lists of words as memory devices, and creative opportunities in the class for each student's unique voice.

CONCLUSION: PAIRING LITERACY AND MOVEMENT IN DANCE CLASSES

Described above, is the look, sound and feel of my creative dance classes for young children. If you are a teacher of young children, I imagine that your classes are already rich in subject matter language and vocabulary. It is my hope that the above descriptions might encourage you to invite dance teaching artists into your classrooms and explore your own ways of integrating dance, language, and literacy across subject areas. The concepts described here can help you extend the work you are already doing by offering young people multiple, multimodal ways of experiencing language, literacy, and movement—some of the most important resources they will utilize throughout their lives.

In returning to the question, "why dance?" as posed in the *Standards for Dance in Early Childhood* (Faber, 2002, p. 2), it is important to remember that, "Preschool children do not conceptualize abstract processes. They primarily learn through physical and sensory experiences. Learning the art of dance helps young children develop knowledge, skill, and understanding about the world." If we indeed care about education, especially *early childhood* language and literacy education, then it is imperative to include movement that invites them to *experience* the joy and magic of language in many rich and varied ways. Integrating multimodal literacies into dance and movement classes is a powerful and enjoyable way to support young people's early cultivation of lifelong literate, artistic and social sensibilities.

Appendix A: Organizations Referenced

National Dance Education Organization (NDEO)
Bethesda, Maryland
www.ndeo.org
(301) 585–2880

Lincoln Center Institute for the Arts in Education
New York, New York
www.lcinstitute.org
(210) 875–5535

Virginia Tanner Creative Dance Program
Salt Lake City, Utah
www.tannerdance.utah.edu/
(801) 581–7374

Luna Dance Institute (formerly Luna Kids Dance)
Emeryville, California
www.lunadanceinstitute.org
(510) 644–3629

University of Utah
Department of Modern Dance
Salt Lake City, Utah
http://www.dance.utah.edu/
(801) 581–7327

University of Utah
Service-Learning Scholars Program
Salt Lake City, Utah
http://bennioncenter.org/serviceLearning/servlearn_scholars.htm
(801) 581–4811

Notes

1. The Dancing Words blog can be found at www.dancingwords.typepad.com.
2. Contact information for organizations referenced in the chapter are listed in the appendix.
3. In *Proust and the squid: The story and science of the reading brain* (2007) author Maryanne Wolf refers to the work of scientist Susan Carey of Harvard, sharing that "most children between two and five years old are learning on average between two and four new words every day, and thousands of words over these early years" (p. 84).
4. See "Dance Concepts—The Elements of Dance" (p. 5) in Anne Green Gilbert's book *Creative dance for all ages* (1992) for a succinct chart of the early childhood dance vocabulary.
5. The seed of this activity came from watching Mary Ann Lee teach at Lincoln Elementary in Salt Lake City, Utah in 1997.
6. The work of Lee, Bossieux, and Kogan cited here is based on observations of their teaching and participation in their workshops.

Works Cited

Armstrong, T. (2003). *The multiple intelligences of reading and writing: Making words come alive.* Alexandria, VA: Association for Supervision and Curriculum Development.

Blecher, S., & Jaffee, K. (1998). *Weaving in the arts: Widening the circle.* Portsmouth, NH: Heinemann.

Burnaford, G., Brown, S., Doherty, J., & McLaughlin, H. J. (2007). *Arts integration frameworks, research, & practice: A literature review.* Washington, DC: Arts Education Partnership.

Dillon, L., & Dillon, D. (2007). *Mother Goose numbers on the loose.* Orlando, FL: Harcourt.

Faber, R. (Ed.). (2002). *Standards for dance in early childhood.* Bethesda, MD: National Dance Education Organization.

Green Gilbert, A. (1992). *Creative dance for all ages: A conceptual approach.* Reston, VA: American Alliance for Health, Physical Education, Recreation, and Dance.

Greene, M. (1995). *Releasing the imagination: Essays on education, the arts, and social change.* San Francisco, CA: Jossey-Bass Publishers.

Greene, M. (2001). *Variations on a blue guitar: The Lincoln Center Institute lectures on aesthetic education.* New York: Teachers College Press.

Griss, S. (1998). *Minds in motion.* Portsmouth, NH: Heinemann.

Hoffman Davis, J. (2005). *Framing education as art: The octopus has a good day.* New York: Teachers College Press.

Kogan, S. (2004). *Step by step: A complete movement education curriculum.* Champaign, IL: Human Kinetics.

Lee, M.A., Cannon A., Wilson, J.U., Smith, L., Ririe, S.R., & Woodbury, J. (1996). *Move! Learn! Dance!* Salt Lake City, UT: Children's Dance Theatre.

Lincoln Center Institute. (2006). *Entering the world of work and art.* New York: Lincoln Center Institute.

Long, J.R. (2008). How to choose a goose. *Horn Book Magazine, January/February,* 49–57.

National Association for the Education of Young Children. (1998). *Learning to read and write: Developmentally appropriate practices for young children.* Washington, DC: National Association for the Education of Young Children.

O'Malley, E. (Ed.). (2004). *Visual and performing arts framework for California public schools: Kindergarten through grade twelve.* Sacramento: California Department of Education.

Opie, I. (1996). *My very first Mother Goose.* Cambridge, MA: Candlewick Press.

Randall, J. Moving through the alphabet: Learning letters through creative dance. Unpublished manuscript.

Reedy, P. (2003). *Body, mind, and spirit in action: A teacher's guide to creative dance.* Berkeley, CA: Luna Kids Dance.

Reitzes, F., & Teitelman, B. (1997). *Wonderplay, too!* Philadelphia, PA: Running Press.

Reitzes, F., Teitelman, B., & Mark, L. A. (1995). *Wonderplay.* Philadelphia, PA: Running Press.

San Francisco Public Library. (2009). *My little rhyme book.* San Francisco, CA: San Francisco Public Library.

San Francisco Public Library's Early Literacy Initiative. (n.d.). *Sharing rhymes: Every day encourages literacy play!.* San Francisco, CA: San Francisco Public Library.

Schickedanz, J. A. (1999). *Much more than the ABCs: The early stages of reading and writing.* Washington, DC: National Association for the Education of Young Children.

Stinson, S. (1993). *Dance for young children: Finding the magic in movement.* Reston, VA: National Dance Association.

The Task Force on Children's Learning and the Arts: Birth to Age Eight & Goldhawk, S. (1998). *Young children and the arts: Making creative connections.* Washington, DC: Arts Education Partnership.

Wolf, M. (2007). *Proust and the squid: The story and science of the reading brain.* New York: Harper Perennial.

CHAPTER TEN

The Paramparic Body

Gestural Transmission in Indian Music [1]

MATT RAHAIM

I am singing at a house concert in California. It is my first performance away from my teacher, and I try to sing as he has taught me. I deliberately choose music that we spent many months working on. Even as I improvise novel melodic material, I recall his repeated admonitions about proper singing: each chunk of melodic action should be well-knit as though it were carefully composed ahead of time; the voice should be clear and open; melodic development should be gradual and methodical. Restraining myself from dashing forward into rapid melodic flights, I will myself to relax my shoulders, take deep breaths, and dwell in a medium-tempo melodic flow, even past the point where my attention wanders. Even when I make a mistake and want to hide my voice behind closed vowels, I remember his relaxed, open voice. All of these small pieces of advice during my training were brought together in a single discipline by my teacher's presence. Singing far away from him, I sometimes recall them one by one; it's easier, however, to simply remember his presence.

One of the guests, a longtime student of Hindustani music, approaches me after I finish. "You sing differently now," she says. I ask her what she means. "You never used to do this," she says, looking at her hands, tracing interlocking ellipses with her open palms. The motion of her body calls my teacher to mind: his open voice; his buoyant, curving melodic flow; his focused gaze. Though she has never seen him, and though I have fallen far short of his ideal tonight, she has caught his presence in the music.

I started attending to how singers move when I began studying Hindustani vocal music with Vikas Kashalkar in Pune in 2000. I noticed that when my teacher was spontaneously improvising melody, his way of moving took on a rather different quality from his way of moving while walking, speaking, or riding a bus. From our earliest lessons, he moved his hands extensively to indicate the shape, structure, and texture of improvised melodic passages. I found that I could make better sense of these passages if I imitated not only what he sang, but how he moved as well. Often I would struggle to piece notes together into melodic phrases while sitting still with my eyes closed in concentration, but when I opened my eyes and moved my hands as I sang, melody sprang to life in the space before me. As I attended more and more concerts, I was surprised to find that my teacher was not alone in moving while improvising. Indeed, every Hindustani vocalist does.[2] Over time, it became clear to me that, just as in extemporaneous speech (McNeill, 1992; Kendon, 2004), in singing, gesture and the voice work together to embody novel ideas.

However, this musical gesture does not amount to a sign language or a systematic code for notes. Singers do not, in other words, place their hands in front of the chest to sing C-sharp, or raise one fist above the head for E-natural, etc. Just as gestures accompany speech without replicating the meaning of every word, the bodily action of musicians complements vocal action without duplicating it, projecting melody into space as dynamic motion: as swooping, looping, and curling; as tension and release; as virtual objects that are sculpted, manipulated, and, eventually, discarded. Unlike the elaborate systems of postures and handshapes mastered by Indian dancers, gesture in Hindustani music is not taught explicitly, deliberately rehearsed, or linked to specific lexical meanings. Melodic gesture embodies a special kind of musical knowledge, transmitted silently from body to body alongside the voice: it is knowledge of melody as motion.

Individual vocalists differ markedly in their gestural, postural, and vocal dispositions. Indeed, a common game among young Hindustani vocalists is to imitate the gestural-postural-vocal disposition of another singer—it is easy to guess who is being channeled within seconds. And yet singers musically resemble their own teachers in ways that are noticeable even to untrained observers (as the anecdote introducing this chapter suggests). Teachers, in turn, were once students; they spent hundreds of hours in front of their own teachers struggling to learn music. The word *parampara* is often used to refer to these chains of transmission. The adjectival form, paramparic, is commonly used to refer to compositions and musical techniques passed down in these lineages with no single recognizable author. In this chapter, the paramparic body is used as a way to address embodied musical dispositions that are passed down through generations of teachers and students with no single recognizable author.

Let us consider one such easily discernible paramparic vocal-gestural pattern. This pattern consists of rotating both hands in a circular trajectory, coordinated tightly with the turns of the vocal melody. Figure 1 shows eminent vocalist Ulhas Kashalkar and two of his longtime students, Omkar Dadarkar and Hrishikesh Gangurde, performing this gestural pattern.

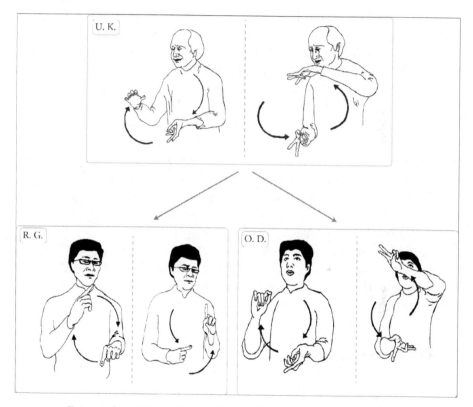

Figure 1. Shared Vocal-Gestural Form: Ulhas Kashalkar (teacher) at top, Rishikesh Gangurde and Omkar Dadarkar (students) at bottom.

This vocal-gestural technique is linked to a specific context of melodic texture and function. The wheeling pattern shown above, among Kashalkar's students, articulates intricate zigzagging melodic motion marked by rapid changes in direction, in which syncopated rhythmic accents dance between strong beats. Note also that each vocalist has a slightly different articulation of this pattern: Gangurde's gestures tend to be smaller than Kashalkar's or Dadarkar's; Dadarkar's gaze, in general, tends to be higher than Gangurde's or Kashalkar's. Despite these differences, teacher and students share a distinctive and recognizable form. Many such shared gestural-vocal routines are obvious to connoisseurs. Students of Jitendra Abhisheki, for example, often combine a precise manual and vocal grip on a note with a characteristic, precise grip of the rings of muscle around the eyes (the orbicularis palpebrarum). Another pattern specific to Jitendra Abhisheki's teaching lineage is a spread-fingered open hand, kept virtually stationary, during rapid, extended vocal phrases on single vowels. There are many possible specific articulations of this gestural-vocal mode. Whereas Jitendra Abhisheki tended to have a very tense handshape, with the fingers spread to their maximum extent, all of his students have looser handshapes. Some use both hands in this situation. But in all of these cases there is a salient kinetic gestalt perceivable in which the steady, seamless texture of the taan is matched by a relatively steady hand and a spread-fingered handshape.

These are neither vocal techniques in the exclusive service of sound nor bad habits that inhibit voice production. As gesture analyst David McNeill stresses, these kinds of gestural performances are "not only expressions of thought, but thought, i.e., cognitive being, itself" (McNeill, 2005, p. 99). This "being," as embodied in gesture, voice, and posture is not an isolated, private world; it is also a social existence, developed in rigorous training and practice. The body of a singer is always already imbedded in social relations, even before its first music lesson. As we will see, they are seldom a matter of deliberate imitation, and, like all gestural forms, are seldom addressed in words. And yet they serve as vehicles for musical values that are transmitted through generations of teachers and students.

TEACHING LINEAGES

Whether performing in a crowded auditorium or practicing alone in a room for many hours, the body of a Hindustani vocalist is always already social; it bears the imprint of training. Gestural and vocal motions are highly disciplined, refined techniques that are nurtured through years of sitting in front of a teacher and extended daily practice. Anthropologist Dard Neuman (2004) aptly describes the great social importance of teaching lineages in modern Hindustani music:

> [O]ne would be hard pressed to consider the world of Hindustani classical music without thinking in turn about musical lineage. Whenever a musician introduces himself, or is introduced to others, he almost always marks his identity through his teacher and the gharana (musical house or lineage) to which they both belong…. [The individual musician] therefore emerges as both a person and a figure, as both an artist to whom we ascribe particular musical features and as a figure bearing the signs of a musical tradition. (pp. 40–41)

Ordinarily, a student encounters traditional, lineage-based musical disciplines through an intensive teacher-student relationship. Such a relationship is often referred to as guru-shishya parampara. This is especially true when the student is not actually a blood relative of the teacher. In the strictest form of this relationship, the guru and shishya are ritually bound to one another as virtual parent and child. This relationship, however, is not simply a means of learning musical techniques or repertoire; a musical ancestry, as noted above, is an important part of a musician's identity. The structure of authority in these musical lineages is similar to other traditions (such as Bhakti sampradayas or Sufi silsilas) that trace their present-day spiritual authority to an originary saint and are overseen by a living torchbearer (known as a khalifa). Though these spiritual and musical lineages very seldom overlap, many musicians trace their musical origins to a great founding figure who often is seen as an accomplished spiritual leader as well—for example Swami Haridas, Gopal Naik, or Amir Khusro. Whether or not these origin narratives are supported by historical evidence, the teaching passed down over the centuries in this way is typically understood to contain esoteric knowledge not available to those outside of the direct lineage. A chain of these relationships, reaching from the past to the present, is called a parampara.

The details of the relationship between teacher and student vary widely from one situation to another. Some call their teachers "guru," others "ustad." Many teachers expect some traditional observances from their students, such as initiatory rites, ritual payment, yearly celebrations at Guru Purnima, or household service such as making tea, doing laundry, and fixing the computer. In return, some teachers house and feed their students, most spend long hours teaching, and nearly all offer instruction that goes beyond repertoire and technique. Nonetheless, the heart of this relationship consists of sitting face to face as the student attempts to reproduce the teacher's phrases in turn. As written notation is seldom used, teacher and student spend hundreds of hours sitting face to face over the course of many years, attending closely to each other. In addition to helping students develop their bodies as memory and learning tools, this extensive one on one experience fosters a close bond sustained by a great deal of time spent together outside of formal lessons. A student's training, however, often also features philosophical discourse, whispered commentary at concerts, corrections from the next room while the student is practicing, and advice regarding elocution, dress, and manners. Other teachers fulfill a role closer to that of a tutor offering private lessons, meeting a student only a few times a month, and accepting an hourly fee.

These teaching practices are shaped by a body of folklore about individual teachers and students, often featuring tales of intense mutual devotion, great sacrifice, and long periods of grueling, non-musical service at the beginning of a discipleship during which no explicit musical instruction takes place. This corpus of folklore serves to reinforce for students the necessity, sanctity and authority of a close bond between teacher and student. It also discursively links the teaching process to ethical values such as faith and humility (Deo, 2011). At the end of this chapter, I will return to the interplay of ethics and aesthetics in the transmission of bodily dispositions. First, though, let us return to our original question: how do students come to move like their teachers when they sing?

Processes of Gestural Transmission

Teachers move their hands vividly in lessons to indicate phrasing, melodic shape, weight, and tension. Although most teachers give copious explicit advice about vocalization, they almost never tell their students how to move. Students learn by singing what the teacher sings, and though the teacher will make a correction in the case of a vocal mistake, the student is generally free to gesture as he or she likes. Although there is often evident (and generally unintentional) gestural mirroring in lessons, the gestures reproduced by students are not replicas of the teacher's. As Mukul Kulkarni puts it, the student is not to replicate the teacher's movements himself but the nuances of lagao, or melodic rendering, of which voice and movement are both vehicles:

> It is not a copy of his actions....He is singing himself, and by gestures, he is also telling that this is the way it should go....Of course it is not intended that you learn from the gestures, but you learn it indirectly....You learn that {sings/gestures Gaud Sarang phrase} is the way you should sing in Gaud Sarang. So your hand also starts making the same design. (personal communication)

Even when the student's gestures resemble those of the teacher, they are often smaller and less overt. Figure 2 shows an example: first Vikas Kashalkar's vocal-gestural rendition of a phrase, followed by Pavan Naik's similar, but somewhat more restrained, rendition of the same phrase a moment later.

In the few cases in which I've seen a teacher give explicit instruction about gesture, a student is simply told to do less of it. Teachers will often chastise their students for making faces or showing visible strain (see Scott, 1997, pp. 456–458). Otherwise, the methods of gestural transmission are oblique; information about melodic motion is foregrounded, a demonstration of a particular melodic nuance is given gestural expression, or a teacher deliberately and clearly traces out a shape in the air as a means of teaching. Once I even saw a teacher shake a student by the shoulders to get them to produce deep vocal oscillations that the student was then able to sing even while holding still. But in none of these cases are teachers telling students how to move.

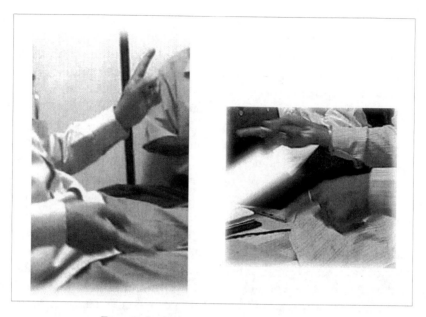

Figure 2. Student reproducing teacher's gesture.

Similarities in gestural performance seem to arise indirectly through a shared understanding of disciplines of melodic motion, of which physical motion is only a part. This, in itself, is not so unusual: speech gesture dialects (for example, the varying gestural traditions of Naples and Northamptonshire described in Kendon, 2004, p. 328) are also transmitted without explicit instruction or straightforward imitation. Sometimes in the course of a lesson, a student will be unable to reproduce a phrase sung by the teacher; the teacher then repeats the sonic content of the phrase for the student using slightly different gestures to model an aspect of melody that the student does not yet perceive. The teacher may also accentuate similarities and differences between different phrases by placing them in contrasting locations in space. The teacher repeatedly provides the same sonic content but uses space to suggest various alternate ways of conceiving the music. These are among the most intense moments in the course of a lesson because they require a student to unlearn a habitual way of conceiving of a melodic fragment, and to reconceive it according to the teacher's demonstration. Even if a student has the sequence of notes right, the particular way of shaping these notes into a phrase may be mistaken and therefore corrected through gestural demonstration.

On one occasion, a fellow student of my teacher told me that he could show the types of taan patterns we had been taught in a series of gestures. He demonstrated them to me systematically: a pattern with varying stresses {such as 12222,

2333, 344, 455} was performed with the hands facing each other loosely, with a twist of the wrists at each point of rhythmic stresses; a zigzagging pattern {such as 132435465} was performed with open palms tracing interlocking loops. Although this gestural taxonomy did not, in fact, account exhaustively for our teacher's gestural repertoire, the power of our shared gestural discipline became clear to me when we were practicing together, and he urged me on through improvisation by making these melodic shapes with his hands. As I was preparing for each taan in turn, he would indicate one of these patterns with his hands, and I clearly understood what to sing. These gestures do not formally or explicitly represent notes as much as letters indicate sounds. In the context of the shared melodic discipline in which we had been trained, these gestural cues clearly implied melodic shapes that I was able to trace vocally and gesturally at will. Gesture analyst David McNeill (2005) calls the sympathy embodied in this shared space of gestural potential the "joint inhabitance of the same state of cognitive being" (p. 159). But inhabiting this shared cognitive state is also inhabiting a shared kinetic discipline—like passing a soccer ball to a teammate who, after months of playing together, can anticipate exactly where and how the ball will come. How did we both end up with this shared melodic-kinetic discipline? How could a singer learn such complex bodily-vocal dispositions without deliberate imitation?

There is ample empirical evidence to show that the apparent contagion of posture, gesture, and subtle facial expression (and their affiliated affective states) can occur without any conscious effort on the part of the recipient (Hatfield et al., 1994; Brennan, 2004; Tamietto & de Gelder, 2009). More importantly, it is easy to apprehend observed motion directly as purposive action. It is quite ordinary, for example, for a student to understand that a teacher is tracing a melodic loop (rather than merely moving her hand in the air) or gripping a note (rather than merely moving her fingers into a bunch). This "action understanding"—the empathetic apprehension of the purpose of another's action as though it were one's own—constitutes rather a different kind of knowing than merely observing the others' hand moving in objective space (Thioux et al., 2008). A tantalizing neurological explanation to account for the link between observation, imitation, and understanding rests on the discovery of "mirror neurons" in macaque monkeys (Rizzolatti & Craighero, 2004; Gazzola & Keysers, 2009). Mirror neurons seem to behave like both motor and sensory neurons, firing in the same way both when an action is observed and when the action is executed. (See discussion of mirror neurons in Kroll's chapter, and the Introduction to this volume.) More specifically, most mirror neuron activity appears to correlate not with the observation of a precise sequence of behaviors (e.g., pinching three fingers together, raising the hand, and then inverting it), but with the observation of intentional actions, with clear goals—e.g., picking up an object and turning it over (Thioux et al., 2008). Mirror neuron activity has been widely celebrated as a likely neural basis for action understanding though there is good reason to remain skeptical that it will account for all intersubjective motor activity (see Hicock, 2009). In any case, learning an action by identifying with the person one is observing seems to be a fundamental capability that underlies face-to-face learning. Michael Tomasello (1993) points out that the ability "to see a situation the way the other sees it…in which the learner is attempting to learn not from another, but through another" seems to be available to most children even before their first birthday (p. 496).

INHERITANCE AND VOLITION

Unintentional musical continuity within a teaching lineage would seem, at first, to suggest an analogy with inheritance (Mukherjee, 1989, p. 5; Neuman, 1990, p. 58; Roy, 2004, p. 12; Qureshi, 2007). For a singer, a musical lineage, reinforced by training and practice, serves both as a way of narrating the past and as an always-available musical discipline in the present.

Although the absorption of individual gestures is mostly unconscious, students are also selective about whose dispositions they absorb. Hindustani vocal students do not go around haphazardly absorbing whatever they see. As Mukul Kulkarni puts it, when "the disciple starts moving hands as his guru," it is a result of "the devotion he has put into learning." The ambiguity in Mukul's phrasing here strongly accords with Tomasello's model of action understanding: moving hands "as the guru" implies both an observed likeness and a process of identity. A close affective connection between teacher and student thus seems to be crucial. Sameer Dublay emphasizes that the full reception of Jitendra Abhisheki's gestural knowledge was possible only within the context of a dedicated, long-term guru-shishya relationship:

> You only know these gestures if you live with him.…For the sake of gesture, if you see this [demonstrates gesture] it might not convey anything. But for us who were learning from him, it immediately brought to mind the exact position of koman rishabh and helped us to reach that level. Now this interpretation is something which you know if you stay with that person. (personal communication)

Young singers are generally expected to commit to the vocal discipline of a singer teacher for many years before developing an individual style. Vocalist Arun Kashalkar describes this process by analogy with developing a handwriting style: everybody's handwriting is different, but in learning to write, a child must commit to a single method of writing each letter and do it a thousand times. Once you follow a discipline for some time, he said, "a light comes to you....Then, the whole world looks different, and you have no interest in other [singers]" (personal communication).

Inasmuch as face-to-face learning is a capacity for encountering music through the body and voice of a beloved teacher rather than a process of passive absorption, the analogy with inheritance starts to break down. In addition to the mere fact of having a teacher and even the sheer length of time that teacher and student spend together, the mutual devotion that bonds the two together seems to be crucial in the embodied transmission of music. Mohan Darekar emphasizes that this respect for the guru is a necessary foundation for adopting his bodily disposition:

> You pick up a person's gesture and posture if you like them....That impression, which you like, you start doing that. If you go under that impression, naturally you will do it....If you like this person, then you naturally pick up these things, not purposefully. And because of that, you learn more. (personal communication)

The relationship between teacher and student is marked through various bodily disciplines. As students approach their guru for a lesson, it is conventional for each to bend down and ritually touch their teacher's feet before beginning. While students may sit casually in chairs along with their teacher, it is generally considered rude to sit on a chair while the teacher sits on the floor. Many musicians keep a small photo of their guru with them while touring; in some cases, a musician will set up a small shrine to a guru centered around a photograph. Homes of musicians often feature at least one framed photograph of their teacher, sometimes marked reverentially with saffron powder or draped with garlands as if it were a photo of a spiritual teacher or a beloved divinity.

These practices and rituals reveal that intense devotion to a teacher is a matter of both intentional commitment and spontaneous affection. A fulsome understanding of the dynamics of musical transmission, likewise, must consider volition as well as inheritance. In most narratives of musical greatness, merely inheriting a style is insufficient. In addition to the deliberate, often heroic devotion to a teacher, a serious musician must, after years of training, become distinct from their teacher (see Napier, 2006).

Only after years of work, once a student has mastered a certain basic musical discipline and become ready to perform, may she freely borrow features from other lineages, as well, or try something new. As Arun Kashalkar put it:

> I keep myself away from the exact singing of my gurus. I always want something of my own. Nowhere you can just tell me that I am just imitating a particular person. I do remember my gurus while singing, no doubt about it....But finally, I will just attach them with my own things, and try to find out a different vista. (personal communication)

Nor is this predilection for a different vista merely a personal preference. It is echoed by other singers as necessary for the development of one's own skills. According to Sameer Dublay, Jitendra Abhisheki was clear in his insistence that his students sing in their own way:

> Completely blind following takes you nowhere. The students with whom I learned…we have our individual singing styles, with predominantly Abhisheki effect in it. We all have our individualities intact. No one sings like one another. We are students of the same guru, but having distinct identities of our own. He used to shout at us! "Don't sing like me. Sing in your own voice!" That has helped us. Each one of us has his own style, his own way of presentation, with distinct elements of Abhisheki in each one of us. (personal communication)

This variety within the discipline, as we might now expect, extends to gestural-vocal practice. Recall the variety of spread-fingered taan handshapes among Jitendra Abhisheki's students and the differences in the way that Ulhas Kashalkar's students performed the "wheeling" gestural routine that accompanies zig-zagging, syncopated melodic action. Just as students may incarnate a particular gestural-vocal feature differently, each student of a given teacher pieces together a unique gestural repertoire from their teacher. For example, Jitendra Abhisheki passed on several gestural-vocal forms, each of which, as far as I can determine, were only picked up by a single student. The first is a moving palms-together form affiliated with delicate slides, which seems to have been only adopted by his son, Shaunak Abhisheki. The second is an idiosyncratic "cupped" grip form for sustained notes with precise intonation.

Gestural repertoires are not passed on in a wholesale, deterministic fashion but appear in various combinations in different students, as suited to their own musical sensibilities. Sameer Dublay notes that this was a special feature of Jitendra Abhisheki's style:

> Abhishekiji's whole being was a message of this pluralist approach. His entire learning process was plural. He learned from different sources…and created his own source. And again, dissemination of information was…person-based. He gave me something which he didn't give to Hemant, he didn't give to Shaunak. He gave something to Shaunak that he didn't give to anyone else. (personal communication)

Mohan Darekar recalls Jitendra Abhisheki saying to him: "Do not think 'this is from this singer or that gharana and I am imitating this style or using that pattern.' Whatever you have got, is yours, and how you combine or merge these building blocks…how you want to sing, you decide and experience the result as one wholeness that is yours.…Your skill decides which elements to choose and how to link them" (Darekar, 2004, pp. 125–126).

Many singers in the twentieth century have learned from more than one teacher, piecing together a way of singing out of the styles of their teachers. Mohan Darekar, though he has studied with both Jitendra Abhisheki and Vikas Kashalkar, has little gesturally in common with the latter. Indeed, he acknowledges the much deeper influence of Jitendra Abhisheki on his singing, as he came to him as a boy and stayed with him for many years, while he approached Kashalkar late in life, as a mature singer, for advice and guidance. These were two different kinds of relationships. Whereas Kashalkar is his "guide," Abhisheki is his guru. Darekar goes on to cite many other influences, of varying importance: he grew up listening to Amir Khan, Bade Ghulam Ali Khan, and Pandit Jasraj; he studied dhrupad (a rather different vocal genre) with Said-ud-din Dagar for many years; he studies the recordings of Ghulam Mustafa Khan for inspiration in taan patterns. In the last five years, he has undergone formal, intensive training with Rajan and Sajan Misra. Darekar describes the relationship of these elements:

> Imitation is very important at the beginning. After that, mixture of the other things, your Guruji's style, things you learn from others, and your own expressions, blending together, a mixture....You have to determine: "how much I can do, what is suitable for me." Otherwise...nobody can help you. Inside you should realize yourself; you should know your personality. (personal communication)

Nor is Darekar unusual in this respect—exposure to a wide range of teachers and recordings has largely become the norm. In the middle of his training, Vikas Kashalkar told Gajanan Rao Joshi that he had come to admire Bhimsen Joshi's singing from listening to recordings. His guru's response was instructive:

> "OK, fine. If you like, you adopt [Bhimsen Joshi's] singing...whatever you like, you can do. But if you want to enrich your singing, you could add the good portion from his singing, and have our [style], too."...This type of leading student on his own path is the best method....So whenever my student Mukul [Kulkarni] sings like me, I get upset. Don't imitate my voice; don't imitate my singing. You take the ideas, and add your own. Nobody should say he is a replica....(Vikas Kashalkar, Interview with Ingrid Le Gargasson, 2008)

A few weeks later, in a lesson, Kashalkar chided Mukul for just this kind of "replication." In singing a note with very delicate intonation, he held the back of his hand up to his mouth to hear his own voice better—an idiosyncrasy of Kashalkar's that both he and Mukul have pointed out to me. Teacher and student burst into laughter, and Mukul dropped his hand and resumed singing.

The problems with mechanically imitating one's teacher are most evident in accounts of students who unthinkingly assimilate their teacher's obvious shortcomings: vocal defects, postural idiosyncrasies, etc. Stories of these serve, in musical folklore, as warnings to young students about blind mimicry (Deshpande, 1973 p. 19). But apart from these obvious defects, students also must make decisions about musical discipline that, while not simply undesirable, may be inappropriate for them as individual singers. Pavan Naik, a student of Vikas Kashalkar, reports that the instruction to find his own path was quite explicitly linked to a difference in body:

> Guruji says . . ."don't forget yourself. Main thing is your identity." Because by birth I have a different body. "Don't follow blindly." Guruji always says that. First naql [imitation] then aql [intelligence]…khuda ko pahechana [recognize yourself.]…Guruji is ready to give me all things, but some of them are not suitable for me.…You have to know yourself. What is Pavan Naik, then Guruji's own style, then in between that, you have to follow the things which suit you.…My pinda [body] is different [from Guruji's].…If you don't want something, then you don't take. You have to take only good things.

The assertion that his pinda (body) is different from his guru's may seem trivial but taken in a musical context in which the student is expected to embody the guru's music, it is actually quite significant. This transmission is not merely a matter of putting on the guru's body like a ready-made suit or simply wishing one's way into an arbitrary singing style; even under the most liberal circumstances, a young singer has only a handful of teachers available for intensive training. This is especially the case within hereditary musical families, in which students may be prohibited in principle from learning from, or even listening to, musicians from different lineages. The extensive training required for the disciplining of a paramparic body takes years. Some great singers have attended music schools, and some have not, but no great singers have done without this intensive period of training with a model teacher. A serious student must develop a disposition suitable for his/her own predisposition out of the limited set of materials given in their training with various teachers.

THE PARAMPARIC BODY

The transmission of musical knowledge from teacher to student, as we have seen, spans the whole volitional spectrum from passive, unconscious absorption of habits to active choices. In the case of Hindustani music training, the stances most readily available to a student are those cultivated by their guru and their fellow students. This dialectic between inheritance and choice within a tight-knit family is captured well by what Katherine Young (2002) calls the "family body":

> . . . [B]odies are passed down in families, not as assemblages of biological traits enjoined on the bodies of children by parents but as intentional fabrications devised by children out of the bodies of parents.…Within families, memory is passed down, not only as oral lore or

material artifacts but also as something that is neither mentifact nor artifact: corporeal dispositions.... Family bodies, like family stories, provide their heirs positions, situated perspectives, on parents' ways of being in the world, out of which children can devise their own
'presentations of self.' (pp. 25–26)

In Young's work, the formation of a family body is seldom fully conscious or
easily articulated in words. Like adapting a guru's disposition to one's own, this
process is both conscious and unconscious, both conservative and innovative. Most
importantly, the process of transmission she describes has not so much to do with
mimicking behaviors as it does with adopting "situated perspectives": stances,
modes of action understanding. To adapt this term to Hindustani music, I use the
term paramparic body to refer to any one of the many gestural-postural-vocal dispositions incarnated by a singer, seen from the point of view of its transmission
through teaching lineages.

ETHICAL PRACTICE AND THE PARAMPARIC BODY

The great variety of paramparic bodies—and thus, the great variety of ways of musically being—may lead us to relegate them to the realm of pure aesthetics: of taste,
of arbitrary preference. And yet we have seen that vocal, postural, and gestural dispositions are also described in terms with undeniable ethical valence: humble versus arrogant, devotional versus erotic, open versus concealed. A beloved teacher's way
of musicking is exemplary (and therefore paramparic) not only because it is beautiful or orthodox or ergonomic but also because it is virtuous. A paramparic body
carries both aesthetics and ethics.

Musical performance, of course, is not the only kind of bodily action that
blends the good and the beautiful. "Good posture," for example, serves both as eval-
uation and prescription, spanning kinesiology, aesthetics, and ethics. Pierre Bourdieu
points out that everyday bodily practices such as table manners and walking gaits
are "capable of instilling a whole cosmology, an ethic, a metaphysic, a political philosophy, through injunctions as insignificant as 'stand up straight' or 'don't hold your
knife in your left hand'" (1977, p. 94). Nor is such a cosmology necessarily coercive
or unconscious. Charles Hirschkind points out that pious Egyptian Muslims deliberately cultivate embodied ethical sensibilities by listening to sermon performance
in Egypt. For example, ishirah (the "opening of the heart" that allows God to
remove sins and implant faith) is linked to a specific gestural routine: "opening up
the arms, raising and relaxing the chest, turning the face upward." The ethical
implications of bodily actions such as these, though deliberate, are not explicitly
taught in words; they are "learned with the body, in all of its kinesthetic and synaes-

thetic dimensions" (Hirschkind, 2006, p. 76). The paramparic body, likewise, is ethically disciplined, not at the level of explicit moral reasoning (e.g., deducing a correct course of action from axioms about natural rights) or conventional emotion (e.g., a public expression of disgust at a political scandal), but at the level of affective stances (e.g., humility, calm, openness) that are known and practiced through habits of posture, gesture, and voice. It is in this sense that paramparic bodies are ethical: a student is disciplined not only to perform beautifully but also to perform virtuously.

Depending on the teacher, the particular ethos that is imparted may vary widely, and the values of different traditions are often fiercely at odds. Indeed, debates about the relative merits of two musicians often hinge on ethical values. Consider the disagreement between V.H. Deshpande and Babanrao Haldankar over the merits of the musical lineage known as the Agra gharana. Deshpande writes that the Agra singer "never even for a moment departs from the rigid observance of the rules" and that their founding figures "exaggerated the importance of discipline and order" (1973, p. 42). Haldankar, positioning himself explicitly against Deshpande's view, sees the great power of Agra singers to derive not from rule-bound rigidity but from "total involvement" and boj (i.e., weightiness, dignity), both of which are manifest in a specific technique of voice production, long breaths, and a preference for extended, weighty melodic phrases (2001, pp. 68–73). Here, as in other debates, music criticism is saturated with ethical overtones but is full of contention over the specific values that apply. Nor are revered musical figures necessarily seen as moral guides in day-to-day affairs. Hindustani musical folklore counts both saints and scoundrels among its pantheon of great musicians, and there is no easy translation between gestural-vocal disposition and moral fiber.

One gestural-vocal practice that bears both aesthetic and ethical weight is khula awaz (open voice). Khula awaz is marked both by relative timbral openness (i.e., richness in overtones) and by relative openness of the lips, tongue, and jaw. The most extreme khula sound is produced with a wide-open jaw and lips, with the back of the tongue lying low, out of the way of the voice. A range of vocal positions can be considered khula; however, for example, Amir Khan's voice is sometimes described as antar se khula (open on the inside: with nasal resonance and lowered tongue) but bahar se band (closed on the outside: lips only slightly open). Within the Gajanan Rao Joshi lineage, khula refers to the moderately open vocal configuration that produces an open /a/ vowel, with relaxed lips, tongue, and jaw. This is often contrasted to band awaz (closed voice) or golia awaz (rounded voice); the English term "false voice" is also used, not only for falsetto but also for a weak, constricted, or breathy tone.

Khula itself has a rich set of ethical connotations beyond phonetics; in addition to open, it also can mean clear, direct, uninhibited, and undisguised. The ethical implications of khula awaz seem to derive partially from the physiology of voice production: singing with open voice requires one to keep the path of the voice unobstructed. Raising the back of the tongue or closing the jaw is the vocal equivalent of standing with one's hands in one's pockets: it conceals the upper overtones, softens the voice, and can hide poor intonation; indeed, beginning singers often resort to closing their voice when they are unsure of what they are singing. Khula awaz, on the other hand, is unobstructed and unconcealed; the defects of the voice are plainly audible. Khula awaz is nearly always linked to a hand shape in which the hand is held open, with the fingers extended and the palm exposed.

In the context of Vikas Kashalkar's gurukul, an open voice is connected to a certain open musical disposition as well: musical elaboration should be straightforward, simple, and clear. Although a soft, closed voice is widely accepted in film and pop songs (and this may be part of why it is marked as it is), many devotional and classical singers seem to prefer khula awaz on principle. The voice should not be hidden behind the tongue or the jaw; likewise there is nothing concealed in the hand. Sudokshina Chatterjee, in an interview conducted by Laura Leante, reports that she was told explicitly about this link: "Ustad Bade Ghulam Ali Khan Sahab used to say you have a open sound if you have a open hand. My teacher also says [that] you should open your hand. Then you will have an open sound" (in Fatone et al., 2011).

Mukul Kulkarni reported that this was the most striking change as he began his studies with Vikas Kashalkar: "he worked hard on the opening of my voice, which was not very powerful, not very khula" (personal communication). Hardly a year went by in the first stages of my own training with Kashalkar when he did not show me an open palm to remind me to open my mouth more singing. And in his own time, in his early apprenticeship with Gajanan Rao Joshi, Kashalkar himself had to work hard to open his voice.

Among the most dedicated adherents to this disposition is Pavan Naik, another student of Vikas Kashalkar. This resemblance across generations was not lost on Vikas Kashalkar. In the video clip from which the picture in Figure 3 was taken, he smiled at me immediately afterwards and said "Gajanan Rao Joshi used to sing this way." Figure 3 shows this open-handed, open-mouthed disposition in Gajanan Rao Joshi, in Vikas Kashalkar, and in Pavan.

On one occasion, I was showing Pavan a video of Gajananrao Joshi performing. Joshi had died before Pavan had a chance to meet him, and this was the first time he had seen a video of him. Very soon after the video began, Pavan remarked, "He looks like me here" (pointing to his open jaw), "and here" (pointing to his flat palm). After watching several more minutes of the video of his grand-guru, Pavan looked at me in amazement and said, "I am the next birth of Gajananrao Joshi," moving his hand along with the video. A few minutes later, as the performance gained intensity, Pavan smiled and said, "Yes, it's confirmed, I'm the next birth."

Gajanan Rao Joshi

Vikas Kashalkar

Pavan Naik

Figure 3. Khula Avaz/Khula Hath (Open Voice/Open hand) lineage

It would miss Pavan's point to interpret his claim of being the "next birth" of Gajananrao Joshi as a claim about the literal transmigration of a living soul into a separate material body. (As Pavan was well aware, he was born several years before Joshi died.) The sense in which Gajananrao Joshi has been reborn in Pavan bridges body and soul: the incarnation occurs continuously in the moment of embodied performance. Pavan's recognition of his own gestural disposition in his grand-guru's musicking was akin to that of a person recognizing his smile in a photograph of a distant ancestor.

But to describe this resemblance merely in terms of passive inheritance obscures the role of volition in this process. Pavan has not simply absorbed this body through his teacher—he has also chosen it. Indeed, he has consciously taken it further than his own teacher does. Even in the early stages of performance, he avoids closed vowels and their attendant gripping gestures. He also deliberately chose not to adopt other features of his teacher's paramparic body. For example, inspired by his drama training, he has chosen an unusually upright orientation of his torso while performing and makes a point of making eye contact with the audience from the beginning. Furthermore, he reports that his original training in khula awaz occurred very early in life, when his teacher repeatedly cautioned him not to sing with closed vowels, like "a girl singing." Kashalkarji, while nurturing this open voice, cautioned him to sing gently as well. This training was specialized for Pavan, though, based on the body he brought to his early training. Different bodies require different discipline. For example, Mukul Kulkarni, in talking about his early training, reports that Kashalkar had to work to get him to sing with more power, as "this gayaki requires a very powerful, very open voice." Mukul and Pavan are visibly in the same musical lineage: they both make wide use of khula awaz, clear phrasing, similar taan shapes, and open-handed, flowing gestures. But the processes by which they arrived at their particular paramparic bodies, owing to their rather different prior training and tendencies, are rather different, and even opposite in some ways.

Through discipline and devoted attention, through vocalization, posture, and gesture, singers incarnate lineages of embodied musicking through their paramparic bodies. Although singers show a striking gestural resemblance to their teachers, different students resemble their teachers in different but musically consequential ways. Students learn to construct and inhabit a paramparic body, full of ethical and aesthetic potential, through sustained, devoted attention to their teachers over many years. These bodies are neither blindly inherited nor arbitrarily chosen.

But there is a danger here. Analyzing a paramparic body usefully highlights the social dynamics by which bodies are trained but also threatens to ossify the dynamics of a moving body into a static disposition. To say that the ethos of one generation is inherited mechanically by the next, that the moral life of our forebears is simply and automatically 'in our blood,' is to posit a world of discrete, self-evident cultures that determine the ethos of their constituents. But, as I have tried to demonstrate, the processes of paramparic transmission require students to discern what is to be accepted, what is to be rejected, and from which exemplary sources. As critical theorist and scholar Carrie Noland (2009) eloquently puts it,

> Despite the very real force of social conditioning, subjects continue to invent surprising new ways of altering the inscribed behaviors they are called on to perform. Individual bodies generate 'tactics' that successfully belie the 'durable' body hexis to which they have been subjected, the disciplining that, if we were to follow a long Marxist tradition, should make humans into gesturing machines. (pp. 7–8)

Every singer, though grounded in a tradition, moves and sings differently. Students choose what to accept and what to reject, choose how to constitute their own musicking bodies, choose how to be musically.

Hindustani musicians are not alone in conceiving of melody as movement or in moving as they sing. Nor is India the only place where ethical and bodily traditions are tightly intertwined. The processes by which gestural dialects (and their ethical resonances) are constructed, transmitted, and modified have significance beyond music performance. No body, after all, moves in a vacuum; no body learns to be itself by itself. Every body, whether speaking, singing, or silent, has a parampara.

Notes

1. Some of the material in this chapter has appeared in Fatone et al. (2011) and in the following publications:

Rahaim, M. (2012). *Musicking bodies: Gesture and voice in North Indian music*. Middletown, CT: Wesleyan University Press.

———. (2008). Gesture and Melody in Indian Vocal Music. *Gesture 8*(3): 325–347.

———. 2010. Music. *The Brill Encyclopedia of Hinduism II*: 574–584.

2. For readers unfamiliar with Hindustani vocal music, there are many fine recordings available online at sarangi.info, musicindiaonline.com, and parrikar.org, though many of these performances are truncated due to the constraints of recording. A YouTube search for any of these vocalists will show the range of gestural action I am describing.

Works Cited

Brennan, T. . (2004). *The transmission of affect*. Ithaca, NY: Cornell University Press.

Bourdieu, P. (1977). *Outline of a theory of practice*. New York: Cambridge University Press.

Darekar, M. (2004). *Pandit Jitendra Abhisheki: A life dedicated to music*. Pune: Mudra Press.

Deo, A. (2011). Alternative windows into tradition: Non-hereditary practices in Hindustani Khyal music. PhD Thesis, Indiana University.

Deshpande, V.H. (1973). *Indian musical traditions: An aesthetic study of the Gharanas in Hindustani music*. Bombay: Popular Prakashan.

Fatone, G., Clayton, M., Leante, L., & Rahaim, M. (2011). Imagery, melody, and gesture in cross-cultural perspective. In *New perspectives on music and gesture*. London: Aldershot, UK: Ashgate.

Gazzola, V. & Keysers, C. (2009). The observation and execution of actions share motor and somatosensory voxels in all tested subjects. *Cerebral Cortex, 19*, 1239–1255.

Haldankar, B. (2001). *Aesthetics of Agra and Jaipur traditions*. Pune, India: Popular Prakashan.

Hatfield, E., et al. (1994). *Emotional contagion*. Cambridge, UK: Cambridge University Press.

Hicock, G. (2009). Eight problems for the mirror neuron theory of action understanding in monkeys and humans. *Journal of Cognitive Neuroscience, 21*(7): 1229–1243.

Hirschkind, C. (2006). *The ethical soundscape: Cassette sermons and Islamic counterpublics*. New York: Columbia University Press.

Kendon, A. (2004). *Gesture: Visible action as utterance*. Cambridge, UK: Cambridge University Press.

McNeill, D. (1992). *Hand and mind*. Chicago: University of Chicago Press.

———. (2005). *Gesture and thought*. Chicago: University of Chicago Press.

Mukherjee, B. (1989). *Indian classical music: Changing profiles*. Calcutta: West Bengal State Music Academy

Napier, J. (2006). Novelty that must be subtle: Continuity, innovation, and "improvisation" in north Indian music. *Critical Studies in Improvisation, 1*(3): 1–17.

Neuman, D. (1990). *The life of music in north India*. Chicago: University of Chicago Press.

Neuman, D. (2004). *A house of music: The Hindustani musician and the crafting of traditions*. PhD dissertation, Columbia University, New York.

Noland, Carrie (Ed.). (2009). *Agency and embodiment: Performing gestures/producing culture*. Cambridge, MA: Harvard University Press.

Qureshi, R. B. (2007). *Master musicians of India: Hereditary sarangi players speak*. New York: Routledge.

Rizzolatti, G., & Craighero, L. (2004) The mirror-neuron system. *Annual Review of Neuroscience, 27*, 169–192.

Roy, A. (2004). *Music makers: Living legends of Indian classical music*. New Delhi, India: Rupa & Co.

Scott, S. (1997). *Power and delight: Vocal training in north Indian classical music*. PhD dissertation, Wesleyan University, Middletown, CT.

Tamietto, M., & de Gelder, B. (2009). Emotional contagion for unseen bodily expressions: Evidence from facial EMG. *Proceedings of the FG 2008 meeting*, Amsterdam.

Thioux, M., et al. (2008). Action understanding: How, what and why. *Current Biology, 18*(10), R431–434.

Tomasello, M., et al. (1993). Cultural learning. *Behavioral and Brain Sciences*, (16), 495–552.

Young, K. (2002). The memory of the flesh: The family body in somatic psychology. *Body & Society, 8*(3): 25–47.

CHAPTER ELEVEN

Literacies of Touch

Massage Therapy and the Body Composed

CORY HOLDING & HANNAH BELLWOAR

This can happen only if my hand, which is felt from within, is also accessible from without, itself intangible, for my other hand, for example, if it takes place among the things it touches, is in a sense one of them, opens finally upon a tangible being of which it is also a part. Through this crisscrossing within it of the touching and the tangible, its own movements incorporate themselves into the universe they interrogate, are recorded on the same map as it; the two systems are applied one upon another, as the two halves of an orange.

—MERLEAU-PONTY (2004: 251)

We are such stuff as dreams are made of, but we are also just stuff.

—LEHRER (2007: XII)

BODY WRITING

It seems that we do not often notice our writing bodies until we must. The co-author of this piece, Hannah, for example, became acutely aware of her typing fingers and wrists eleven years ago, just after finishing college. A tightness, she recalls, that came with every mouse click and keystroke was quickly diagnosed as carpal tunnel syndrome. At first, the pain could be alleviated with simple treatment—Ibuprofen, mousing with her left hand. But in graduate school, the sensation became stronger and less easily managed. In order to continue to write, Hannah turned to physical therapy and yoga, which helped only slightly. While writing her dissertation, which, of course, entailed copious note taking, page turning, mouse clicking and typing, Hannah had to buy wrist braces. To sleep at night, she had to have a prescription for muscle relaxers. And more recently, while writing about Bryan—the massage therapist who is the main subject of this chapter—Hannah had to massage her own shoulders, making sure to get up and walk around the room, and regularly stretch in order to keep writing.

As writers and writing researchers, we find troubling the extent to which tactility is left out of descriptions of writing processes. The points of contact that constitute literate activity are overlooked: where skin meets (reads and writes) the physical world, tracing the interface between the composition and sensory activity of composing. We believe, as Haas and Witte (2001) do, that writing is always an embodied practice: "Hence, in labeling writing as an embodied practice, we mean that its recurrent nature, its goal directedness, and its intimate linking with technologies and with knowledge are always enacted in part through bodily and sensory means" (Haas & Witte, p. 416). Haas and Witte call attention early in the essay to the extent to which the body is under-theorized in relation to its integral role in the writing process. It is remarkable, they say, that although the fields of Rhetoric and Composition and Writing Studies have spent years exploring aspects of the composition process, we have yet to address the writing body on its own terms (cf., Sauer, 2002; Emig, 1971; Fleckenstein, 1999). To this end, Haas and Witte explore collaboration over a technical document on engineering standards, exploring how writing is "accomplished by means of the human body"—how it is gestured, moved, and etched into being (p. 415).

Though they do not use the word, the process of writing that Haas & Witte describe is "multimodal." In this chapter we build on their important work to consider multimodal composition at its most visceral: in relation to tissues, bones, and organs, by way of massage therapy. We begin by observing that in ten years, Haas and Witte's call to attend to writing bodies has been largely ignored. Most studies of writing, even those that focus integrally on the writing process—new forms of technology, pedagogical practice, etc.—write the writing body out of the story methodologically and substantively. Although it could be argued that the body is "implied" in such accounts, we suspect that this writing-out is deliberate and reflects discomfort among writing researchers with the legitimacy of the kinaesthetic—what Perl (2004), following Eugene Gendlin, calls the "felt sense" characteristic of writing acts.[1] This erasure also reflects our continuing obsession as researchers and teachers of writing with the verbal and the lingering notion that multimodal composition can still somehow be reduced to words. Some, like Williams (2001b), critique composition's obsession with the word, arguing that writing is multiform as well as multimodal. Although Williams builds his case for teaching composition through a design model, we believe his call focuses too much on the visual and too little on the kinesthetic and tactile.

We would also add that "writing" continues to be defined and prescribed in traditional, pen-to-paper, artifact- and text-centric ways. Although we have not yet developed vocabulary/research methods to capture the body's role in invention and composition, or in reception to texts, our chapter calls attention to tactile aspects of multimodal composition by way of an ethnographic portrait of Bryan, a massage therapist who uses his sense of touch not only to write in the customary sense (to make notes on clients, etc.), but also to perceive, analyze, and subsequently compose the course of the therapy session itself. Through this case study, we argue that there is something multimodal not just in the product of writing—that as teachers, it is not enough to require students to produce multimodal products—but also in the process of writing, and that this is important to attend to both in theory as well as in pedagogy. Like Haas and Witte (2001), Perl (2004) and Prior and Shipka (2003), we wonder what will happen in the field of composition when we move beyond the verbal/visual in our conception of multimodality to structure student projects not just around what the composition will "look like," but around its tactility, what the composition "feels like" not only as it forms but also as it circulates—in essence, how the composition *moves*.

Like Rose (1999), we see the tactile as data. Rose's research participants—physical therapists in training—had to get useful tactile information about their patients' conditions in order to provide the most effective and efficient treatment. Similarly, Bryan sees tactile information as central to his massage practice; in addition to his training and his accumulated experience with the individuals he sees, Bryan must continue to obtain tactile data throughout the course of each session in order to provide the most effective treatment for his clients. He can draw on what his body and his mind already know about massage and about the particular client but that is only part of what makes the massage effective in the moment. He also uses his body, in particular his hands, moving in certain ways to obtain information about the client's muscle tension, and then using that tactile data to cater the massage to the needs of the client. Thus, Bryan's composition is an ever-shifting one. He calls obtaining this data "reading" the bodies of his clients at "the point of contact."

POINT OF CONTACT

This chapter explores the pedagogy of touch. Putting into conversation the case study of Bryan, a massage therapist, with contemporary theorists on sensation

(Serres, 2009; Paterson, 2007; Classen, 2005) and gesture (Noland, 2009; Streeck, 2009; Noland & Ness, 2008) we explore how embodiment, touch and kinesthesia intertwine to comprise learning at the interface of bodies. Specifically, we argue that not only does Bryan read muscles/pain/tightness through touch, but also, in the process of reading it, he simultaneously composes (rewrites) the body as he changes the feeling of muscles through those points and patterns of contact. We take the indivisibility of "reading" and "writing" through touch, and the way that touch interconnects with talk and gesture to exemplify the extent to which literacy learning happens multimodally and should be theorized as well as taught with multimodal dimensions in mind.

To approach this multimodality of literacy learning, we've rooted our research methodology in the transdisciplinary field of Gesture Studies. Our data are comprised of footage from a videotaped 2-hour interview as well as documents from Bryan's training, including his main textbook. Bryan's data are taken from a larger study that examines the multimodal practices of patients and practitioners engaging with documents as a part of healthcare. Bryan participated in a semi-structured discourse-based interview in which he gave a tour of his workspace: touching, moving, and explaining the equipment, the texts, and the uses of his body as he practices massage therapy. In this way, we were able to analyze the gestures Bryan made by focusing on more than those that fit the customary definition of gesture—airborne, impractical, with "manifest, deliberate expressiveness" (Kendon, 2004, p. 15)—i.e., gestures like those described below, which draw upon the client's body in an iconic sense. In addition, we also analyze the gesture that extended to touch: connections between Bryan's hand and his own body, between his hands and tools/equipment in the room and what these connections conjure of his practice that his words may not.

We wish that we could depict this primary source material "in real time"—to the gestures' full extent, from relative beginnings to endings. However, instead, this print medium requires us to rely upon still images and in-text transcriptions/descriptions for "capture," a format borrowed from other studies of gesture in print (e.g., the journal *Gesture*). Ultimately, our analysis suggests that *bodily contact is necessarily compositional*, and that Bryan, through touch, is writing (composing) the body itself. Although touch is integral to any composition practice and represents a control over tools/material, no matter how seemingly invisible (i.e., the pen or the computer), we use the example of massage therapy to underscore the keen intuition of hands and fingers, the body as sense-making tool and resource. As Bryan says, "you can give a massage blindfolded without a problem" because muscles are not visible on the body's surface. Bryan describes not only contact points of massage—collaboration through touch, gesture, and talk with the client, and the learnability of his own hands—but also his training, which required students to move from visualizing parts and connections within another's body to feeling and maneuvering them through touch. This intuition of the hands, he says, is honed through "internalization" and practice.

Below, we track Bryan's gestures and the pedagogy of touch they suggest across three contact zones. The first focuses on Bryan's training, on the transposition of visual information from textbook onto and into Bryan's feeling body. The second renders Bryan's engagement with other bodies by way of touch, lingering especially upon the boundary between what he describes as his "intent" and what the client's body seems to ask for by way of response. The third takes up the rituals Bryan uses to break what he calls the "subtle connection" established with the client's body through the give and take of talk and touch. To conclude, we gloss another site of "body writing" in order to return to the question of what the implications of this research might be for writing classrooms.

MAPPING THE BODY

The interview begins with Bryan's tour of the room. He points out the shelves with books, which line the wall. It is important, he emphasizes, that the space not just look but also sound, smell, and feel "rejuvenating." There is an adjustable light, although he most prefers to conduct sessions in candlelight. A corner shelf holds a music player while the table spans the middle of the room. The tour also previews what emerges as Bryan's reliance upon touch to gather and communicate information from and to the client's body.[2] As Bryan tours the room, he also tours the massage table. Describing how he invites clients to lie in a particular position, Bryan makes with his hands the form of what would be the client's shoulders at the top of the table (see Figure 1). When he says "full bodied," he traces the form of a back over the table, before verbalizing the important opening moments of a session. These first moments play a large role in establishing rapport between client and therapist: "you first warn them, and tell them what you are about to do." You describe where you will place your hand, and how heavily. What Bryan calls "reading the client" ensues tactilely; Bryan's hands establish the spatial location of the body on the table and suggest the direction of his movements. "That's when I put the bolster under their ankles." He makes as though to lift feet and insert the pillow while continuing his procedural description.

Briefly, Bryan summarizes the elements of a typical massage. "And," he uses gestures rather than words for the most part, running his open hands in circles over the imagined area, "the upper back."

Figure 1. Imagining the upper back.

"Then," moving his hands down the table as though to press, he says, "the strip…around the spine," and his hands land with a beat at the table edge, "and then I do one arm, and then the other." His words trail behind his movements.

It becomes evident early in the interview that Bryan requires his gestures and the would-be body on the table in order to explain in a very basic way what it is that he does. In a sense, then, he cannot tell the story without the motions—without, at least, the suggestion of another body that they produce. Part by part, he shapes the invisible client upon the table. He refers to this invisible body while he shares how he learned to navigate between texts and sensation during his education as a massage therapist. The training, he says, centered on honing not only his understanding of human musculature but also his physical sensitivity. His certification included reading textbooks, memorizing anatomy, learning to articulate between pictures in textbooks and the sensation of the same body parts through skin, and, finally, practicing and receiving massage from fellow learners.

Bryan emphasizes that he had to "practice" touch. That is, although textbook study was crucial, the majority of his expertise was accrued extra-textually. Textbooks had always to be used in conjunction with a partner's body, because none of the structures depicted is visible through skin. The exercise, he explains, was to transpose what you saw visually on the page onto your partner's body through your fingers. Describing this process, he holds a favorite textbook—one he likes because it is "specifically designed for massage therapists to *feel* muscles." The book is open on his knee, the cover held with his left hand. With his right hand, he elaborates how his partner would lie supine while Bryan tactilely searched for particular muscles on his partner's body. For example, he explains, "Working with a partner…find" (reads from textbook) "*rectus abdominis.*" He repeats the name, appearing to consider where he would find these muscles on his partner or perhaps on how he would describe their location for the interviewer. After repeating the words, Bryan's right hand goes to his own abdomen, just over his ribcage, and with an open clench, he traces a line down his own body where part of this muscle would be.

The gesture stops at Bryan's lower abdomen, as he says, "which would be . . ." imagining spatially and verbally as he tries to find a way to describe this in words for the interviewer. His hand changes direction, the open hand moving across his abdomen perpendicularly to the first line, as he at last settles on language to convey his thoughts: "you have these muscles that go up and down" [he retraces the first gesture for demonstration], "and you also have muscles that go this way [he now traces the perpendicular line, from his left to right], called *transverse abdominis*." In this example, we see not only Bryan's hand layer the textbook image as well as his imagined partner's abdomen (on which he had to locate this muscle) onto his own body but also Bryan's hand reaching and contouring the description of this muscle before his words.

This capacity of the hands—and body as a whole—to express concepts independent of, or alongside (or even assisting) spoken language has been a central tenet of the recent resurgence of interest in studies of gesture (see Kendon, 2004; McNeill, 1996). For example, Goldin-Meadow (2003), in *Hearing Gesture: How Our Hands Help Us Think*, suggests that the body saves the speaker cognitive effort in speaking: "gesturing may not only reflect a speaker's cognitive state but may, by reducing cognitive load, also play a role in shaping that state" (p. 157). This capacity is central to Kendon's (2004) encapsulation of what gesture is: "a label for actions that have the features of manifest deliberate expressiveness" (p. 15). While this definition has operated as a popular definition for gesture within the field of gesture studies for some time, it seems to restrict the qualification of gestures to those "being done for the purpose of expression rather than in the service of some practical claim" (p. 15). We feel that this binary breaks down in the context both of Bryan's descriptions and in his work.[3] Bryan's gestures not only appear to assist him with the description and communication of concepts during the interview, as above, but they also serve as navigational devices, to map for us muscle coordinates, illustrating the layering of content from textbook, onto the body of the partner, onto Bryan's own body. That is, the hand stands in for the muscle itself as it communicates that muscle's direction to the interviewer. Note that this is something that gestures can do which words cannot. We would argue that the massage itself is, in this sense, gesture-full—it articulates information that Bryan has learned about the inner workings of the body even as it "answers" the client's body in a specific way. Gesture simultaneously comprises the learning and the massage.

Put another way, Bryan not only conveys ideas through gesture, but the gestures are doing their own important, generative work. Gestures are means by which the body inscribes its world, and are representative of that which the world inscribes upon it (Noland, 2009; Goldin-Meadow, 2003). To return to the example at hand, Bryan continues to read to us from the textbook, demonstrating how he learned to move from the illustrations of muscles on the page to finding them on his partner's body. The textbook explicates how to find certain landmarks under the skin's surface—parts of bones, joints—and then to move from these landmarks to particular parts of muscles. Bryan reads: "Locate the xiphoid process."[4] Bringing his hand to his own breastbone, using his first two fingers to fumble around, Brian searches for the answer (see Figure 2). He tries to apply words, saying, "which is, uh"—his fingers continue probing, as the pause extends.

The fingers seem to find what he is looking for, rooting beneath the base of his sternum. His hand wobbles around the anchored fingers as though to emphasize the point. He then says: "the bone that sort of sticks out the bottom of where your ribs connect." At the word, "where," his fingers unroot and he draws a circle across the bottom of his rib cage. The fingers then re-root. He continues, saying, you find the pubic crest (which he gestures more loosely toward), "and then you place your hands between them, and you just sort of"—he stops to move, returning to the two original *abdominis* gestures—"feel the muscles." Through this combination of gesture and talk, Bryan evidences not only the deeply embodied pathways to understanding but also the critical medium for his learning from both the textbook material and others' bodies: his own "felt sense."

Figure 2: Locating the xiphoid process.

"I am a big fan of the doing, instead of just the reading and memorizing," Bryan offers. But he admits that there are muscles in the textbook that he was made to learn that "you're never gonna feel" because they are too deep, too small, or off the beaten path.

INTERVIEWER: "So why do they put some things in there that you'll never feel?"

BRYAN: "Because it still shows you how things are connected. See, that's the thing about massage and muscles, is...it helps emphasize that the human body is connected...everything is connected."

Engaging Bodies

Until now we have talked generally about Bryan's education, how he learned to map out the muscles and invisible parts of the body, using images and text and bringing those things with him to the massage using his body's imagination. In this section, we talk about Bryan's engagement with specific bodies during his practice as a massage therapist. Before we turn to Bryan's gestures, it is important to note that when we talk about bodies here, we do not mean to imply body parts. As Bryan is feeling with his fingers, he is using his whole body to feel with his fingers, and as his clients receive a massage on particular body parts (neck, back, arms, legs, etc.), they are receiving a massage with their whole bodies.

Bryan speaks about how subtle the connection is between therapist and client as he discusses the concept of "intent." He compares physical pain to emotional pain, claiming that both are elusive to the therapist; it is possible to feel sympathetic towards a client's pain, but it is difficult to assess and understand what the client is experiencing: "it's a lot about how you feel."

In order for Bryan to treat pain that he cannot truly understand, he has to figure out how to assess pain levels. He says that, "Normally the way you test [a muscle for pain] is you *feel* it. A lot of massage is *intent*, about how *deep* into the tissue you're going." Bryan not only talks about intent through words but also through gestures. When he says the word "feel," for example, he brings his hands together, touching the fingers of his left hand on the palm of his right. To demonstrate "deep," Bryan uses his index and middle fingers to press into the palm of his left hand, demonstrating a massage technique of pushing into the muscle.

Intent is not just about something that occurs before the massage but during it as well. Bryan says, "That sort of thing is hard to describe and hard to figure out in an empirical evidence way." In other words, it is subtle and difficult to describe in words, because it is a question of feeling and sense. Bryan uses a motion with his right hand to describe intention; he moves his palm from his shoulder down to his lap when he says, "intend to go," demonstrating the progress that "intent" implies. Intent, then, is feeling muscles to assess pain, and going a certain depth into the muscle tissue to treat pain.

Bryan uses his whole body to engage a client's pain. He discusses how important the differences are in the way you feel when you are receiving the massage, versus when you are giving it. The therapist can learn from receiving massages but only what the client needs to do in order to make the massage effective—not necessarily what the therapist needs to do. How the therapist uses his or her whole body to conduct the massage is too subtle and too complex for the client to discern from the table. Elaborating, Bryan says, "Part of that's because the point of contact"—here, he opens his left hand and touches his right fourth finger onto the palm flesh—"and the rest of the movement of what the person is doing are two different things."

At this moment, Bryan stands abruptly for the first and only time during this portion of the interview. He assumes the posture of giving a massage, widening his stance, feet spread apart and rooted firmly on the floor, demonstrating how the motions are full bodied, continuous, and emergent. "You know, knowing how someone is standing," he says, "or to achieve a certain point of . . ." He repeats the gesture for "point of contact" while standing but does not complete the sentence.

"I don't know why I'm doing that," he says, returning to a seated position.

Although Bryan says that he does not know why he stands, it seems that part of the reason is that he cannot describe this nuanced difference—the richness of the movement—only through words. His explanation and his own ability to articulate appear contingent on finding the gesture itself.

INTERVIEWER: "You can stand up if you need to."

On invitation, Bryan again rises to demonstrate the range of momentum that he can use to procure leverage and depth during a massage. Holding his arms before him, he moves his fingertips across the coffee table. Then he lowers, even squats, shifting his legs as the range of his motion extends. He says that doing the first motion is not the same as the second because "you get more power out of your legs to get into the movement." When he involves his whole body, he feels the mus-

cles differently, and he can get deeper into them, engaging better with the client.

Ideally, the client, too, must engage through the whole body. Bryan suggests that clients often try to "help" him by extending their arms or legs when they feel him move to that part, basically activating the muscles that he is trying to massage. When that happens, he encourages the client to give up the control of the muscles they are used to administering—in general, he encourages clients to think less.

A SUBTLE CONNECTION

INTERVIEWER: "We're talking about how you make a personal connection [with the client]. It sounds like a lot of that is a combination of both text and talking at the same time?"

BRYAN: "Yeah; it's also—like it's a subtle—it's kind of a subtle connection…it's hard to determine what exactly causes people to feel in certain ways."

Talk is integral to the bond, Bryan admits. For example, it is needed to forewarn the client about what you are going to do and when. It is helpful for acquiring feedback during and after the massage (although this also happens tactilely). And the act of talking can itself help the client to relax. But talk can be confounding in its own right. Imagine trying to describe how, as a client, you would like for a particular sensation to change slightly. "It can be frustrating to try and explain exactly what you want," Bryan says, speaking from experience as both therapist and client. "Sometimes, if it's not *exactly* right, it's not worth going to the effort of trying to say it, because you're relaxed otherwise." And feeling has a certain ineffable aspect: trying to put the request into words can actually lead to more muscle tension.

To further explain the complex relationship of talk to touch in the context of "subtle connection," Bryan offers the example of someone who talked about work during a session. As a general rule, Bryan feels that he should follow the client's lead in terms of how much talking should be involved. Some people, he suggests, have to get something "off their chest" verbally before they can become still. For them, talk is "part of their relaxation process." But in this particular situation, talk interfered with relaxation. "She came in," he recalls, "started getting a massage, started talking about all the problems at work, and…it was almost too late by the time that I realized it was a really bad idea." Bryan felt her muscles clench as she spoke. "I tried to taper it off, but she just kept getting more and more tense, talking about all the problems at work." Ultimately, because she was not engaging in the massage with her thoughts or by relaxing her muscles, the massage was less effective.

On the other hand, Bryan says that sometimes he can get so caught up in conversation during a session that he will, as he joked, "massage the same part ten times" or apply the wrong amount of pressure. He explains that to a degree, his own ability to listen to a client through touch becomes less acute with talk (whether the subject is massage or something else): "my focus shifts," he says. "I'm not paying attention to how the body *feels*."

What Bryan feels principally comprises and sustains the subtle connection seems to manifest in a gesture. Describing the end of a massage, Bryan says, "I always say thank you, and I usually do a last, like—pause." The gesture he offers to complete the utterance happens during the em dash. It begins on the plane that he has been using to demonstrate contact with the client's body. He stills his hands on that plane and then lifts them "off." In this gesture, Bryan communicates how touch marks the end of the massage, the moment to end the connection and return from the bodily experience of the massage to a conversational relationship between the massage therapist and the client. The subtle connection made throughout the massage must end eventually, and Bryan feels it is best to mark that moment through touch to allow the client to gently return to more conventional relations.

THE PEDAGOGY OF TOUCH

One afternoon, we are at a coffee shop discussing the current project with a friend who is pregnant. What we are trying to describe as the complexity of talking about massage in relation to "writing the body," our friend associates with a website about "spinning babies" (*SpinningBabies.com*). The project of the program, she explains, is to help women learn to identify—and to manually shift—the position of the baby inside the womb. This maneuvering, the website claims, aims at "optimal fetal positioning" to make birth easier and safer. But our friend says that although she has tried following the complex maps and diagrams for discerning which part of the baby is which, she really cannot tell head from foot.

The three of us pore over the extensive website, which boasts, among techniques and testimonials, an extensive section on "belly mapping." This particular section includes the three steps that our friend describes as having lost her. Step one suggests diagramming the belly onto a piece of paper. Four quadrants are to be marked, and within each one is to be description of what is happening there, like "kick" or "wiggles." Step two is visualizing the baby or figuring out which part is which. Clues are offered, for example, "When baby is head down, wiggles in the lower front are hands" (*SpinningBabies.com*). Step three is titling the position, and here are a host of illustrations from which to choose (e.g., "left occipital traverse"). Further down this page, we see a woman who appears to have actually drawn the illustration of her baby's fetal position on her skin.

Our friend admits, gently pressing different parts of her belly, that she just doesn't get it. Everything feels about the same to her fingers. She notices (and, of course, touches) her baby constantly—its weight, its shifts—but the sensation is diffused throughout her body. Even the kicks are hard to pin to an exact place. All the same, she jokes, she *should* be able to map her belly. It is, after all, her own body, which she presumes to know quite well.

We offer this as a concluding anecdote for a few reasons. Firstly, it reemphasizes the primacy of vision in our culture, which we feel does extend also to how we talk about composition as well as define what comprises multimodal learning. Just as even this website requires women to figure out how to feel by way of diagrams, maps, and metaphors of sight (e.g., "Baby can make a triangular shape when straightening the legs" [*SpinningBabies.com*]), we tend to conceive of writing as bound not just to "verbal media," as Williams (2001a) says, but to the production of a particular kind of visible artifact (p. 22). Even what many conceive of as multimodal writing assignments center on seeing, on movement between words and images.

Secondly, to that point, this anecdote highlights the confounding nature of trying to shunt sensation into representation. The lack of verbiage as well as mode available to richly engage the language of touch is plain (see also Paterson, 2007; Classen, 2005; Serres, 2009). Thus, we think there is a need to imagine what a different kind of composition (as well as a medium for "conversation") could look, sound, or feel like. What would it mean to engage touch in its own terms? To recalibrate our language according to touch?

Thirdly, this anecdote suggests the productivity of touch as well as the complexity of any endeavor to ask, prescribe or calibrate its outcomes. As Merleau-Ponty suggests in the epigraph at the beginning of this chapter, contact is dynamic, inevitable, both gives and receives, forms and is formed, torques to the proximate, while largely ineffably "its own movements incorporate themselves into the universe they interrogate" (Merleau-Ponty, 2004, p. 251). Even as our friend cannot recognize the baby's foot, contact by its own virtue explores as it creates.

With Bryan, we perceive the creativity of touch amid the massage practice he depicts as well as the interview he gives. The subtle connection is a kind of manifest composition. It elaborates through touch: Bryan using his whole body to engage, the client using their whole body to receive the massage (and our making sense of this). It is a delicate balance of the complex relationships between talk, movement, and touch that Bryan describes both with his words and his gestures, which both recall movement and touch as well as move and touch themselves.

Conclusion

As teachers of writing, we cannot and should not ignore the writing body. This chapter emphasizes the embodiment of writing, the write-ability of the dynamic human form, and the intelligence of intuition. It suggests that gesture analysis as a methodology offers an enriching way to study the multimodal dimensions of composition practice in writing studies; the need to expand the scope of gesture in such cases to incorporate contact (with tools and the rest of the material world); and, certainly, experiment with kinesthetic learning styles and projects in the classroom. Finally, we suggest that touch itself is a mode of invention in writing and composition studies that merits our attention if we are to engage writing through the tangible world.

Notes

1. Perl quotes Eugene Gendlin, who describes this as "a body-sense of meaning"; to work with this body-sense, Perl adds, "we need to attend to our bodies and discover just what these inchoate pushes and pulls, these barely formed preverbal yearnings or leanings, are beginning to suggest to us" (Perl, 2004, p. xiii).

2. Rose concludes that there are three main reasons why practitioners use talk, visuals, and their bodies (touch) to communicate with and provide treatment to their clients: 1) these methods are a part of the educational system of the practitioners 2) people learn in different ways, so having all three methods available will aid in learning, and 3) which Rose considers most significant, in order for practitioners to develop a "coherent conceptual structure" of practice and integrate what in our culture are segmented systems, practitioners learn to move what seems almost seamlessly amongst these multimodal ways of knowing.

3. Prior and Holding in *Inscriptional Gestures: Writing as Embodied Activity* (in process) suggest that this binary also breaks down in the context of writing-as-gesture.

4. This is the hardened cartilage that connects the diaphragm to the sternum.

Works Cited

Classen, C. (2005). Handshakes. In *The book of touch*. Ed. C. Classen. Oxford, UK: Berg.

Emig. (1971). *The composing processes of twelfth graders*. Urbana, IL: NCTE.

Fleckenstein, K. S. (1999). Writing bodies: Somatic mind in composition studies. *College English, 61*, 281–306.

Goldin-Meadow, S. (2003). *Hearing gesture: How our hands help us think*. Cambridge, MA: Belknap Press of Harvard University Press.

Haas, C., & Witte, S. P. (2001). Writing as embodied practice: The case of engineering standards. *Journal of Business and Technical Communication, 15*, 413–457.

Kendon, A. (2004). *Gesture: Visible action as utterance*. Cambridge, UK: Cambridge University Press.

Lehrer, J. (2007). *Proust was a neuroscientist*. New York: Houghton Mifflin.

Marks, L. (2002). *Touch: Sensuous theory and multisensory media*. Minneapolis: University of Minnesota Press.

McNeill, D. (1996). *Hand and mind: What gestures reveal about thought*. Chicago: University of Chicago Press.

Merleau-Ponty, M. (1968). *The visible and the invisible: The intertwining-the chiasm*. In Thomas Baldwin (Ed.). *Maurice Merleau-Ponty: Basic writings* (2004). London and New York: Routledge, p. 251.

Noland, Carrie. (2009). *Agency and embodiment: Performing gestures / producing culture*. Cambridge, MA: Harvard University Press.

Noland, C. & Ness, S. A. (2008). *Migrations of gesture*. Minneapolis: Minnesota University Press.

Paterson, M. (2007). *The senses of touch: Haptics, affects and technologies*. Oxford and New York: Berg.

Perl, S. (2004). *Felt sense: Writing with the body*. Portsmouth, NH: Boynton/Cook.

Prior, P. (2010). Remaking IO: Semiotic remediation in the design process. In *Exploring semiotic remediation as discourse practice*. Eds. P. Prior & J. Hengst. Pp. 206–234. New York: Palgrave Macmillan.

Prior, P. & Shipka, J. (2003). Chronotopic lamination: Tracing the contours of literate activity. In *Writing selves, writing societies: Research from activity perspectives*. Eds. C. Bazerman & D. R. Russell. Pp. 180–283. Fort Collins, CO: WAC Clearinghouse.

Rose, M. (1999). "Our hands will know": The development of tactile diagnostic skill—Teaching, learning, and situated cognition in a physical therapy program. *Anthropology & Education Quarterly, 30*(2), 133–160.

Sauer, B. (2002). *The rhetoric of risk: Technical documentation in hazardous environments*. New York: Routledge.

Serres, M. (2009). *The five senses: A philosophy of mingled bodies*. Trans. M. Sankey & P. Cowley. London: Continuum.

Shipka, J. (December 2005). A multimodal task-based framework for composing. *CCC, 57*(2), 277–306.

SpinningBabies.com. (2008). Maternity House Publishing. Web. June 2011.

Streeck, J. (2009). *Gesturecraft: The manu-facture of meaning*. Philadelphia: John Benjamins.

Streeck, J., & Kallmeyer, W. (2001). Interaction by inscription. *Journal of Pragmatics, 33*(4), 465–490.

Tully, G. (2004). Belly mapping: Using kicks and wiggles to predict posterior labor. *International Doula, 2004*. http://www.spinningbabies.com/research-and-references

Williams, S. D. (2001a). Part 1: Thinking out of the pro-verbal box. *Computers and Composition, 18*, 21–32.

Williams, S. D. (2001b). Part 2: Toward an integrated composition pedagogy in hypertext. *Computers and Composition, 18*, 123–135.

CHAPTER TWELVE

The Embodiment of Real and Digital Signs

From the Sociocultural to the Intersemiotic

JULIE CHEVILLE

With the emergence of new media, users are able to integrate multiple symbol systems in ways that pose distinct analytic challenges for writing researchers. In the case of video gaming and streaming video, moving images may appear in activity sequences that involve little linguistic mediation. As this chapter will indicate, the language-based analytic approaches that have traditionally framed investigations of language and literacy often do not acknowledge contexts of signification represented by many new media. The risk of these "sociocultural" perspectives is that by placing primacy on linguistic sign use, oral and print, researchers may not recognize contexts of signification in which spatially situated signs, like bodies and images, exert predominant ideational influence (Wartofsky, 1973).

In this chapter, I consider spatial, perceptual, and sensory operations that appear to guide *spatial* signification, a communicative context constituted by syntactical units that are visual rather than linguistic in their expression. As Tchertov (2002) asserts, "...spatial semiosis allows syntactic structures to be built in an essentially other way than the successive ordered chains of discrete signs, known for linguistics" (p. 443). Specifically, I will consider how the human body and the image function as spatially situated signs in real and simulated activity, respectively. In my analysis of the human body's ideational influence in real activity, I will suggest how human bodies are mobilized to communicate meaning through collective production of a visual-spatial code (Tchertov, 2002). I will then shift to interactive virtual game play, a context in which the succession of images constitutes visual-spatial expression.

Based on emerging research in the area of biosemotics and social cognitive neuroscience, I will argue that in communicative contexts mediated primarily by spatial signs, distinct perceptual and neural processes unfold that are largely overlooked by methodologies attuned to social practice. I will conclude by suggesting how an emerging connection between spatial and sensory signification welcomes a shift from a sociocultural approach born of Vygotsky's (1987) primary concern for language to an intersemiotic framework that recognizes how social, spatial, sensory, and other signifying systems intersect.

HUMAN BODIES AS SPATIALLY SITUATED SIGNS IN REAL ACTIVITY

Recently, select researchers of the social semiotic have urged greater interest in the influence of the human body on social practice (Leander, 2001, 2002; Leander & Sheehy, 2004; Lemke, 1997; Whitson, 1997). Leander's (2002) fascinating study of activity in one high school classroom discloses how students' social and spatial practices recombine to situate identities. In its function as an "identity artifact," the human body is at once semiotic (or constitutive of meaning) and material (an object of signification). Important to Leander's account are the ways that interactants mobilize their bodies to redirect social activity toward specific ideological ends. What Leander investigates is a communicative context in which bodily activity influences but does not *recode* a verbal plane of expression. In other words, Leander's concern for the human body is restricted to how its activity reinforces, impedes, or redirects language, the primary mediational means.

Although Leander provides an innovative and thorough analysis of how spatial orientations influence social practice, his method does not reveal the body's full potential as a sign. As I've noted elsewhere (Cheville, 2006), language-based perspectives necessarily restrict the human body to materiality, a condition of "having mass or matter and occupying physical space" (Haas, 1996, p. 10). Indeed, in the *social* semiotic (Halliday & Hasan, 1989; Halliday & Matthiessen, 1999; Hodge & Kress, 1988), where language mediates thought, the body's activity remains material because its semiotic potential does not exceed that of language, thereby leaving a predominant "audio-temporal" sign system intact (Tchertov, 2002). The risk is that over-attribution of materiality to the human body prevents us from recognizing its primacy in the *spatial* semiotic, a communicative domain constituted by a visual-spatial syntax (Cheville, 2006).

For the purposes of illustrating spatial signification in the context of real-world activity, I briefly report on a qualitative investigation of female basketball players' athletic learning (Cheville, 2001). This study documented how embodied activity on the court gave rise to embodied mental schemata (Johnson, 1987). In addition, it examined how perceptual habits and cognitive operations shifted when athletes entered classrooms where pedagogies were often disembodied and where athletes worried that professors and students held latent assumptions about race, sexuality, and/or somatic type that might undermine their academic performances.

In this chapter, I focus strictly on the semiotic features of athletic play in order to disclose the human body's relevance as a sign vehicle. To frame analysis, I draw on the work of C.S. Peirce, whose semiotic theory supports the interpretation of visual-spatial signs. Peirce's conception of the triadic sign involves the dynamic relation of three elements: object, sign (representamen), and meaning (interpretant). An important feature of Peirce's semiotics is the notion of meaning as the *effect* of the sign-object relation, or meaning in activity, as opposed to meaning inherent in discrete linguistic signs (de Saussure, 1966). Peirce also acknowledged that semiotic systems could be verbal or extraverbal, insuring the relevance of the theoretic frame to investigations of semiotic domains as diverse as "matter, energy, or information" (Lemke, 1997).

For the intercollegiate athletes I studied, engaging the body as a sign vehicle involved three degrees of signifying competence. First, players were expected to encode meaning sensible to teammates. Whether one occupied the position of point guard, forward, or post on the basketball court, her most basic rhetorical burden was to enact movements (dribbling, jumping, passing, shooting, footwork, and/or ball handling) that teammates could decipher. Early in the first year of my study, the entire team faced perceptual struggle when the head coach moved Nadine, a freshman guard, to a permanent position on the wing, an area of the court nearest the sidelines. The wing position demanded that Nadine revise much of her positional knowledge as a point guard, adjusting to new vectors of movement and ball rotation.

In moments of confusion, particularly in offensive sets, she compensated by enacting one-on-one moves that were foreign to teammates, thus disrupting the rotation of the ball from one body-sign to the next. While in possession of the ball, a player held her greatest signifying potential, and idiosyncratic movements only jeopardized teammates' capacity to produce a smooth, synchronic chain of body-signs. When it occurred, her eruptive play earned the redress of her coach, "Nadine, I don't think there's a day that goes by that you don't try to do things all by yourself!" No option existed for Nadine but to abandon many of the moves she had acquired on the public playgrounds of her home community, the very moves that had garnered her blue-chip status as a high school athlete. In her intercollegiate career, Nadine was expected to encode meaning in the context of relational, interanimating body-signs. If Nadine could not score, she was expected to move in ways that insured the ball's fluid rotation to another player who could.

In addition to encoding meaning through their bodies, players were expected to become accomplished "readers" of other sign-vehicles on the court. Signifying competence demanded that players agree in their interpretations of and responses to sign activity. As an auxiliary sign, the basketball and its pathway through space were the objects of each player's perception. "Following the ball" visually extended players' perception beyond the dermal limits of their body to joint haptic activity cued by the ball's trajectory. Decoding necessitated an anticipatory sense not just for where the ball would rotate but also how a new sign vehicle, the body of a teammate, might encode meaning once the ball was in her hands. Players were expected to know and anticipate teammates' signifying activity, including but not limited to the height of jumps, shot preferences, and posting maneuvers. Jenny, a junior reserve center, explained the process of decoding this way:

> After you've been playing with the same people for a while, you almost start to get on the same brain waves....You get really confident and, 'Well, they understand. They understand what I'm thinking, and I understand what they're thinking.' I can lob a pass up to Tan and expect her to catch it. I know her timing on her jump and how high she is going to jump or if she is going to be up higher in the lane when she posts. I think that's what makes a team really successful. If you know that person is going to be there without even having to look at them. You can always depend on them being there. If you can't expect this person to do this, then you....'Well, yesterday you cut out to the wing and today you're cutting up to the top. Which way is it? I don't know what to expect with you.' You don't know how to deal with it. Once you start playing with a person you understand their moves. You understand what they're thinking. (Cheville, 2001)

Contradictory interpretations of a single body-sign jeopardized spatial signification, in many cases inviting linguistic mediation, either through more frequent sign calling or through time outs that allowed coaches and players to verbally align their perspectives. In the end, one's decoding of spatial signs was only productive if it was shared. Successful players developed particular strategies for rehearsing the interpretation of sign relations. In the locker room before games, these women often sat, eyes closed, in silent periods of visualization that allowed them to rehearse offensive plays. What they were "reading" was the visual-spatial code of the ideal "text" they hoped to embody on court.

The third plane of signifying competence, contingent on successful embodiment of the first two, involved meaning exchange so fluid in its production that players were no longer conscious of their discrete encoding and decoding behaviors. The concept of "presence" (Lee, 2004) has become increasingly important to those interested in highly interactive contexts of semiotic activity in which participants enter into the "illusion of non-mediation" (Lombard & Ditton, 1997). I employ the concept of presence rather than "flow" (Csikszentmihalyi, 1990), given its greater relevance to the analysis of semiosis, particularly in disclosing users' relation to the medium mediating their experiences. Presence is a condition that relates both to the mediational means (the body) and to a participant's state of mind (Schroeder, 2002).

For the athletes I studied, presence occurred during stretches of play when a participant was so engrossed in her emergent sign activity that she was no longer conscious of the signifying demands of encoding and decoding. Related to the immersive condition of presence was "co-presence" (Schroeder, 2002), and the experience of multiple participants caught up in intersubjective sign relations. Of the two, co-presence was the ultimate objective and achievement for the team. As Jackson and Delehanty (1995) write, "Basketball is a sport that involves the subtle interweaving of players at full speed to the point where they are thinking and moving as one" (p. 17). In the condition of presence or co-presence, the human body as mediational means was transparent. At this most sophisticated level of signifying competence, the visual processing of spatial signs was characterized by wide visual scan paths across court space with rapid and reversible eye tracking across the entire field of play. Rather than fixating on gaze targets, players' vision was multi-radial, and response to abrupt onsets of activity anywhere on the court was rapid and jointly enacted. Within a single practice or game, presence and co-presence might never be achieved or might occur and cease any number of times. Presence-inducing stimuli were generally unpredictable given the distinctive contextual features shaping each performance, and stimuli for one player's presence did not necessarily trigger co-presence. Certainly, an athlete's preoccupation with physical pain, with the inability of her body to sign effectively in the context of play, mitigated the onset of presence and of co-presence (Cheville, 2001).

In this section, I have reported the spatial signification characteristic of gross motor activity in a real-world context for which language did not serve as chief mediational means. To illustrate spatially situated sign relations in activity sequences mediated primarily by the human body, I have not addressed the influence of other sign vehicles familiar to any spectator. Certainly, in practice and in game situations, the visual-spatial code players enacted was periodically halted or interrupted by visual and acoustic signs that included hand signals and talk, whistles and buzzers, and peripheral sign activity of coaches and teammates. In addition, any number and configuration of these additional signs could function as presence-inducing stimuli. Although participants' play was thus always multimodal, it would not have proceeded in the absence of a predominant visual-spatial code.

DIGITAL IMAGES AS SPATIALLY SITUATED SIGNS AND THE NEURAL CORRELATES OF ACTION OBSERVATION

In this section, as in the last, I consider presence to be an experience of perceptual and psychological immersion (Biocca & Levy, 1995). Here, I turn from spatial signification in one context of action execution to that characterizing action observation in digital spaces, specifically virtual game worlds that allow users to select or design full-bodied avatars, or digital body signs, whose movements can be cued by mouse clicks, arrow keys, joysticks, or head mount displays. In in-role activity, the avatar is chief among spatially situated signs that include other figures, objects, and landscapes. Of the avatar's significance, Taylor (2002) writes, "It is in large part through these avatars that users can come to bring real life and vibrancy to the spaces. Through avatars, users embody themselves and make real their engagement with a virtual world....The bodies people use in these spaces provide a means to live digitally—to fully inhabit the world" (p. 40).

As was true for the athletes in real world sign use, a virtual game often integrates multiple sensory channels, including the inscriptive (text-chat features) and the acoustic (voice, music, and other audibles). That activity sequences in simulated game activity are grounded by a visual-spatial syntax is supported by research indicating the potential effects of virtual motion activity on users once they exit the graphical space. "Simulation sickness" affects sensory processes associated with spatial perception and includes the symptoms of "dizziness, eyestrain, disorientation, dysphoria, unsteadiness standing and walking, even nausea, reduced hand-eye coordination, illusory sensations, and 'flashbacks'" (Lombard & Ditton, 1997, p. 20).

In an *Educational Researcher* article, Squire (2006) cites the remarks of an elementary student attending a Serious Games Summit. The child was an active user of the educational game "Civilization," a software program that allows users the opportunity to assume the avatar of an emperor or empress in various historical periods and to mobilize material resources to enhance the wealth and security of their domains. The child's rhetorical question "Why read about ancient Rome when I can build it?" acknowledges what we know about the agency associated with in-role game activity (Gee, 2003). In light of recent research in social cognitive neuroscience (SCN), however, the remark also begs us to consider how the intense experience of presence may involve particular neural processes that make engagement with spatially-situated signs different and, for many, more efficacious than interaction with linguistic signs.

At present, the designers of virtual game systems that employ avatars are focused on improving computational algorithms that control the avatar's eye and head motions, facial expressions, reach, and locomotive behaviors. One design challenge results from the fact that graphical space is "perceived" differently by humans and avatars (Chopra-Khullar & Badler, 2001; Peters & Itti, 2006). Human users are guided by action monitoring systems located in the real world. These include visual, auditory, and proprioceptive processes that don't necessarily align with the algorithms that guide the behaviors of virtual agents. Heightening users' experiences of presence necessitates the design of avatars that respond to, even anticipate, users' activity (Schroeder, 2002). Aligning the action-monitoring systems of humans and avatars ensures the synchronized embodiments required of presence and avoids the phenomenological glitches between self and other that Taylor (2002) describes this way: "Seeing people inadvertently walk through the walls or suddenly disappear are persistent problems in many systems. This feeling of being suddenly pulled back out of the virtual world highlights the fragility of multiple forms of embodiment, especially in relation to the digital" (p. 44).

Researchers in the area of social cognitive neuroscience are currently using brain-imaging technologies to document the neural correlates of agency, "the feeling that we can cause an action" (Farrer et al., 2003, p. 618). Agency is a core concept in simulation theory, a framework attentive to neural processes underlying real, imagined, and simulated motoric activity (Jeannerod & Pacherie, 2004).

What seems clear, even this early in brain research, is the significance of mirror neurons (Rizzolatti, Fogassi, & Gallese, 2000; Gallese, 2005), which appear to be activated during the observation of complex body movements (Decety & Chaminade, 2003; Gerardin et al., 2000; Lotze et al., 1999) when a subject feels as if he or she is actually anticipating and initiating observed action (Decety, 1996; Decety & Jeannerod, 1996; Jeannerod, 1995, 2001; Pellegrino et al., 1992). In the observation of imagined, real, or simulated activity, mirror neurons activate only when subjects view motion sequences they perceive as purposeful and possible. "[B]iomechanically impossible movement paths" do not trigger these neurons (Decety & Chaminade, 2003, p. 582). They also fail to activate during the observation of still objects and images. As Favareau (2002) reports, "the simple presentation of objects, or their manipulation in 'meaningless' or non-goal directed ways by hand (whether witnessed or performed) will not evoke the neuron to discharge" (pp. 74–75). Although much SCN research has involved the observation, imagination, and imitation of real body activity, the activation of mirror neurons appears to occur during the observation of goal-oriented *simulated* activity as well (Decety & Jeannerod, 1996; Perani et al., 2001).

Central to our understanding of motor imagery and the experience of agency is the finding that those neural pathways triggered in goal-oriented observation of motor activity are precisely those that activate in the execution of these movements. As Decety and Chaminade (2003) report, "…during the observation of actions produced by other individuals, and during the imagination of one's own actions, there is specific recruitment of the neural structures which would normally be involved in the actual generation of the same actions" (p. 584). The shared neural pathways for action execution and observation in spatially situated sign activity have been corroborated in additional studies (Cochin et al., 1999; Fadiga et al., 1995; Gallese, 2005) and have important implications for how we understand and document the embodiment of real and digital bodies. The findings have led Gallagher and Meltzoff (1996) to suggest that, "understanding of the other person is primarily a form of embodied practice."

In his article "Beyond Self and Other: On the Neurosemiotic Emergence of Intersubjectivity," Favareau (2002) uses an emerging theoretic frame known as "neurosemiotics" to analyze the communicative function of mirror neurons. Interest in the broader field of "biosemiotics" emerged in the Soviet Union and the province of Estonia during the second half of the twentieth century as semioticians began to shift their attention from a cultural semiotics to other "secondary modeling systems" that semiotic principles appeared to explain. Although the term "biosemiotic" originated in 1962 in Rothschild's work in psychiatric medicine (Kull, 1999), Yuri Lotman provided the analytic framework that stimulated widespread interest. Drawing on his own understanding of the hermeneutic relation of text and context, as well as von Uexküll's (1864–1944) concept of "Umwelt," Lotman began to consider the interaction of organism and environment on semiotic terms (1977, 1990). By the 1970s, he wrote of the "semiosphere" to explain a context of intersecting semiotic processes that mediate meaning exchange. At the same time, familiar with the semiotic conception of life processes introduced in Uexküll's *Theoretical Biology* (1926), American semiotician Thomas Sebeok began to contemplate a framework for biosemiotics. Characterizing it later, he wrote:

> Biosemiotics proper deals with sign processes in nature in all dimensions, including the emergence of semiosis in nature, which may coincide with or anticipate the emergence of living cells; (2) the natural history of signs; (3) the 'horizontal aspects of semiosis in the ontogeny of organisms, in plant and animal communication, and in inner sign functions in the immune and nervous systems; and (4) the semiotics of cognition and language. (1991, p. 55)

Peircean semiotics orients biosemioticians to the transactional relation of sensory signification across cells, cellular pathways, and motoric processes to extradermal spatial signification. Neurosemioticians interested in the intersection of sensory and spatial sign relations hold to Hoffmeyer's (1995) view that "the sign rather than the molecule is the basic unit of life" (p. 369).

For its mechanistic and reductive character, Favareau (2002) bemoans the neural conduit model that has long been used to explain neural message transfer as "flow[ing] through the circuitry of neurons in much the same way as electricity flows through a computer motherboard (i.e., in ways in which neither the signal nor the vehicle of its transmission are [is] understood to be themselves interactive participants in the creativity of semiosis)" (p. 68). As a result, he suggests that neuroscientists have grossly underestimated how the interpretant (meaning) that is mirror neuron activity originates in the perception of spatially situated signs. In Favareau's words,

> The totality of this systemic and incessant sign activity…is an ongoing, dynamic process of sign-exchanging cells embedded in sign-exchanging brains embedded in sign-exchanging bodies embedded in sign-exchanging worlds, the eternal interplay of self-organization and symmetry-breaking that characterizes the moment-to-moment experience of this recursively interactive system that constitutes, in a very real sense, the very essences of 'knowing' and 'the mind.'…Properly seen, body, brain, mind and cell are but levels of the same one endlessly interacting complex system….(2002, p. 67)

Emerging interest in Peircean semiotics as a unified framework for explaining the communicative activity of life systems (plant, animal, human) and human sub-systems (cells, pathways, motoric processes, inter-dermal schematic orientations) promises to enrich our comprehension of meaning exchange and understanding, particularly our attention to the neural processes underlying production and interpretation of the visual-spatial code in new media compositions.

Gee (2003) has suggested that virtual games present compelling problems that require the level of attention, rehearsal, collaboration, and immersion characteristic of the most efficacious learning tasks. Social practices aside, I suggest that it is the experience of presence induced by *spatially situated* signs in digital and real activity that triggers the neurons most responsible for agency, presence, and co-presence. Put simply, users' intense engagement with new media may have neural origins that produce the affective features we may underestimate when considered through sociocultural theoretic frames. It seems imperative that analyses of new media recognize the intersemiotic character of sign use, namely how social, spatial, sensory, and other sign systems intersect to form a broader "semiotic ecology" (Lang, 1997).

IMPLICATIONS FOR THE INTERSEMIOTIC ANALYSIS OF NEW MEDIA LITERACIES

Some have argued that new media literacies have initiated a transformation in cultural and cognitive activity that will prove as profound as the shift from orality to literacy (Bolter, 1991; Poster, 1995). As a researcher and practitioner, I have begun to consider how interest in the intersemiotic orients me to the broadest notions of text, composer, and creative process. Although this chapter's concern for spatially situated bodies in real and digital space has focused on specific contexts in which a visual-spatial code predominates, sign relations in new media texts are often more balanced in their use of verbal and extraverbal elements. Nevertheless, many of the issues raised here invite empirical and conceptual questions relevant to the analysis of literacy practices in all forms of new media.

The immediate concern, of course, is the access that literacy and composition researchers have to semiotic frameworks and institutional niches that consider the relation of social, spatial, and sensory signification in new media engagement. What seems clear is that a new generation of young scholars is already deeply engaged in semiotic studies. At the 2007 National Council of Teachers of English Assembly for Research Conference, the theme "What Counts as Literacy: Living Literacies of the Body and Image" invited a large number of doctoral students and junior faculty who addressed new media practices not only with rich conceptual frames but with life histories shaped by evocative new media experience. In response to National Science Foundation imperatives, colleges of education have also begun to invest in innovative faculty positions and interdisciplinary institutes dedicated to the intersection of teaching, learning, and creative expression. The University of Washington's Institute for Learning and Brain Studies (ilabs.washington.edu) is a particularly important resource for those interested in the intersemiotic dimensions of multimodal learning.

Several questions seem important as we consider the neural underpinnings of embodiment in real and simulated activity. What neural affordances and constraints characterize highly interactive multimodal, computer-mediated literacy practices? From an intersemiotic standpoint, how might social, spatial, and sensory signifying practices be organized, and in what media, to best support engagement and learning? What resources and instructional opportunities might we begin to provide for students whose literacy practices and preferences involve high-presence media?

One imperative for new media researchers is the need for continued definition of presence. As Lee (2004) indicates, varying conceptions exist. Most scholars agree that any medium can mediate the experience of presence, but there is little sense for the neural processes activated in immersive experiences with "low presence media" (Lombard & Ditton, 1997) like written texts. Comparative analyses of the experience of presence in real and virtual narrative "worlds," for instance, would assist us in identifying the neural correlates of "inferential and participatory behaviors" (Gerrig, 1993) common and distinct to both. Although there is much current interest in bridging adolescents' virtual and conventional literacies, it may be that inducing stimuli for presence in real and virtual "reading" are distinct and thus complicate this instructional aim. Finally, what are the neurophysiological and developmental implications for children whose earliest and most pervasive interaction is with high presence media?

A second imperative is the need for continued application of brain imaging to the study of composing (Berninger & Richards, 2002; Berninger & Winn, 2006; Winn, Windschitl, Fruland, & Lee, 2002). Most necessary now are semiotic conceptual frameworks that assist researchers to shift their focus from the study of graphomotor sequences to other motor output activity, including composing via head mount displays. I use "composing" rather than "writing" to indicate an entirely new set of multimodal demands that brain imaging must begin to document. Goldfine (2001) has noted how the technological features of word processors can interrupt the metacognitive behaviors central to planning. How, then, might new media designed to support basic composers involve real time, semiotically diverse interventions (eye-tracking technologies, for one) that sustain and/or prompt working memory and planning? Unfortunately, the emerging technologies most often licensed to schools at the moment are automated scoring technologies that align with mandated writing assessments. Criterion is just one example of Internet-based writing programs that feature real time, non-adaptive diagnostic response. The software is merely the newest iteration of skill-and-drill writing instruction. As Joyce (1995) reminds us, ineffective hypertexts "assuage the hunger for automaticity with the full-bellied inertia of tradition. We know the bulk of this stuff; we have chewed on it for years" (p. 43). What are linguistic, spatial, and sensory processes that underlie interaction with constructive (as opposed to productive) hypertexts? How do new media technologies invite alternative planning, organizational, and revising strategies?

A third imperative for literacy and composition scholars is to make their methodological expertise known to emerging working groups within and beyond the academy. Even a brief foray into computational accounts of multimodal engagement reveals that researchers in this area rely on methodological tools that do an injustice to case reporting. Abbreviated questionnaires that ask computer users to report on their interactions with new media limit our capacity to identify intersections between social, spatial, and sensory data. What literacy and composition researchers possess are the deep developmental understandings and rich case study methodologies required of instructive description.

Works Cited

Alvermann, D. (Ed.). (2005). *Adolescents and literacies in a digital world.* New York: Peter Lang.

Berninger, V., & Richards, T. (2002). *Brain literacy for educators and psychologists.* New York: Academic Press.

Berninger, V., & Winn, W. (2006). Implications for advancements in brain research and technology for writing development, writing instruction, and educational evolution. In C. A. MacArthur, S. Graham, & J. Fitzgerald (Eds.), *Handbook of writing research* (pp. 96–114). New York: Guilford Press.

Biocca, F., & Levy, M. (1995). *Communication in the age of virtual reality.* Hillsdale, NJ: Lawrence Erlbaum.

Bolter, J. (1991). *Writing space: The computer, hypertext, and the history of writing*. Hillsdale, NJ: Lawrence Erlbaum.

Cheville, J. (2001). *Minding the body: What student athletes know about learning*. Portsmouth, NH: Boynton/Cook.

Cheville, J. (Jan./Feb. 2005). Confronting the problem of embodiment. *International Journal of Qualitative Studies in Education*, *18*(1), 85–107.

Cheville, J. (2006). The bias of materiality in sociocultural theory: Reconceiving embodiment. *Mind, Culture, and Activity*, *13*(2), 25–37.

Chopra-Khullar, S., & Badler, N. (2001). Where to look? Automating attending behaviors of virtual human characters. *Autonomous agents and multi-agent Systems*, *4*(1), 9–23.

Cochin, S., Barthelemy, C., Roux, S., & Martineau, J. (1999). Observation and execution of movement: Similarities demonstrated by quantified electroencephalography. *European Journal of Neuroscience*, *11*, 1839–1842.

Cope, B., & Kalantzis, M. (Eds.). (2000). *Multiliteracies: Literacy learning and the design of social futures*. London: Routledge.

Csikszentmihalyi, M. (1990). *Flow: The psychology of optimal experience*. New York: Harper and Row.

Decety, J. (1996). The neurophysiological basis of motor imagery. *Behavioural Brain Research*, *77*, 45–52.

Decety, J., & Chaminade, T. (2003). When the self represents the other: A new cognitive neuroscience view of psychological identification. *Consciousness and Cognition*, *12*, 577–596.

Decety, J., & Jeannerod, M. (1996). Mentally simulated movements in virtual reality: Does Fitts law hold in motor imagery. *Behavioural Brain Research*, *72*, 127–134.

Emig, J. (1971). *The composing processes of twelfth graders*. Urbana, IL: National Council of Teachers of English.

Fadiga, L., Fogassi, L., Pavesi, G., & Rizzolatti, G. (1995). Motor facilitation during action observation: A magnetic stimulation study. *Journal of Neurophysiology*, *73*, 2608–2611.

Farrer, C., Franck, N., Paillard, J., & Jeannerod, M. (2003). The role of proprioception in action recognition. *Consciousness and Cognition*, *12*, 609–619.

Favareau, D. (2002). Beyond self and other: On the neurosemiotic emergence of intersubjectivity, *Sign System Studies*, *30*(1), 57–100.

Gallagher, S., & Meltzoff, A. (1996). The earliest sense of self and others: Merleau-Ponty and recent developmental studies. *Philosophical Psychology*, *9*, 213–236.

Gallese, V. (2005). Embodied simulation: From neurons to phenomenal experiences. *Phenomenology and the Cognitive Sciences*, *4*, 23–48.

Gallese, V., Fadiga, L., Fogassi, L., & Rizzolatti, G. (1996). Action recognition in the premotor cortex. *Brain*, *119*, 593–609.

Gallese, V., & Keysers, C. (2001). Mirror neurons: A sensorimotor representation system. *Behavioral Brain Sciences*, *24*, 983–984.

Gee, J. (2003). *What video games have to teach us about learning and literacy*. New York: Palgrave Macmillan.

Gerardin, E., Sirigu, A., Lehéricyl, S., Poline, J.-B., Gaymard, B., Marsault, C., Agid, Y., & Le Bihan, D. (2000). Partially overlapping neural networks for real and imagined hand movements. *Cerebral Cortex*, *10*, 1093–1104.

Gerrig, R. (1993). *Experiencing narrative worlds: On the psychological activities of reading*. New Haven, CT: Yale University Press.

Goldfine, R. (2001). Making word processing more effective in the composition classroom. *Teaching English in the Two-Year College*, *28*, 307–315.

Haas, C. (1996). *Writing technology: Studies on the materiality of literacy.* Mahwah, NJ: Lawrence Erlbaum.

Halliday, M., & Hasan, R. (1989). *Language, context, and text: A social semiotic perspective.* London: Oxford University Press.

Halliday, M., & Matthiessen, C. (1999). *Constructing experience through meaning: A language-based approach to cognition.* London: Cassell.

Hodge, R., & Kress, G. (1988). *Social semiotics.* Ithaca, NY: Cornell University Press.

Hoffmeyer, J. (1995). The semiotic body-mind. In N. Tasca (Ed.), *Essays in honor of Thomas A. Sebeok* (pp. 367–383). Lisbon, Portugal: Almeida.

Jackson, P., & Delehanty, H. (1995). *Sacred hoops: Spiritual lessons of a hardwood warrior.* New York: Hyperion.

Jeannerod, M. (1995). Mental imagery in the motor context, *Neuropsychologia, 33,* 1419–1432.

Jeannerod, M. (2001). Neural simulation of action: A unifying mechanism for motor cognition. *Neuroimage, 14:* 103–109.

Jeannerod, M., & Pacherie, E. (2004). Agency, simulation, and self-identification. *Mind and Language, 19,* 113–146.

Johnson, M. (1987). *The body in the mind: The bodily basis of meaning, imagination, and reason.* Chicago: University of Chicago Press.

Joyce, M. (1993). *Of Two Minds: Hypertext Pedagogy and Poetics.* Ann Arbor: University of Michigan Press.

Kellogg, R. T. (1994). *The psychology of writing.* New York: Oxford University Press.

Kull, K. (1999). Biosemiotics in the twentieth century: A view from biology. *Semiotica, 127,* 385–414.

Lang, A. (1997). Non-Cartesian artifacts in dwelling activities: Steps toward a semiotic ecology. In M. Cole, Y. Engeström, & O. Vasquez (Eds.), *Mind, culture, and activity: Seminal papers from the laboratory of comparative human cognition* (pp. 185–204). Cambridge, UK: Cambridge University Press.

Lankshear, C., Snyder, I., & Green, B. (2000). *Teachers and technoliteracy.* Sydney: Allen and Unwin.

Leander, K. (2001). "This is our freedom bus going home right now": Producing and hybridizing space-time contexts in pedagogical discourse. *Journal of Literacy Research, 33,* 637–680.

Leander, K. (2002). Locating Latanya: The situated production of identity artifacts in classroom interaction. *Research in the Teaching of English, 37,* 198–250.

Leander, K., & Sheehy, M. (Eds.). (2004). *Spatializing literacy research and practice.* New York: Peter Lang.

Lee, K. (2004). Presence, explicated. *Communication Theory, 14*(1), 27–50.

Lemke, J. (1997). Cognition, context, and learning: A social semiotic perspective. In D. Kirshner & J. Whitson (Eds.), *Situated cognition: Social, semiotic, and psychological perspectives* (pp. 37–56). Mahwah, NJ: Lawrence Erlbaum.

Lombard, M., & Ditton, T. (1997). At the heart of it all: The concept of presence. *Journal of Computer-Mediated Communication.* Retrieved from http://jcmc.indiana.edu/vol3/issue2/lombard.html.

Lotman, J. (1977). Myth—name—culture. In D. Lucid (Ed.), *Soviet Semiotics* (pp. 233–252). Baltimore: Johns Hopkins University Press.

Lotman, J. (1990). *Universe of the mind: A semiotic theory of culture.* A. Shukman (Trans.). London: I.B. Tauris.

Lotze, M., Montoyaa, P., Erba, M., Hülsmanna, E., Florb, H., Klosec, U., Birbaumerc, N., & Groddc, W. (1999). Activation of cortical and cerebellar motor areas during executed and imagined hand movements: An fMRI study. *Journal of Cognitive Neuroscience, 11,* 491–501.

Luke, C. (2000). Cyber-schooling and technological change: Multiliteracies for new times. In B. Cope & M. Kalantzis (Eds.), *Multiliteracies: Literacy learning and the design of social futures* (pp. 69–91). Melbourne, Australia: Macmillan.

Metzinger, T., & Gallese, V. (2003). The emergence of a shared action ontology: Building blocks for a theory. *Consciousness and Cognition, 12*, 549–571.

New London Group. (1996). A pedagogy of multiliteracies: Designing social futures. *Harvard Educational Review, 66*, 60–92.

Pellegrino, G. di; Fadiga, L., Fogassi, L., Gallese, V., & Rizzolatti, G. (1992). Understanding motor events: A neurophysiological study. *Experimental Brain Research, 91*, 176–180.

Perani, D., Brunelli, G. A., Tettamanti, M., Scifo, P., Tecchio, F., Rossini, P. M., & Fazio, F. (2001). Remodelling of sensorimotor maps in paraplegia: A functional magnetic resonance imaging study after a surgical nerve transfer. *Neuroscience Letters, 303*(1): 62–66.

Peters, R., & Itti, L. (2006). Computational mechanisms for gaze direction in interactive visual environments. In *Eye Tracking Research and Application: Proceedings of the 2006 Symposium on Eye Tracking and Application.* Retrieved from Portal.acm.org/citation.cfm?id=1117315.

Poster, M. (1995). Postmodern virtualities. In M. Featherstone & R. Burrows (Eds.), *Cyberspace, cyberbodies, cyberpunk: Cultures of technological embodiment* (pp. 79–96). London: Sage.

Rizzolatti, G., Fogassi, L., & Gallese, V. (2000). Cortical mechanisms subserving object grasping and action recognition: A new view of the cortical motor functions. In M. Gazzaniga (Ed.), *Handbook of cognitive neurosciences*, 2nd ed. (pp. 539–552). Cambridge, MA: MIT Press.

Ruby, P., & Decety, J. (2003). What do you believe versus what do you think they believe?: A neuroimaging study of perspective-taking at the conceptual level. *European Journal of Neuroscience, 17*, 2475–2480.

de Saussure, F. (1966). *Course in general linguistics.* (Trans. W. Baskin). New York: McGraw-Hill.

Schroeder, R. (Ed.). (2002). *The social life of avatars: Presence and interaction in shared virtual environments.* London: Springer.

Sebeok, T. (1991). *A sign is just a sign.* Bloomington: Indiana University Press.

Squire, K. (2006). From content to context: Videogames as designed experiences. *Educational Researcher, 35*, 19–29.

Taylor, T. (2002). Living digitally: Embodiment in virtual worlds. In R. Schroeder (Ed.), *The social life of avatars: Presence and interaction in shared virtual environments* (pp. 40–62). London: Springer.

Tchertov, L. (2002). Spatial semiosis in culture. *Sign Systems Studies 30*, 442–453.

Uexküll, J. von. (1926). *Theoretical biology.* (Trans. D.L. Mackinnon). New York: Harcourt, Brace.

Vygotsky, L. (1987). Thinking and speech. In R. Rieber & A. Carton (Eds.), *The collected works of L. S. Vygotsky, Volume 1: Problems of general psychology* (pp. 39–288). New York: Plenum.

Wartofsky, M. (1973/1979). *Models: Representation and the scientific understanding.* London: D. Reidel.

Whitson, J. (1997). Cognition as a semiotic process: From situated mediation to critical reflective transcendence. In D. Kirshner & J. Whitson (Eds.), *Situated cognition: Social, semiotic, and psychological perspectives* (pp. 261–280). Mahwah, NJ: Lawrence Erlbaum.

Winn, W. (2003). Learning in artificial environments: Embodiment, embeddedness and dynamic adaptation. *Technology, Instruction, Cognition, and Learning, 1*, 87–114.

Contributors

Hannah Bellwoar is an Assistant Professor of English at Juniata College, where she teaches professional and multi-media writing. Her research explores literate activity of alternative and traditional medical professionals as well as laypeople. Her work has appeared in *Technical Communication Quarterly*, *Kairos*, *Rhetoric Review*, and *National Women's Studies Association Journal*.

Julie Cheville is an Associate Professor in the Department of English Studies at Illinois State University. Her research interests include the social and spatial origins of perception and cognition. Her publications include an ethnographic study entitled *Minding the Body: What Students Athletes Know about Learning* (Boynton/Cook, 2001), as well as articles and research handbook chapters that consider spatial signification in relation to contexts of virtual embodiment.

Eliot Fintushel is a creator and performer of mask, mime, and clown theatre, with incursions into puppetry, improvisation, and performance art. Having twice received the NEA Solo Performer Fellowship, Eliot has performed nearly four thousand shows at schools, theatres, and community centers, including solo performances at the National Theatre in Washington DC and at various international festivals. He is also a consultant and teacher of performance for professional companies, universities, and for special projects among diverse populations. In addition to acting, and writing about theater, Eliot also writes science fiction, which has appeared in numerous magazines and anthologies. He is currently a contributing editor to *Tricycle* magazine.

James Paul Gee is the Mary Lou Fulton Presidential Professor of Literacy Studies at Arizona State University and a member of the National Academy of Education. His books include: *Sociolinguistics and Literacies* (Fourth Edition 2011); *An Introduction to Discourse Analysis* (Third Edition 2011); *What Video Games Have to Teach Us About Learning and Literacy* (Second Edition 2007); *How to Do Discourse Analysis* (2011); and the following books co-authored with Elizabeth Hayes: *Women and Gaming: The Sims and 21st Century Learning* (2010) and *Language and Learning in the Digital World* (2011). Jim's latest book *The Anti-Education ERA: Creating Smarter Students through Digital Media* appeared in 2013. He has published widely in linguistics, psychology, social science, and education journals.

Nina Haft's work in new Jewish performance has been profiled in *Dance Magazine* and supported by the Djerassi Resident Artist Program and Margaret Jenkins' Dance Lab, where she developed "Mit a Bing, Mit a Boom! A Klezmer Dance." Her company is known for its site-specific performances in libraries, synagogues, dockyards, parking lots, cemeteries and other liminal spaces. Nina received her MFA in Dance at the University of Wisconsin, Milwaukee, where she was a Javits Fellow. She is currently Associate Professor of Theatre and Dance at California State University, East Bay, where she is also affiliated with the new Jewish Studies Program. She also teaches at Shawl-Anderson Dance Center in Berkeley, where Nina Haft & Company is in residence.

Elizabeth Carothers Herron's poetry and prose have appeared in *Orion, Ions, EarthLight, Parabola,* and *Jung Journal of Culture and Psyche.* Her books include: *While the Distance Widens* (short fiction) and *Desire Being Full of Distances* (poetry) along with four chapbooks. Her new and collected poems are forthcoming from Risk Press (2013). A former professor in Sonoma State University's School of Expressive Arts and later in the School of Arts & Humanities, Elizabeth is now Professor Emerita at SSU.

Cory Holding is an Assistant Professor in the Department of English at the University of Pittsburgh, where she specializes in composition. Her interests include bodily invention, prison literacies, and performance theory. She greatly appreciates the lessons in tactile composition she learned from working with students in "Staging the Argument" at the University of Illinois's Education Justice Project. Cory's current research focuses on the rhetoric of gesture.

Mira-Lisa Katz earned a PhD in Education in Language, Literacy and Culture from the University of California, Berkeley. A recipient of U.C. Berkeley's Outstanding Dissertation Award in 2000, NCTE's Promising Researcher Award in 2001, and the Robert Bowne Foundation's Edmund Stanley Jr. Research Grant in 2006, she has presented research internationally on literacy, reading, dance, and multimodality. Mira is a co-author of the California State University's ERWC (Expository Reading and Writing Curriculum); published jointly by the California Department of Education and the CSU Chancellor's Office (2008; 2013) and taught in over 500 public high schools throughout California, the ERWC is designed to facilitate the transition from high school to college. As Professor of English at Sonoma State University, Mira offers undergraduate and graduate courses in literacy theory and practice, applied linguistics, English education, and literature. Her scholarship has appeared in *Linguistics and Education*; *Research in the Teaching of English*; *Canadian Modern Language Review*; *The California Reader*; *Leadership*; the *International Journal of Innovation in Language Teaching*; *Afterschool Matters*; and *Open Letter: Australian Journal for Adult Literacy and Research*. In addition to teaching and writing, Mira has been a performing artist in the San Francisco Bay Area for over 35 years. She is currently a member of SoCo Dance Theater, based in Sonoma County, California.

Catherine Kroll is an Associate Professor of English at Sonoma State University in California, where she teaches courses in modern African literature, English education, and composition pedagogy. Her published work includes essays on critical pedagogy and transcultural perspectives in the classroom, as well as studies of Boubacar Boris Diop's *Murambi: The Book of Bones* and Patrice Nganang's *Temps de chien*. Her article "The Tyranny of the Visual: Alex La Guma and the Anti-Apartheid Documentary Image" was published in the Fall 2012 issue of *Research in African Literatures*. "Bodies of Evidence: South African Gothic and the Terror of the 'Twice-Told Tale'" appears in *Textus: English Studies in Italy*, special issue on Gothic Frontiers (2012). Her book chapter "Inversion Rituals: The African Novel in the Global North" was published in *Teaching Africa: A Guide for the 21st-Century Classroom*, edited by Brandon D. Lundy and Solomon Negash (2013).

David Leventhal is a founding teacher and Program Manager for Dance for PD®, a collaborative program of the Mark Morris Dance Group and Brooklyn Parkinson Group that has now been used as a model for classes in more than 100 communities in eight countries. He leads classes for people with Parkinson's disease around the world. Since 2007, he has trained more than 350 teachers in the Dance for PD® approach in 18 cities on three continents. Along with Olie Westheimer, he is the co-recipient of the 2013 Alan Bonander Humanitarian Award from the

Parkinson's Unity Walk. He has written about dance and Parkinson's for such publications as Dance Gazette and Room 217, and has a chapter about the program in *Creating Dance: A Traveler's Guide* (2013, Hampton Press). He is a frequent guest speaker at Parkinson's conferences and symposia, and serves on the Board of Directors of the Global Alliance for Arts and Health. He danced with Mark Morris Dance Group from 1997–2011, performing principal roles in Morris' *The Hard Nut, L'Allegro, il Penseroso ed il Moderato,* and *Romeo and Juliet: On Motifs of Shakespeare* and received a 2010 Bessie (New York Dance and Performance Award) for his performing career with Mark Morris. A graduate of Brown University with honors in English Literature, David lives in Brooklyn, NY with his wife Lauren and son Zev.

After earning a BS in Speech Communications from Northwestern University, **Tori Truss** became a founding member of Bloomsburg Theater Ensemble in Pennsylvania and subsequently spent five years training and performing in New York. At NU, Tori studied with Readers Theater pioneers, Frank Galati and Leland Roloff, and, after moving to California, became Artistic Director of Bay Area Youth Theater, where she worked closely with public alternative K-8 schools. As a professor at Sonoma State University for over 15 years, she taught acting and theatre courses, and has also directed operas and musicals, and created original works in settings ranging from classrooms and large stages to arts camps, beaches, army barracks, and recycling centers. A performer throughout the San Francisco Bay Area, Tori currently teaches drama at an independent K-8 School in San Rafael, California.

Matt Rahaim is Assistant Professor of Ethnomusicology at the University of Minnesota. A longtime student, teacher, and performer of Indian vocal music, his book, *Musicking Bodies: Gesture and Voice in Hindustani Music* (2012, Wesleyan University Press), focuses on the transmission of the bodily disciplines of melodic knowledge through generations of Indian vocalists. His current project is about the ethical dimensions of South Asian vocal techniques. Matt's articles have appeared in *The Journal of Asian Studies, Gesture, World of Music,* and *New Perspectives on Music and Gesture* and authored the article "Music" in the *Brill Encyclopedia of Hinduism.* Before coming to UMN, he taught Religious Studies, Asian Studies, and Music at the University of California, Berkeley, as well as at Stanford and St. Olaf College.

A professional dancer, teaching artist, and writer, **Jill Homan Randall** received her BFA in Modern Dance from the University of Utah in 1997. Over the past 16 years she has taught extensively in K-12 public schools, preschools, and community dance centers. From 2004 to 2006, Jill was Director of Education for the Lincoln Center Institute Program in Berkeley, and for four years thereafter she was Program

Director of Berkeley's Shawl-Anderson Dance Center. She currently teaches dance at The Hamlin School in San Francisco, where in 2013, she received the Herbst Foundation Award for Teaching Excellence. Jill has performed with many Bay Area choreographers including Nina Haft, Dana Lawton, and Randee Paufve. She has published in the *Horn Book Magazine*, *In Dance*, *Teaching Artist Journal*, and has written educator guides for "Spark" for KQED (National Public Television). Jill authors three blogs: "Dancing Words," a blog on children's books about dance; "Dancers Using Technology," about the many intersections between the arts and technology; and "Life as a Modern Dancer," a 'living textbook' for college students about careers in modern dance.

Erica Tom is a doctoral student in American Studies at Rutgers University. She holds a BA in English with a minor in Classical Studies from the University of Washington, and an MA in English Literature from Sonoma State University, where she taught lower division composition, tutored in SSU's Writing Center, and co-founded the feminist discussion group, Locating Lysippe. She has worked with non-profit equine programs, gentling feral horses and collaboratively developing educational programs for young women and adults, and has presented her interdisciplinary work on embodiment and power—and how it is mediated with and through the body of the horse—at conferences across the United States. Her current research focuses on Mounted Police. She enjoys working within and beyond the academy as an educator, editor, equine trainer, and poet, and her poetry has appeared in *Volt*.

Keli Yerian earned a PhD in Linguistics from Georgetown University. Currently the Director of the Language Teaching Specialization MA Program in the Department of Linguistics at the University of Oregon, Keli offers various language teacher education courses as well as English as a second language in the American English Institute at UO. She is most interested in how teachers use both language and the body in interaction with students, and how users of English from different language backgrounds may integrate modalities in different ways, especially in their use of gestures that have pragmatic functions. Other teaching-focused research interests include investigating the goals and experiences of international graduate students in US language teacher education programs, and the use of graphics in course materials.

Colin Lankshear & Michele Knobel

*General Editor*s

New literacies emerge and evolve apace as people from all walks of life engage with new technologies, shifting values and institutional change, and increasingly assume 'postmodern' orientations toward their everyday worlds. Despite many efforts to take account of such changes, educational institutions largely remain out of touch with the range of new ways of making and sharing meanings that increasingly mediate and shape the lives of the young people they teach and the futures they face. This series aims to explore some key dimensions of the changes occurring within social practices of literacy and the educational challenges they present, with a view to informing educational practice in helpful ways. It asks what are new literacies, how do they impact on life in schools, homes, communities, workplaces, sites of leisure, and other key settings of human cultural engagement, and what significance do new literacies have for how people learn and how they understand and construct knowledge. It aims to challenge established and 'official' ways of framing literacy, and to ask what it means for literacies to be powerful, effective, and enabling under current and foreseeable conditions. Collectively, the works in this series will help to reorient literacy debates and literacy education agendas.

For further information about the series and submitting manuscripts, please contact:

Michele Knobel & Colin Lankshear
Montclair State University
Dept. of Education and Human Services
3173 University Hall
Montclair, NJ 07043
michele@coatepec.net

To order other books in this series, please contact our Customer Service Department at:
(800) 770-LANG (within the U.S.)
(212) 647-7706 (outside the U.S.)
(212) 647-7707 FAX

Or browse online by series at:
www.peterlang.com